Political Hysteria
in America

POLITICAL HYSTERIA

in AMERICA

The Democratic Capacity for Repression

MURRAY B. LEVIN

BASIC BOOKS, INC., PUBLISHERS

NEW YORK LONDON

Library of Congress Catalog Card Number: 71–174826
SBN 465–05898–1
Manufactured in the United States of America
DESIGNED BY THE INKWELL STUDIO

TO

Harry Rand AND *Howard Zinn*

DIFFERENT TRUTHS IN DIFFERENT WAYS

BOTH LOVELY MEN

ACKNOWLEDGMENTS

While writing this book I became aware of my debt to Louis Hartz, who was my tutor in Harvard College years ago, and to Franz Neumann, who directed my graduate work at Columbia. I learned much from both of them. But, more than that, they were the first men who showed me the pleasures of study. This has made a big difference in my life.

Two graduate students and two colleagues—all dear friends—talked with me, it seems endlessly, about the ideas in this book. Edward Berger and Harvey Boulay argued, instructed, clarified, and sometimes annoyed and distracted me. Some of the ideas in this book are really theirs. Professors Robert McShea and Howard Zinn read the manuscript and, much to the benefit of this book, suggested changes. I thank them for their help and their many kindnesses.

A few months after I began this book—three years ago—I met Doris Kearns—a lovely and wise woman—who talked with me and helped me with several drafts of this book. I cannot possibly thank her adequately for her help and caring—except to say simply, thank you.

Joan Agri, Linda Lees, Betsy McBurney, and Cathy Tabor typed the drafts that preceded the final version of the book. Again—many thanks.

Three students were of special help to me, so I thank Claudia Ives, David Solomon, and Bruce Wolpe.

My editor at Basic Books, Erwin Glikes, translated parts of this book into English, fed me much spaghetti carbonara, and became my friend.

CONTENTS

Political Hysteria
in America

INTRODUCTION

CERTAIN EVENTS in a nation's history, frequently of brief duration and generally regarded as peripheral or freakish, may reveal profound forces that customarily lie below the surface. The Dreyfus Affair was such an event in France. The Monkey Trial, McCarthyism, and My Lai were such events in America. These events were not aberrations outside the nation's history, but the result of a mix of elements essential to the culture and always present, not aberrations, but exaggerations of the commonplace, not the actions and reactions of psychotics or paranoids, but those of so-called normal men. Like verbal slips in everyday life, they reveal powerful but repressed fears and desires.

The great Red scare of 1919–1920 was such an event in American history. Its essence was almost universal belief in the imminent destruction of American civilization by a highly organized, brilliantly directed, and well financed Bolshevik conspiracy in America, which, in fact, did not exist. It was a dramatic although not a unique phenomenon—millions of people, an entire nation, frantic, anxiety-ridden, fearful of an illusionary threat perceived as apocalyptic. This is poor "reality testing" on a grand scale—panic without real cause—and it raises many questions about the America which produced it, and which may produce it again.

This national panic without real cause was political hysteria, and political hysteria in America is my subject. Although I will use the Red Scare, the most dramatic explosion of political hysteria in American history as an example, I am not interested so much in the Red Scare, as I am in the underlying forces that can produce this hysteria and the repression it breeds. What is it about America that creates the successes of A. Mitchell Palmer and Joseph McCarthy? What produces the witch hunt when there are so few witches? Why do so many Americans—who usually claim to be so pragmatic and passionless in their politics—suddenly become so frightened, vicious, and irrational that they applaud the pursuit of ephemeral and ghostly enemies with such obvious pleasure? There must be much passion and fury somewhere below the calm surface of American politics. And there must be men who know this, who know how to excite it, and who attempt to exploit it.

Political hysteria involves an extreme loss of customary political self-control and a very high degree of misperception —a passionate crusade to eliminate an imaginary threat. Millions become convinced that evil conspirators exist and have the capacity to destroy them. This conviction arouses intense anxiety—anxiety so widespread that a national panic is discernable. The conspiracy is fabricated by elites out of bits and pieces of reality, but the bits and pieces never add up to the whole. The dangers are vaguely defined by the elites. The perceived danger and its unspecific quality are used by elites to escalate anxiety. The anxiety induced among the masses—their anticipation of future danger—leads them to yearn for the elimination of these dangers. The yearning leads them to approve extreme means which elites might select to eliminate the danger.

Political hysteria, therefore, is a peculiar combination of conscious elite contrivance and spontaneous and largely unconscious mass response. Elites are active during tht hysteria. The people are largely passive and approving. The active participation of the people in the process of repression is not even necessary. Their approval and noninterference is enough to permit elites to promote and administer repression. If

Fascism came to America it would not require popular participation—merely popular nonopposition.

Elites may be tempted to promote political hysteria and repression when they believe their power is seriously threatened or when they believe their self-interest can better be served by hysteria than the usual allegedly pluralist channels. In either case the intended political and economic consequences are almost always the strengthening of existing elites. Promoters of political hysteria usually intend conservative consequences by eliminating a challenge to existing power. Political hysteria is usually a technique for managing tension and maintaining an existing economic and political system—a technique designed to halt and reverse challenges to power or the decline of power.

We are aware of three kinds of situations which have excited elites to step beyond the usual exercise of power. One is a rapid and dramatic decline in the strength of the more entrenched political party—the Federalist party's search for conspiracy and promotion of repression when confronted with a Jeffersonian onslaught. Another is a serious challenge by labor to the power of giant corporations—the great steel and coal strikes of 1919 and labor's proposal of "one big union" played a major role in leading U.S. Steel and other corporations to promote the Red scare. Political hysteria can be a form of strikebreaking. Yet another situation is the temptation of achieving notoriety and building a power base for future political moves through leading an antiradical hysteria—true of A. Mitchell Palmer, Joseph McCarthy, and, in lesser degree, George Wallace and Spiro Agnew. A sharp and dramatic increase in the spread of communism abroad often serves as a catalyst to political hysteria in America.

In contemporary America, defeat in war, or a costly stalemate, or a major cultural deviance might excite hysterical potentials once again.

Regardless of the causes, numerous pay-offs for many groups are available through political hysteria—pay-offs which are neither obvious nor publicly stated. Those who promote the idea that America is in imminent danger of destruction at the hands of evil conspirators always justify their actions by claiming that their only aim is the preservation of the American way of life. Selflessness and the courageous defense of America was the public posture of A. Mitchell Palmer and Judge Gary of U.S. Steel, of Joseph McCarthy, and of Richard Nixon of the House Un-American Activities Committee. But there are many and significant benefits available to promoters of the conspiratorial perspective. Among them have been strikebreaking, sterotyping opposition leaders as alien and radical, the justification of military expenditures, and additional personnel for law enforcement agencies, expanding newspaper circulation, profits and fees for superpatriotic societies and speakers, and, among others, the creation of scapegoats so that failures of the economy and policy will be neither traced to the party in power nor to dominant American values. The latter function preserves the purity of the American identification with the values in the tradition of John Locke and Adam Smith—rarely perceived as a possible source of American difficulties.

For elites, political hysteria may be very profitable. For the American people, it may be very pleasurable. Reaffirming one's American identity by smashing America's enemies may be delightful. Projecting one's secret, despised, and wished for inner-self onto filthy sexually lascivious enemies of America may be a great relief and source of renewal.

The conspiratorial enemy is invariably portrayed as germ, infection, vermin, lice, rat, or snake in the grass. The growth of the conspiratorial power is likened to a plague or epidemic —a flooding of hideous and pestilential sickness and evil which can only be halted by extraordinary precautions and extreme solutions. Some have speculated that perhaps the evil conspirator on the march is the hated and feared secret self, finally out of control. And perhaps this projection is one source of the anxiety/upon which the hysteria builds and it explains the pleasure and intensity of the pursuit.

Thus, the crusade to purge evil, unrestrained righteous passion, and mass orgiastic release in political action can be hugely satisfying, particularly when it is promoted and legitimized by the state and the "best people" in society.

Political hysteria mixes crass self-interest and intangible psychological pleasure. The motivation is very complex. Many who actively promote the hysteria genuinely believe in the conspiracy and the threat, perceive themselves as patriots, and, simultaneously, utilize the hysteria for private political and economic gain which they hide—perhaps unwittingly—behind facades of patriotic and communal rhetoric. Sincere public spiritedness and private greed operate side by side in the same individuals without a hint of doubt or contradiction.

Political hysteria and repression are potential American responses to stress, but they are only potentials. American elites are usually able to sustain their power without resort to hysteria and the fantasy of conspiracy. The techniques for managing tension, and for preventing the emergence of alternatives to the dominant liberal perspective are numerous and remarkably efficient. The absence of serious challenges to liberalism from the left or the right is testimony to the power and pervasiveness of the American way. After all, he who is not a Republican is invariably a Democrat—all liberals, all Lockians, all Smithians. The continuity and changelessness of American values and institutions is impressive.

But occasionally elites do become panicky and feel seriously threatened. Then they may be tempted to cry conspiracy and excite the democratic capacity for repression. And that capacity can be substantial, for the American people passionately identify with the principles of political and economic liberalism as they have become transformed into American cliches, dogma, and ritual. The identity of Americans is framed by these liberal cliches—this Americanist nationalism. When elites can convince millions that their identity, their dogmas, and their

America, are threatened by imminent and apocalyptic conspiratorial demons, the anxiety and rage that ensue prepare the
people to applaud and delight in the pursuit of America's
enemies by America's leaders.

The hysteria and the repression can also be very seductive
because, as it unfolds, it looks very American—pluralist, fundamentally lawful, not particularly violent, and absolutely pragmatic. Elites promote the hysteria by traditional ways, by
applying pressure on legislatures in the traditional American
way and by influencing media in the traditional American way.
Political hysteria is promoted within pluralist groupings and
uses public relations men and lobbyists. Like every attempt to
sell a product with a national market, it is promoted by a
nationwide advertising campaign. The "pluralism" of its rise
and progress makes it American, and seductive.

Our brand of hysteria and repression is American and seductive because it is, with few exceptions, a lawful operation. It
unfolds in, through, and around constitutional procedures.
Radicals and deviants, with a very few exceptions, are not shot
in the streets; they are rarely pursued by vigilantes; they are
rarely the victims of new "emergency" legislation—although at
the height of the frenzy such legislation is often proposed; they
are not forced to wear the Star of David; and they are not
sent to concentration camps. They are investigated by lawful
committees and duly constituted administrative agencies, indicted in a more or less lawful way and tried by a jury of their
peers before a duly appointed judge on the charge of violating
laws enacted long before the alleged violation occurred. During
the Red Scare and McCarthyism perhaps not more than a total
of seven or eight thousand persons had their civil rights
violated—probably much less than occurs during an average
two year period in the South alone. Our home grown brand of
repression is seductive because it customarily uses the law and
requires only the slightest increase in the level of violence. The
pluralism, the lawfulness, and the nonviolence by which the

hysteria and repression unfold can make the purge appear very purifying, honorable, pleasurable, profitable, and wholly within the American tradition—as, in fact, it is.

Most scholars who have analyzed political hysteria or extremism in America—or the so-called paranoid style in American politics—argue that, although these phenomena recur periodically, they are essentially aberrant, abnormal, and peripheral—not an integral part of "mainstream America." Such interludes are perceived as temporary responses to social and/or economic dislocations—responses of Americans who are either predisposed to such behavior because they are characteristically disturbed or because they are being socially or economically bypassed. This view of political hysteria and repression as the gross exception needs examination. Just as it is important during the hysteria to exorcise evil, to deport aliens, and purify the country, so, too, after the hysteria, the American people and American historians tend to exorcise the memory of such times by treating them as alien, aberrant, "exceptions" to the rule. Thus they attempt to purify American history and perhaps, exorcise their complicity.

I will suggest here that these predispositions and excitements are not in the least "un-American." They are not merely exotic episodes of temporary abnormality or madness in the American body politic. They involve millions of people from all social classes. They have deep roots in the interstices of American culture. They are the hidden underbelly of American politics. The deeply felt intolerance that springs from our intense commitment to Americanism, the irrational and compulsive need to defend the assumptions of John Locke and Adam Smith, the anti-Semitism, the nativism, the antiintellectualism, the vigilantism, the racism, the xenophobia, the pursuit of self-interest under the guise of superpatriotism, and the profound antiradicalism that can be observed "in extremis" during the hysteria have always been and are today the working assumptions of millions of Americans.

In normal times, however, they operate in much more subtle and covert ways than they do during a fit of national hysteria.

Here we will first observe some of these forces in their excited state—in their less subtle, more vulgar, but no less American manifestations. We will examine the passion below the bland surface of American politics, the courtship of that passion, the suitors, the courted, the foreplay, and the climax.

It must be asked whether political hysteria is an archaic phenomenon. It is, among other things, a technique used by elites to manage social tension and maintain the system that provides them with power. It can be argued that the techniques of tension management in America have become so sophisticated and plentiful that elites may have little need to resort to political hysteria in the future. Social control has become an increasingly complicated and computerized business. It appears that elites weathered the storms of the nineteen sixties without resorting to anything like the Red scare or McCarthyism, and the sixties were substantially more turbulent than 1919 or the fifties. The deep forces in American culture that made political hysteria an American potential continue to exist, but the ability of modern nations to contain qualitative change without resorting to political hysteria has become great. So we will ultimately consider what these deep forces are and how they produce the modified forms of repression whose effect is not very different from the overt, primitive political hysteria which precede them. We will examine the conditions which might produce, even today, a national regression to political hysteria in its purest form. And then we will close with some considered speculations of the circumstances which might lead to eventual liberation from the largely unrecognized by uniquely powerful democratic capacity for repression.

But first, a close look at the phenomenon in its undiluted and undisguised purity—political hysteria in America in full hue and cry.

1

AWAKE AMERICA!
A MEDLEY OF POPULAR
AMERICAN TUNES

Here is a sampling of the voices of American superpatriots, a collage of their cries of warning to their countrymen in 1919 and 1920. Their voices are shrill—and their claims may strike us as merely ridiculous. But these statements are recurrent themes of American political discourse and they have influenced our lives—and our fate as a civilization—more deeply than we care to know.

☆

The Red Threat to America

There is, in this nation, a large well-organized, skillfully managed and liberally financed movement that has for its purpose the overthrow of our form of government and the destruction of our business enterprises, peacefully if possible, by force if necessary, that there may be erected on the ruins a purely socialistic form of government and a purely communistic form of business, a form of government and a form of business that would—

FIRST—Destroy property rights;

SECOND—Take away all personal initiative in industrial activities;

THIRD—Abolish civil government and the political state;
FOURTH—Destroy the church and religious institutions; and
FIFTH—Abandon the family relations.[1]

This is the doctrine that a thousand missionaries are preaching in
season and out of season—in mills and machine shops, in stores
and factories, among the telephone girls and the newsboys, among
the bellhops and the bootblacks in hotels. This is what they have
taught even in the trenches. This is what they propose to teach in
your public schools. And we have been indifferent. We have not
believed it possible. Like the traditional ostrich, we have buried
our heads in the sands, while the more prominent parts of our
anatomy have ornamented the landscape.[2]

The world is in turmoil; the relationships of men in industry
and commerce, and in business generally, were never so upset as
they are today. Conditions are much worse in Europe than they
are in America: crises are coming and have come over there—
and they will come over here within five or maybe ten years unless
all of us take some real interest in our country's affairs and try
seriously and conscientiously to solve some of these problems.[3] The
lure of Bolshevism and Marxian Socialism is at once the most
powerful and dangerous that ever tempted rotten-hearted and sinful
men. "Stolen property" is its bait and Ignorance is its favorite
agent. Whenever its foes are commanded by General Apathy, the
robbers win.[4] The evidence which has been collected by the Department of Justice is so conclusive of a gigantic conspiracy to
destroy the government of the United States that it is really alarm-
ing[5] "The time has come," says Nicholas Murray Butler, President of Columbia University," to mobilize all the resources of
America, material and human, for war against the red menace,
not overseas, but here at home." In a recent address he said:

It is an amazing thing that after 125 years there should
appear the necessity of re-defining Americanism, but today
we hear the hiss of the snake in the grass, and the hiss is
directed at the things that Americans hold most dear.[6]

What Is Bolshevism?

Bolshevism is not indigenous to American soil. It is a disease that,
like influenza and cholera, comes from overseas, and with which no

native-born American would be likely to be afflicted unless there were something about him congenitally abnormal.[7]

For our purpose Socialism, I.W.W. 'ism, Syndicalism, and Bolshevism are one and the same menace. While these bodies vary in their methods and machinery, they all mean the same thing: the expropriation of private property, factories, mines, farms, banks, mills, railroads, telephone and telegraph systems, etc.—in fact the dictatorship of the proletariat—and Karl Marx's "Capitalism" ("Das Kapital") is the bible of them all.[8] There is ample and convincing evidence that the movement had its inception some time prior to the beginning of the world war in 1914, and that it was started here and elsewhere by paid agents of the Junker class in Germany as part of their programme of industrial and military world conquest.[9] A raid on I.W.W. headquarters in Portland, Oregon, according to a dispatch in New York "Illustrated Daily News," brought to light "a letter proving German money was paid to I.W.W. leaders to spread German propaganda";[10]

What we are witnessing today in Europe as well as in the United States is the culmination of one hundred and fifty years of continuous and implacable scheming.[11] The history of the development of Bolshevism and of its present control in Russia forms the darkest and deadliest record in the annals of government. In comparison with its manifold atrocities, all other revolutions seem almost humane.[12]

The Reds In Russia

The Czar of Russia was too wise to throw the doors of Russia open to the German hordes; he knew it meant suicide—the Germans would take and hold. Neither could he withdraw without ample excuse to the allies, for they had Japan ready to strike if Russia made a treacherous movement. The Czar needed a revolution as an excuse to withdraw from the World's War. *Russia had to have a revolution.* The revolution was planned by the Czar of Russia and the Kaiser of Germany. The German War Machine perfected the plans. First, starvation, then an Ism for all the people to follow. Then their intentions were, when the revolution became sufficiently extensive, that Russia could withdraw from the war to take care of her own internal troubles, and the Czar would then use his army to put the civilian population again under his tyrannical control. But the German War Machine had a different idea, for they wanted Russia, her territory and wealth. So they maliciously helped the Czar make a sizable revolution such as he nor any other man could put down, Lenin and Trotzky, paid German agents, were being directed in their work from Berlin by the great German War Machine which was supplying them with an endless amount of money that was being used to form soldiers peasants and workers into soviets (councils) in all parts of Russia.[13]

Robert Wilton, the correspondent of the *London Times* in Russia for a number of years has recently stated that the 384 Bolshevik Commissars which ruled Russia right after the Bolshevists took charge of it were composed of two Negroes, thirteen Russians, fifteen Chinamen, twenty-three Georgians and Armenians, and over 264 men who had come out of the United States from the Lower East Side—Trotsky among them.[14] Those men, known to our authorities, were not only permitted, but assisted, to go into Russia in the midst of an ally who was at arms with us fighting a common enemy, and bringing their ally down. Trotsky himself was held up in Canada and not permitted to go through by the Canadian authorities and was released and sent on his way at the earnest request of our State Department. Sixty percent of the officials of the State Department in Washington are socialists.[15]

The Reds In America

Both the labor and political programs of the Bolshevist movement are most capably and systematically organized and promoted by 2,500 trained and paid agitators. The leaders of Bolshevism in this country claim the sympathy and support of more than 5,000,-000 of the 9,000,000 industrial workers within its borders.[16] In the United States the anarchists have found a fertile field and for many years they have been working without any particular opposition. The great War gave them encouragement, and recent events, not only in Europe, but also in this country, have confirmed them in the belief that a minority, active and well financed, can control the majority. They were given an example of the possibility and power of minority control by Germany. This was followed by the control of Russia by a comparatively few active anarchists. In the

United States, the anarchists had the example of what can be accomplished by the determined leadership of minorities in the success of prohibition and women suffrage.[17]

A sample of the teachings brought to light by the Government's raids is the Manifesto of the Federation of Unions of Russian Workers of the United States and Canada. Assistant Attorney General Garvan characterized it as "the most dangerous piece of propaganda ever disseminated by any radical organization in the United States." It advocates, according to a Washington dispatch published in the New York "Globe," these things:

Capture of all products and means of production.
Liberation of all political prisoners.
The blowing up of all barracks.
The murder of law-enforcing officials.
The burning of public records.
Destruction of fences and all property lines.
The destruction of all instruments of indebtedness.[18]

The great number of violent disturbances that are happening in our country—bomb outrages, revolutionary strikes, murders and sabotage—could not be ascribed to mere chance, that there is a direct relation between the bomb throwing outrage in Los Angeles, the constant preachment of the "revolution" by radical agitators, the attempts at revolution in Seattle and Winnepeg, in fact did occur as a result of an actual plan conceived and carried out by a central organization made up of bold, cunning and dangerous men.[19]

"Toleration"? "Let them talk." "They can't do anything." "They are only a handful, of agitators." "No danger to civilization." "They can't hurt the United States." Is it not high time to realize the folly of such indifference, contempt and passive toleration? Such an attitude is precisely what these revolutionists against all constituted authorities of government are relying upon our taking. They have carefully seen to it that as many of us as possible shall be lulled and doped into a false sense of security. They count on our doing nothing towards effectively interfering with them until they are ready to fire the bomb which will find us unprepared, indifferent, non-active. Lloyd George has just declared to the University of Oxford, "The next war will blot out our civilization. The Dove of Peace is perched on an ammunition dump." Indications point that the next war will be directed by the Communist headquarters from Moscow and their ablest coadjutor will be the Communist Party of America. We are facing the direst peril that has ever confronted our government. Pacifism is a deadly menace. Indifference and contempt are fatuous follies. We have been steadily doped for a quarter of a century. We have been so blind that we would not see. The time has come when we must throw off this lethargy and prepare ourselves to meet a danger in comparison with which all other perils we have encountered dwindle into insignificance.[20]

Americanism stands for Liberty;
Bolshevism is premeditated slavery.

Americanism is a synonym of self-government;
Bolshevism believes in a dictatorship of tyrants.

Americanism means equality;
Bolshevism stands for class division and class rule.

Americanism stands for orderly, continuous, never-ending progress;
Bolshevism stands for retrograding to barbaric government.

Americanism stands for law;
Bolshevism disdains law.

Americanism stands for hope;
Bolshevism stands for despair.

Americanism is founded on family love and family life;
Bolshevism is against family life.

Americanism stands for one wife and one country;
Bolshevism stands for free love and no country.

Americanism means increased production and increased prosperity for all;
Bolshevism stands for destruction, restriction of output, and compulsory poverty.

Americanism believes in strength;
Bolshevism teaches premeditated weakness and inefficiency.

Americanism has taught, and Americans have practiced morality;
Bolshevism teaches and its votaries practice immorality, indecency, cruelty, rape, murder, theft, arson.

Americanism stands for God and good;
Bolshevism is against both God and good.[21]

☆
Who Are the Reds in Our Midst?
What Are Their Plans for America?

Socialists never have anything good to say about the country they
live in. They enjoy all of its rights and privileges and benefit from
its protection and its opportunities, and still they nurse a grudge.
They say the country is all wrong and has been headed wrong for
the past 130 years.[22]

Whenever the Bolsheviki are in power the Christian church is
persecuted with even greater ferocity than in the first three centuries of the Christian era. Nuns are being violated, women made
common property, and license and the lowest passions are rampant.
One sees everywhere death, misery and famine.[23]

The atheism that permeates the whole Russian dictatorship
clearly reflected in the activities of their revolutionary confreres in
the United States, and in their publications they have denounced
our religion and our God as "lies." This gives added significance
to the revolutionary attitude toward the Christian church and the
Christian religion. The prohibition of religious schools and the
teaching or studying of religion, except in private, would necessitate
the abolition of 194,759 Sunday schools in the United States
and a great number of seminaries, colleges and universities from
enjoying the institution that has become an important part of their
lives and is one of the great moral influences of the nation. Catholic
schools, colleges and seminaries to the number of 6,681 would be
suppressed. Church property of the value of $1,676,600,582
would be confiscated and 41,926,854 (census of 1916) members

of 227,487 church organizations would be subjected to the domination of an atheist dictatorship.[24]

Of the arrested and suspected anarchists and communists in
America, nine out of every ten are foreigners. They come from
different parts of Europe—a large proportion coming from Russia,
however; and some of them have spent many years in the United
States. Of the American element, it is said that as a class they are
less bloodthirsty and less given to violence than the foreigners.
Many of them border on the verge of insanity; many others are
women with minds gone slightly awry, morbid, senseless and seeking the sensational, craving for something, they know not what.[25]

More menacing because more infectious, and less amenable to
any sort of treatment, is this Bolshevism of romance—of imagina-
tive adventure. It is this Bolshevism of restless souls who are forever
trying to escape the actual and the obvious by winged journeys
into the realm of the remote and the wonderful. Its disciples are
utopians, Greenwich Villagers, wealthy persons with idle hands
and still more idle brains, dilettante of various sorts, young persons
freshly out of college, editorial writers on our so-called liberal
journals of "ideas and opinions"—an indescribable assortment of
the fitful and fretful worshippers of the "Cult of Something
Else."[26]

It was announced in the papers last week that "a score of
wealthy New York women are said to be under espionage by the
Department of Justice 'because they are entertaining and giving
comfort to the criminals who have been convicted of offenses against
the federal statutes.' " It is also stated that "this same group of
women have been financing the publication of radical newspapers
which openly demand a revolution for the purpose of seizing all
industries. 'Parlor Radicals' are accused of providing the funds
for the publication of some of the most expensive pamphlets and
booklets ever published, all carrying propaganda in opposition to
the American form of government. Let us hope that the Department
of Justice will not only be successful in its attempts to bring to
public view and execration these educated and criminally sentimental notoriety-seeking women, but will lock them up, if not in
jails, at least in psychopathic wards.[27]

The Bolsheviki Government of Russia issued a decree that

nationalized all women between the ages of 18 and 45 years. This so-called nationalization process was nothing other than marrying them collectively to the State. This law made them public property for all Bolsheviki Government citizens. (n.b.caos.) They termed it, "giving women their freedom," but instead it was nothing more than enslaving them.

In some parts of Russia today, it also is "help yourself" to your neighbor's young wife and daughters, and change them once a month, if you like![28]

This free love idea is undoubtedly the greatest attack against the female sex that has ever been devised. Even the lowest form of savages who indulge in the wildest spirit of cannibalism is far superior to such barbarism as this indecent, hellish state license. Never before has any portion of the world made such a retrograding step in civilization as Russia in her reign of Bolshevism. Purity of mind and body, which the world idolizes today, which was built up by religious teachings and sensible governmental laws, is cast in the dust-bin of history by them. What has free love done for Russia? Every woman can be a legalized prostitute. Homes are wrecked, the joys of the fireside with the children's mirth when at play are gone. Everybody does as he or she likes. The woman who is your wife today, may be another man's wife tomorrow.[29]

The attack upon the family as an institution finds expression not only in libidinous literature, but "birth control" movements engineered by radicals. The American people discovered that the recently proposed constitutional amendment ostensibly aimed at child labor had the united support of reds and pinks because it gave the state complete control over youth during the entire period of parental control as it has heretofore existed, namely, up to eighteen years, and that the ultimate purpose, as proclaimed in communist journals was to make all children wards of the state.[30]

The American people are persistently, even viciously prone to be too generous, too magnanimous, and to "chide mildly the erring" even when the erring deserves the swift kick into outer darkness.[31] Under the fatal spell of our perfectly idiotic eagerness for quantity in immigration, we have flung aside nearly all considerations making for quality! America has become the dumping ground for the ashes and cinders of all nations. For every betterment that has come to us from across the sea, we have received at least one deterioration. Presently the Anglo-Saxon stock will disappear, by submergence, and the result will be a nation of indecipherables, mongrels, with the mental handicaps and the vices of all contributors sharply accentuated. We have tolerated a fast-growing colony of rattlesnakes that now in a crisis boldly crawl out in the open and defy us.[32]

People are inclined to look upon communists as an army of crazy fanatics, and they say "Although in a country under despotic rule it may succeed, yet in this republic where one man is as free as another, though communism may cause some trouble, it will certainly not be long-lived.

But men should not allow themselves to be lulled into such false security. The signs of the times are full of portents. By the flames of Pittsburg we can discern approaching a terrible trial for free institutions in this country. The communist is here. His presence means something. Never tiring, never ceasing, he is today filling men's minds with his theories. Communistic societies have grown up. Their secret meetings are everywhere held. They have regiments of soldiers in constant drill, prepared with arms and ammunition. They have their newspaper organs, their politicians. Their cause is pleaded in Congress by ranting demagogues. Are these signs of peace? Are these indications of death to communism? Indeed, at the present time they may not be causing trouble, but, during this season of delusive quiet, they are gaining strength and preparing themselves for the next contest; and the longer they are left at rest the more formidable an enemy will there be to contend with.

These men ridicule life and laugh at the earnest efforts of men whose life-time toil has resulted in continuous, permanent advancement of the human race. They believe in the achievement of Paradise in a day—yes in an hour! Force, violence, uproar—a continuous Donneybrook Fair—is their idea of progress! They are the hurry-up, get-it-over-quick boys, who have retarded the progress of the human race more than all the oppressors of the centuries.

They are against all government. They are against all morality. They are against all progress. They are against all decency. They preach no doctrine of construction and their policy of destruction is futile, weak, ignorantly vicious and ineffective. From Bakounin to Haywood they have taught every vile act, every despicable deed, to be right if it is done by one of their members.[33]

Poisoning canned food by placing rodents in the cans, destroying vineyards, placing spikes in logs, burning mills, causing industrial accidents, forging checks—as they do in Russia: all these things are holy in their sight! They look upon the government (the State) as an exhaustless mine from which each one may draw according to his desires.[34]

Joined to the radicals, or so-called reds, are the "parlor socialists"—the "pink bolshevists," or, as they prefer to be called, "the intelligentzia." These people are dangerous. They lend their names and their support to groups and movements which will destroy organized society if their end is accomplished. Few of them really realize the character of the destructive force with which they are playing. They patronize and support certain disloyal and pink radical sheets which presume to carry on a program of "higher criticism" of politics and religion—publications which were devoted to pacifism and pro-Germanism during the war and are now dedicated to the Red cause, but in such a manner as to mislead the uninformed. These prints, which can easily be identified, find their way through their false front into thousands of homes which would not receive them in their true colors. These same misguided persons join forces with the aiders and abettors of the Red cause—societies organized to pledge men and women to refuse aid to their country in any way in the event of a future war; at the same time they demand pardon of the slackers, traitors and assassins of our country whom they characterize as "political prisoners."

Under the guise of advocating freedom of speech, they seek the repeal of laws which today hold in check the mad dogs of society. Every true, intelligent supporter of the Government knows that the real purpose behind the efforts to repeal these laws is to give greater scope to the efforts of the revolutionists to undermine society and destroy our Government.[35]

The men and women who are behind this conspiracy are not amateurs; they are skilled in creating distrust and stirring up disorder. They have a record of what they persist in calling a success in Russia—and it was successful destructively. They are dedicated to this work and their hours are twenty-four a day for seven days every week. They are bitter, envious, determined and cruelly vicious. Beware of them![36]

What Is to Be Done—to Save America?

Now the question must arise in the minds of everyone. "What can be done to meet the exigencies of this critical time?" And it behooves every citizen and true patriot, every lover of liberty, to rouse himself so that with concerted action all the moral and political forces of the nation may be brought to bear on this common enemy; and this terrible conflagration extinguished.[37]

Believing, as we do, that Socialism menaces all that Christian civilization has achieved and that it should therefore be extirpated, root and branch, from every soil where it has found a foothold, we face some very serious questions.[38]

Every citizen is either a constructive or destructive unit in the national organism. If indifferent or inactive he automatically becomes an ally of destructive elements. In this fight, which has been wholly lost to civilization in Russia and partly lost in other European nations under our very eyes, you are either on one side or the other.[39] Not infrequently, for example, the claim is made by our little brothers of the bolsheviki that the United States Government is under the "domination of big interests" though every department of the law-making and law-enforcing branches of our government is dominated by public servants chosen by the American people themselves.

Americanism means nothing more or less than a government by law as contrasted with a government by mob violence. It means a government, not by statute, not by legislative action whether subject to a referendum or otherwise. It means a government, so far as statutory enactments are concerned, by legislation which observes the rules established by the fundamental law, constitutional and otherwise, governing the property and personal rights of individuals. It means a government which is founded upon the individual right of private property and of certain personal rights and liberties, including the right to contract and be protected in the contract made; the right of freedom of religious worship; the right of every individual to acquire, to own and to hold as his own, the fruits of his initiative, his capacity, his effort and his thrift. It is a government which holds out encouragement and incentive to individual effort and thrift because it is a government which has established an independent judicial department whose function it is to declare invalid any legislation which is repugnant to those rights.[40]

Ours is a poorer soil for social injustices to grow in than you will find anywhere else in the world. There is a sense of the "square deal" among us and a freedom to fight for one's rights that stand guard against injustices.[41] We wail about our 47 cent dollars, but our dollars are the best values in the world at the present time.

We are not in want; we are all employed; we are, in fact, the most fortunate people in the world with the least reason for being discontented.[42] Here in this great open field of opportunity called America, its very soul vibrant with the largest measure of human liberty consistent with orderly government, every man carves out his own fortune, makes his own way in the world, and if he fails it is because he did not find his job and stick to it.[43] The "RED" is not a righteous or honest protest against alleged defects in our present political and economic organization of society. It does not represent the radicalism of progress. It is not a movement of liberty-loving persons. It is a distinctly criminal and dishonest movement in the desire to obtain possession of other people's property by violence and robbery. A justification of such a course necessarily means the destruction of government and the destruction of religion.[44]

For instance, how many people know that frequent and loud assertion that the great bulk of the wealth of the nation is held by a small number of rich men, is wholly false; and that the fact is, on the contrary, that seven-eighths of our national income goes to those with incomes of $5,000 or less, and but one-eighth to those with incomes above $5,000.[45]

There is no reform which cannot be had by honest, patriotic work in this representative democracy—the first successful democracy the world has ever seen. The American people, when properly approached, and properly educated along the lines of justice and right, will banish every injustice, and open every man to the fullest opportunity for the attainment of all things of which he is worthy.[46]

Therefore, please note that our p.esent national problems are not primarily political and are not primarily economic. These are important phases, but they are secondary. *Our problems are primarily spiritual, since they concern the spirit of the American people.* Loyalty to America is essentially loyalty to its ideals. Defensive loyalty is the defense of these ideals when they are in danger; constructive loyalty is the application of these ideals to new problems of national life.[47]

A Program To Save America

Let us restore the freedom of the old America, the freedom that enabled the young man to look into the future with confidence, knowing that the only limitations to his achievements were the boundaries of his intellect and the measure of his energy. America is worth saving, not only as a land in which men and women may be free and increasingly prosperous, but as a land and a government under which character can be built, individual capacity given opportunity for free exercise, and cooperation on the widest scale promoted not only for private advantage but for the public good.[48]

Nothing so confounds the socialist or Bolshevist who is denouncing "the terrible industrial conditions of this country" as to confront him with the facts regarding the industrial and political progress actually made. When we see that eighty percent of the "ill-smelling sweatshops" and the "reeking tenement houses" have been abolished and also that ninety-five per cent of all child workers under fourteen years of age have disappeared from the factories, mines, and mills of the country, we have a showing that constitutes one of the most important antidotes to the revolutionaries.[49]

The real Americans of our country now must keep wide awake, alert and on guard to meet any and every emergency that may arise through the traitorous and seditious elements who abhor all restraint and duty, and live as blood-sucking parasites on the country that they curse with their baneful presence. Beware of treachery and sabotage; and when either are found, strike, and strike hard![50]

It is the general opinion that the menace has become acute, and that if we would save our institutions every American individually must help combat the forces of revolutionary radicalism, in schools, in colleges, churches, charitable and philanthropic institutions and wherever found. If it is impossible to clear these organizations of radicals by individual protest, the majority of writers agree that the time has come for united and organized action on the part of all who believe in the Constitution and our forms of government.[51]

1. We must enforce our educational laws and make them compulsory, and see not only that this is done, but that education is conducted in the English language and is thoroughly American in its character. We believe that only so shall America become the hope of the world.

This will not come about, however, until treason-texts have been removed from our schools; for the ideals instilled in childhood always become the inspirations of later years. The heritage of our past and the spiritual treasures handed down to us, can only be preserved by guarding our school doors against the vile propaganda which is being so persistently urged among us, by the use of historical and other text books which are not based upon anything but perverted and distorted facts.

2. We should not allow foreigners changing their names, to assume names belonging to long-established American families. They should be compelled to choose names as they would be permitted to take in the lands from which they came. Nor should we allow public meetings to be held where addresses in foreign tongues, extolling foreign culture and customs, and criticising our own, are the feature of the occasion. Our aims and ideals are distinctly dissimilar and on a higher plane from those of most foreign nations, and it is not only unpatriotic but disloyal to countenance in any way acts which lower these ideals.[52]

3. Deny the use of the mails to all propaganda advocating a revolution.

4. Perpetually prohibit Bolshevik teachers from teaching in any American schools, colleges or universities.

5. Expel from the country all alien Bolsheviks, socialists, and

anarchists. (Arrest and deportation of these Bolsheviki are as necessary as cauterizing a wound to prevent gangrene.)[53]

6. Prohibit Bolsheviks from holding public office.

7. Make it unlawful for any employer of labor to appoint or
keep a Bolshevik in his employ.

8. Prohibit the use of the red flag in processions and in as-
semblages.

9. Promote the Americanization of aliens.[54]

Let us line up our national defenses against anarchy and chaos,
and see what they look like. Here they are:

1. The American Press
2. The old Republican Party
3. The old Democratic Party
4. The Churches, of all dominations
5. The American Federation of Labor
6. Native-American women, everywhere.
7. The Service Men, of the Army and Navy
8. The Boy Scouts
9. The Police of all cities

The above forces make a goodly array. If they are all awakened,
and aroused to the point of vigorous action, the American Bolshevists can be held in control, without any revolutions of civil
war.[55]

There has never been in the history of the world a stronger, more
active, better financed or more thoroughly organized coalition, military or otherwise, menacing the peace, prosperity and democratic
ideals of the world, than these which are now allied in purpose
and in activity to divorce forever from every form of government
all regard for individual rights which were established as part of
English and American civilization.[56] We have a government truly
representative of the people themselves—a government under which
all have equal opportunity. *Our* propaganda, *our* truths, are hidden
away in our hearts and minds. A propaganda of lies will stand
unless it is answered by truths plainly and bluntly told. We must
tell the truth to remain free.[57]

What are we going to do about it? We know that we have
partriotism and plenty of it. All of us are ready to fight and die
for our ideals. We have proved that. God gave us the clear-eyed

sight to discern the danger signals and common sense to read their meaning. Thanks to the Benign Power which has safeguarded the destinies of America, in spite of our easy-going tolerance and our sublime belief in our own sanity, it is not yet too late. But the menace is great; the crisis is imminent. And let thanks be given again that at last America is waking up.[58]

2

RED SCARE:
WHAT DID HAPPEN?

IN 1920 a salesman in Waterbury, Connecticut, was sentenced to six months in jail for having remarked to a customer that Lenin was "the brainiest" or "one of the brainiest" political leaders in the world. In 1919 a citizen of Indiana, in a fit of rage, shot and killed an alien who yelled, "to hell with the United States." The jury deliberated for two minutes before acquitting the killer. In Weirton, West Virginia, during the great steel strike of 1919, a mob of enraged citizens forced 118 aliens, who were on strike, to kiss the American flag. In western Pennsylvania, steel workers were tried and fined in cases where the charge was "smiling at the State Police." In New York City a riot ensued in the Waldorf Astoria hotel when a man shouted, "to hell with the flag." The American Legion, in that year, demanded that "enemy aliens" who were buried in Arlington Cemetery "be removed . . . and given proper burial elsewhere." In the state of Washington, school teachers were forbidden to answer student's questions concerning Bolshevism or "any other heresies." Twenty-eight states passed laws banning the display of Red flags. The vice-president of the United States cited as a manifestation of the growth of radicalism the fact that Radcliffe College debators upheld the affirmative: "Resolved that the recognition of labor unions by employers is essential to collective bargaining." In Centralia, Washington, after radicals shot and killed three members of the American Legion, local citizens removed a member of the IWW from jail, castrated him, lynched him by throwing him off a bridge with a rope around his neck, and then riddled his body with bullets. Senator McKellor of Tennessee argued that native-born American citizens who were radical should be sent to a penal colony in Guam. In 1920 the legislature of the state of New York expelled five duly elected members of the Socialist party.

The great Red Scare of 1919–1920 was in progress—a nationwide antiradical hysteria provoked by a mounting fear and anxiety that a Bolshevik revolution in America was imminent— a revolution that would destroy property, church, home, marriage, civility, and the American way of life. The essence of the hysteria was the disparity between the enormous anxiety induced by the fear of a Red conspiracy and the fact that no Red threat of any serious capability existed in the United States. The fear was based on fantasy. The origin and nature of this fantasy and the extraordinary response to it is the subject at issue.

Less than three months after the armistice was signed in 1917 thirty-five thousand shipyard workers in Seattle, Washington, struck for higher wages and shorter hours. When management refused to negotiate, the Seattle Central Labor Council, which contained a number of radicals, voted to wage a sympathy strike. Local AF of L unions agreed to cooperate. *The Seattle Union Record*, a labor publication, asked the public to be calm, and assured the city that the strike committee would feed the people, care for the sick, and preserve law and order. Seattle, which was a stronghold of the Industrial Workers of the World (IWW or Wobblies), became so terribly frightened that department and grocery stores were deluged with customers purchasing the necessaries of life in anticipation of a long and bloody siege. Owners of hardware stores reported that they could not satisfy the sudden demand for guns. *The Seattle Union Record* did not calm the public fear when it editorialized: "We are undertaking the most tremendous move ever made by labor in this country. . . . We are starting on a road that leads

—NO ONE KNOWS WHERE." *The Seattle Star*, however, urged union men not to resort to the general strike: "Stop before it's too late. You are being urged to use a dangerous weapon— the general strike . . . this is America—not Russia." In a front page cartoon the *Seattle Post Intelligencer* depicted a red banner flying above the American flag, with the caption, "Not in a thousand years."

On February 6, sixty thousand workmen struck, and the economic life of Seattle came to a halt. The strike committee permitted essential public services to continue. Public safety was not endangered. No one was arrested. The city was not left without food, coal, water, heat, or light. There was no violence. Some Wobblies distributed pamphlets urging revolution, but it was clearly a strike for higher wages and better hours. It was not a revolution.

Yet the mayor of Seattle, Ole Hanson, referred to the strikers as "scoundrels" who "want to take possession of our American government to duplicate the anarchy of Russia." Hanson requested federal troops and ensured the good people of Seattle that he could guarantee the safety of their city, which was, in fact, quite "safe." "The time has come," he said, "for the people in Seattle to show their Americanism . . . the anarchists in the community shall not rule its affairs." The revolutionary threat had been sounded.

For a variety of reasons the strike committee terminated their activities. The Mayor announced that, "the rebellion is quelled, the test came and was met by Seattle unflinchingly." *The Seattle Star* notified its readers: "FULL STEAM AHEAD . . . today this Bolshevik-sired nightmare is at an end." A replica was published of the cartoon with the Red banner in shreds and the American flag waving. The caption read: "Our Flag is still there."

Headlines in the national press echoed the Hansonian alarm: "Reds Directing Seattle Strike—to Test Chance for Revolution," "The Seattle Strike is Marxian," "a revolutionary movement aimed at existing government," "The stepping stone to a bolshevized America." *The Chicago Tribune,* advocating the domino theory, warned that "it is only a middling step from Petrograd to Seattle." Senators and congressmen followed the line. Senator King of Utah was sure that the strike organizers were Bolsheviks and announced, "From Russia they came and to Russia they should be made to go."

Shortly after the strike Mayor Hanson, who had become a national celebrity, resigned his office and toured the country. In dozens of lectures he warned of the dangers of Bolshevism and the infiltration of the Reds into the labor movement. In seven months he earned $38,000 in lecture fees—more than five times his annual salary as mayor of Seattle.

The Red scare was underway and organized labor was its first victim.

During the next six months of 1919 it became commonplace for major American newspapers to describe strikes—violent or nonviolent—as "crimes against society," "conspiracies against the government," and "plots to establish communism." The press had ample opportunity to make the charge because 175 strikes occurred in March of 1919, 248 in May, 303 in June, 360 in July, and 373 in August.

By March of 1919, newspapers, in increasing numbers, began to publish rumors of bomb plots uncovered by the police and police reports of secret radical conspiracies. These reports rarely cited sources other than the customary "reliable" ones. The stories were rarely supported by facts. The plots were usually presented as ominous, and often, as foreign inspired. The Department of Justice, in April of 1919, disclosed an alleged anarchist conspiracy to seize a government arsenal in Pittsburgh. The department reported that captured explosives were to be used to "lay the city in ruins." The capture of anarchist plotters was announced. No additional details were reported to the public.

On April 28, 1919, a bomb was found in Mayor Hanson's

mail. The following afternoon, a servant in the home of former Senator Thomas Hardwick of Georgia opened a package that contained a bomb which exploded. The servant lost both hands, and Mrs. Hardwick was badly burned. Although Hardwick, as chairman of the Committee on Immigration, had proposed legislation to exclude alien agitators, he was generally known as a liberal.

The next day a clerk in the parcel post division of the New York Post Office read about the Hardwick bomb. The newspaper described the package in which the bomb was sent as being approximately six inches long by three inches, wrapped in brown paper, and, like the Hanson bomb, having a return address marked Gimbel Brothers of New York. The clerk remembered that he had seen packages that day which he had not mailed because of insufficient postage. He returned to the post office and found sixteen such packages addressed among others, to Attorney General Palmer, Justice Holmes, Judge Landis, the postmaster general, the secretary of labor, the commissioner of immigration, J. P. Morgan, and John D. Rockefeller. The police department examined the packages and found bombs in every one. Some of the packages had been mailed. The total number ultimately accounted for was thirty-six. Some of the addresses were ultraconservatives or prominent antiradicals. Others, like Justice Holmes, were regarded as liberals.

None of the men who mailed the packages were ever found. With some exceptions the press drew the conclusion that the bombs were part of a gigantic radical plot: "Reds Planned May Day Murders." Many congressmen joined the chorus. A very few papers thoughtfully observed that the bombs were probably the work of a few deranged anarchists. One paper opined that to perceive a Bolshevik plot in the attempted bombing was "to convict ourselves of a mild form of hysteria." A few radical journals suggested that the bombs were a plant, designed to produce an hysterical antiradical public opinion. But officials of the New York Police Department stated that the bombings looked like an IWW and Bolshevik plot. Officials of the Justice Department theorized that the bombings signaled that May Day would initiate a reign of terror. Their view would turn out to be the more popular interpretation.

On May Day, 1919, radicals in several cities staged rallies, mass meetings, and paraded with red flags. Riots ensued in Boston, New York, and in Cleveland where one person was killed, forty injured, and one hundred and six arrested. In New York City, mobs broke up dozens of radical meetings and 1700 policemen were needed to prevent a mob invasion of a radical meeting in Madison Square Garden. Mounted policemen charged and dispersed paraders in Chicago, Detroit, and other cities. In Cleveland, army tanks and trucks, policemen and mobs attacked 20,000 people who were listening to speeches in a public square. More than one hundred were shot or beaten and two men died. Many newspapers throughout the country now warned that the riots were probably dress rehearsals for a revolution. The move to "curb Bolshevism" spread. *The Salt Lake Tribune* editorialized, "Free speech has been carried to the point where it is an unrestrained menace." Papers in New Orleans, Seattle, and Detroit, however, pleaded for tolerance and urged that fear of a Red revolution in America was unwarranted. A historian of the period has written that for many Americans, "the May Day riots provided evidence both of the strength of American radicalism and of the radical's willingness to use force to achieve their ends."

One month later, on June 2, explosions killing two people shattered public and private dwellings in eight cities. The intended victims included the mayor of Cleveland, a Massachusetts state legislator, a Paterson silk manufacturer, a Boston municipal judge, New York City and Pittsburgh federal judges, a Philadelphia jeweler, and Attorney General Palmer, the front of whose home was demolished. None of the intended victims— if that is what they were—were injured. Fragments of a body

were found near Palmer's home along with about fifty copies
of an anarchist pamphlet titled "Plain Words."

> Class war is on and cannot close
> but with a complete victory for the
> international prolitariat . . .
> There will have to be murder;
> we will kill . . . there will have to
> be destruction; we will destroy . . .
> we are ready to do anything and
> everything to suppress the capitalist
> class.

None of the alleged bomb throwers were apprehended. Although, again, some newspapers argued that it was folly to see
a massive revolutionary uprising behind the bombings, this is
precisely what most papers suggested. The attorney general
publicly stated that the bombings were part of a planned effort
by radicals to take over the United States.

The press intensified its demand that the government begin
an all out antiradical attack. The attorney general responded
and readied the Bureau of Investigation for an antiradical assault.
All of the agencies of the federal government concerned with
crime were placed at the disposal of the bureau. Congress began
to make preparations. Senator King of Utah prepared a bill
making it a capital offense to transport bombs in interstate
commerce. Senator Walsh of Montana proposed a sedition bill
which provided for a $5000 fine or five years in prison, or both,
for urging the overthrow of the United States government, displaying, in public or private, the symbols of revolutionary
socialism, or distributing anarchist literature through the mails.
The attorney general proposed similar legislation and informed
the Senate that the wartime Espionage and Sedition laws could
not be used to curb radicals operating in peacetime. Congress
responded by appropriating an extra $500,000 for the Justice
Department to ferret out radicals.

While the bombings and May Day riots were taking place

during the spring of 1919, radical and liberal labor groups were planning a nationwide strike to protest the conviction of Thomas Mooney, a radical labor organizer who had been sentenced to death for a bombing which occurred during the San Francisco Preparedness Day Parade. Because there was substantial doubt about Mooney's guilt, he became a symbol of the union's fight for social justice.

The general strike was scheduled for July 4. For several weeks prior to Independence Day papers throughout the country predicted that the strike would cripple the country, cause great suffering, and unleash a reign of violence and terror. On July 4, the *San Francisco Examiner* and the *Cincinnati Enquirer* featured bold headlines: "Reign of Terror Planned;" "Stolen Explosives to Be Used;" "Plans for Widespread Violence and Murder." These headlines and the stories that followed—like almost every rumor of apocalyptic destruction that appeared in 1919—were unsubstantiated.

The anxiety created by these continuous warnings must have been substantial. Private citizens and public officials took emergency precautions for what they assumed would be a holocaust. In Chicago, the entire police force and one thousand private volunteers were placed on emergency standby and two army companies were moved into the city. Federal agents were deployed across large areas of the Northwest in anticipation of IWW uprisings. In Oakland, California, known radicals were jailed on July 4 as a precautionary measure. Police forces in Boston, Philadelphia, San Francisco, and other cities were in full force or on standby alert. The mayor of New York City suspended all meetings scheduled for July 4 which he thought might cause trouble or incite riot—including meetings of patriotic societies. The police—about eleven thousand men—were maintained on twenty-four hour duty guarding the Stock Exchange, the homes of some prominent public figures, and Federal, State, City, and County buildings. Many hundred private citizens were sworn in as special deputies. The fear and precautions were truly national in scope. Each apparently fed the other.

On Independence Day nothing extraordinary occurred—except these extraordinary precautions and an extraordinary nationwide wave of anxiety. There was no general strike.

A few newspapers then suggested that the "crisis" was precipitated by conservative interests to create a more strident antiradical public opinion. Most newspapers, however, made an attempt to recoup by claiming that the widespread precautions which they urged, did, in fact, prevent the planned disorder.

The summer of 1919 passed quietly, as though the proponents of the Red scare and the radicals had taken a holiday. Then, on September 9, the Boston police struck. The police, whose maximum salary was $1600, had attempted on several occasions to raise wages and improve conditions of work—without success. Finally, they made plans to affiliate with the AF of L. In part, because of the rapidly escalating belief in the radicalism of unions, and in part, because policemen just did not join unions, the move was bitterly opposed by city officials, the public, and the press. Police Commissioner Curtis declared that "a police officer cannot consistently belong to a union and perform his sworn duty." The police asked for and were given an AF of L charter. Nineteen strike leaders were tried and found guilty of violating the commissioner's orders. By a vote of 1134 to 2 the police decided to strike. Although there is absolutely no evidence that the police had any radical aspirations whatsoever, one Boston newspaper predicted that the strike was doomed to fail because "behind Boston in this skirmish with Bolshevism stands Massachusetts and behind Massachusetts stands America." This was no doubt comforting to Bostonians, if somewhat puzzling to their policemen. *The Boston Herald* announced, with sorrow and sobriety, that it was simply inconceivable that Bolshevism should be permitted to explode in the city which gave birth to the American Revolution.

The press frightened Bostonians so severely that a panic ensued. Private security guards were posted all over the city. Many ex-soldiers and American Legionnaires volunteered their services and a voluntary police force was quickly formed. President Lowell of Harvard assured students who volunteered that their grades would not be affected.

On the first evening of the actual police strike, small groups of hoodlums removed tires from automobiles and knocked hats off pedestrians. One group forced a trolley car to stop by throwing stones at it and then forced the passengers to exit. In the downtown shopping area windows were smashed, goods were looted, and fruit stands were overturned. There were small riots in three sections of the city and some of the volunteer policemen were pelted with mud. In more serious incidents about the city, three men were killed. The total damage from two days of looting amounted to about $34,000. At no time was the flow of life-supporting goods and services endangered and at no time did the number of rioters or looters exceed small numbers. Nothing approaching anarchy or even widespread disorder occurred. What disorder there was seemed more related to fear than actual threat. Yet on the day after the strike began every Boston newspaper suggested that radicals were behind it. Prominent citizens were quoted who characterized the strikers as "agents of Lenin" and "bolshevists." *Life*, a magazine directed toward middle class audiences, stated that the police had "lined up with the Bolsheviki."[2]

Robert Murray, who wrote the most comprehensive narrative of the Red scare, summarized the press's interpretation of the strike.

. . . the local press exaggerated the real extent of lawlessness in the city. *The Evening Transcript* carried large pictures showing several looted stores and implied that the destruction on Tremont Street, opposite Boston Common, was worse than on Nevsky Prospect, Petrograd, during the Bolshevik Revolution. Other papers described the night just passed as a "Bolshevist nightmare filled with such lawlessness, disorder, looting . . . as was never known in this city. . . ."

Newspapers outdid one another in the amount of editorial excretion heaped upon the Boston strikers. They immediately took up the cry of "radicalism" emanating from the Boston press, and vied with each other in pointing out the most "facts" which proved the strike was nothing less than revolution. Scare words such as "Bolshevist," "Soviet," "radical," "chaos," and "terror," were used indiscriminately and served as the framework around which exaggerated stories were built. Cartoonists depicted Boston as being completely under the control of thugs as the city's police stood idly by, and editorial phrases such as "Boston and Bedlam," "Sovietism in Boston," and "Desertion—Not A Strike" were commonplace. The policemen, agreed the press, had absolutely no right to strike and by their action indicated what would happen all over the country if more workers became inspired with communistic ideas. "Bolshevism in the United States is no longer a spector," warned *The Philadelphia Public-Ledger.* "Boston in chaos reveals its sinister substance." "Lenin and Trotsky are right on their way," screamed *The Wall Street Journal.*[3]

The word spread to San Francisco where the *Examiner* reported in an eight column headline: "POLICE STRIKE: RIOTS IN BOSTON—Gangs Range Boston Streets, Women Are Attacked, And Stores Are Robbed, Shots Are Fired." Other newspapers had their own versions. *The Rocky Mountain News* headlines reported "TROOPS TURN MACHINE GUNS ON BOSTON MOBS." *The Salt Lake Tribune* reported, "TERROR REIGNS IN CITY."

Just as the Seattle strike had been converted by the press into a Bolshevik holocaust, so too was the Boston police strike. The transformation, as in the case of Seattle, included dire predictions of future anarchy and revolution. *The New York Times* suggested that the police strike provided ". . . not merely a glimpse, but a long look at the fires of anarchy and crime that smoulder asleep under civilization."[4] Warnings of potential doom, a stock in trade of the press during the fall of 1919, raised the level of public anxiety upon which the growing hysteria fed.

As in the Seattle strike, high ranking public officials aided the transformation and increased anxiety with apocalyptic predictions. Senator Myers of Montana warned that unless immediate steps were taken to curb radicalism in America, "the nation will see a Soviet government set up within two years" Calvin Coolidge became a national figure when he refused to negotiate with the police and cabled Samual Gompers: "There is no right to strike against the public safety by anybody, anywhere, anytime."

The issues of the strike, like dozens of other issues in 1919, were being defined in terms of an apocalyptic confrontation between American civilization and Bolshevik terror and anarchy. This characterization was the joint product of the press and government officials. The government lent its legitimacy to the myth of the Red conspiracy. President Wilson himself not only called the strike "a crime against civilization," but he described Bolshevism as a fatal "poison." Despite the fact that a few newspapers and liberal journals saw the strikes for what they were—legitimate demands to redress grievances—the great majority of newspapers insisted that many of the strikes were preliminary coordinated attempts to foment a Bolshevik revolution in America.

Although the number of strikes during the winter and spring of 1919 was unusually large, and although a few strikes involved as many as twenty or thirty thousand strikers, the productivity of American industry was not seriously lessened, and the productive apparatus was not seriously damaged. Then in September of 1919, the month of the Boston Police strike, about 365,000 steel workers walked out. The strike—the largest in American history —was enormously effective and left the steel industry crippled.

Working and living conditions among steelworkers were appalling. The average work week for the entire industry was about sixty-nine hours. Approximately half the work force put in a twelve hour day and worked seven days a week. The average annual income of unskilled steelworkers was $1,460. The estimated minimum subsistence level for a family of five in 1919 was $1,575.

The strike was organized under the leadership of the American Federation of Labor—not the IWW. The overwhelming majority of the organizers and strike leaders were old-time AF of L organizers—not radicals. Almost all the strike literature was concerned with immediate demands for wages, hours, and conditions of work—not with socialist objectives or with the need for an American revolution. The right to bargain collectively was the root demand. In addition to this demand, the strike committee asked for an eight hour day, a six day week, abolition of the twenty-four hour shift, double pay for overtime, the abolition of company unions, seniority, and the reinstatement of all men who were discharged for union activities with full salary for time lost. Almost every would-be radical leader was excluded by the union from a position of responsibility. The strike leadership even opposed the "one big union" idea—the one truly radical proposal then current in labor circles.

Some strike leaders had been socialists and would become communists after the strike. A very small number of organizers were radical and a small amount of radical literature was distributed. A few AF of L leaders had talked about socializing America's basic industries, but the idea did not proceed beyond idle speculation.

The U.S. Steel Corporation and its President, Judge Elbert Gary, attempted to break the strike by creating the impression that it had little to do with demands for wages and hours but was instead a communist conspiracy and part of a larger plan to cripple American industry and foment a Bolshevik revolution. This succeeded, and played a major role in escalating the national antiradical hysteria. Building upon the fears of communist infiltration previously generated by the Seattle and Boston strikes, Judge Gary initiated a nationwide public relations campaign to create the stereotype of rampant Bolshevism in the steel industry. Testifying before the Congress, Judge Gary predicted that a victory for the strikers would be a first step toward "industrial upheaval and perhaps social upheaval" and "the control of the government and the established rule of the minority in American politics." Miles Poindexter, one of the many senators who concurred, remarked on the floor of the Senate, "I am convinced that the increasing number of strikes is based on a desire to overthrow our government, destroy all government, and establish communism."

In his efforts to create this impression, Judge Gary was aided by the executives of many major corporations, hundreds of private detectives and labor spies, agents of the Justice Department and Military Intelligence, senators, representatives, local police departments, vigilantes, superpatriots, American Legionnaires, the secretary of labor, presidential advisers, the attorney general, local newspapers controlled by U.S. Steel, and many distinguished national newspapers including *The New York Times*. A former employee of the Library of Congress, J. Edgar Hoover, who had recently been appointed chief of General Intelligence (antiradical) Division of the Bureau of Investigation of the Department of Justice contributed to the portrait of the strike as a Bolshevik tactic. He dispatched "captured" radical documents to the press as "proof of the Red conspiracy" and initiated the first large scale attempt by the United States government to maintain a centralized file of radicals in the headquarters of the Department. This file became a major source of information, and will be discussed, in greater detail, in a later chapter.

U.S. Steel was one of many American corporations that used large numbers of private detectives as labor spies. The labor spy would infiltrate unions, urge laborers not to join unions, and promote antistrike activities. For many corporations, U.S. Steel included, the spy was the major source of the information upon which labor policies were formulated. The authors of the most comprehensive and reputable study of the steel strike concluded that "it is undeniable that labor policies in the steel industry rest in considerable part on the reports of 'undercover men' paid directly by the steel companies or hired from concerns popularly known as 'strike busters'." The "operatives" make money by detecting "unionism" one day and "Bolshevism" the next.[5]

Investigators for this study of the steel strike interviewed a federal agent who reported that "90 percent of all radicals arrested and taken into custody were reported by one of the large corporations, either of the coal or steel industry . . ."[6]

One aspect of the process by which "evidence" of Bolshevism among steel workers was pieced together is illustrated from reports on the files of Monessen Foundry and Machine Company —a subsidiary of U.S. Steel. The information was gathered by investigators of the Interchurch World Movement who published "The Report On the Steel Strike of 1919."

A letter was found in the Monessen files which, according to the investigators, was written on "a scrap of dirty paper the size of one's palm."

Charleroi, Pa., Oct. 13th 1919.

Dear Sir:

I am an employee of the Pitts Steele Proct of Allenport. I went to work last Fri and would like to work so I will give you some names of some Belgian dogs that made it so hard for me and my family I had to quite they are a menace to our country so Please keep their names in mind

Yours truly
Over

Charle Ballue
   209 Shady Ave. Charleoi Pa.
Arthur Ballue
   Oakland ave between 3 and 4 st Charleroi Pa.
Tony Jarruse
   208 Shady ave Charleoi Pa
Gus Vanduzene
   312 Shady Ave Charleoi Pa
Albert Balue
   3 st Charleroi Pa
Make these suffer as they are making other just now when you start your mills.

Besides the original letter in the file there was another letter sent on October 15 by the general superintendent of the Pittsburgh Steel Products Company to executives of other companies in the same city. This letter contained the contents of the original anonymous letter—corrected for punctuation, grammar, and spelling—along with the comment, "this is for your information and files."

On the same day, another general superintendent, obviously in receipt of the first letter, sent another letter to the original sender, two other original addressees, and two "new" addressees in which the phrase "leading agitators" was used to describe the "Belgian dogs".

PITTSBURGH STEEL COMPANY
Mill Office
Monessen, Pa., October 15, 1919.

C.J. Mogan, Gen'l Supt.
D.P. King, Ass't Gen'l Supt.
A. Allison, Ass't Gen'l Supt.
Messrs.,
    M. Wilstrom, Pgh. Steel Products.
    U.S. Smiley, American Sheet & Tin Co.
    F.D. Bumbaugh, Monessen Fdry. & Mach. Co.
    J.L. Hoffman, Carnegie Steel Co.
    G.A. Paff, Page Steel & Wire Co.

Dear Sirs:
Enclosed is a list of men who are some of the leading agitators in keeping the men from going to work by all kinds of threats.

Yours very truly,
(Signed) C.J. Mogan,
General Superintendent.

CJM/C

One of the more unusual examples of how U.S. Steel created the portrait of the Steel strike as a Bolshevik conspiracy relates to William Z. Foster, a strike leader. Foster had been a radical prior to the strike and did join the Communist Party after the strike. During the strike, however, he fully supported the immediate demands and did not agitate for revolution. Foster was even attacked by the IWW as an emasculated radical.

Several years prior to the strike Foster wrote a syndicalist pamphlet which had been out of print for years. Thousands of copies were reprinted during the strike—by whom, is not clear —but U.S. Steel officials did distribute copies. Prior to this reprinting, no mention of the pamphlet as a factor in the strike had been made.

The use to which this pamphlet was put in creating the portrait of a Bolshevik strike, along with many other events of the Red Scare, will be analyzed in the next chapter which deals with the larger questions of the process of mythmaking and the creation of pseudoevents. The task at hand, however, is not the detailed analysis of the process, but the description of specific events. Here is how the authors of The Interchurch World Movement Report on the steel strike describe the results of their investigation of the Foster pamphlet:

. . . What induced the newspapers in many states in the first week after September 22 to print on their front pages extensive extracts of a pamphlet called "Syndicalism" by Wm. Z. Foster? Why was "radicalism" charged? Were ideas of political radicalism as inextricably mixed with ideas of industrial radicalism in the actual situation as they were in the published charges? Was there industrial radicalism, that is, ulterior strike aims for something beyond orthodox trade union demands on hours, wages, conditions and organization?

The first facts persistently brought up were: Mr. William Z. Foster, Secretary-Treasurer of the National Committee for Organizing Iron and Steel Workers, and his "Red Book," the above mentioned tract on "Syndicalism." The two must be separated. The "Red Book's" actual relation to the strike is undisputed. No copy of the original book, out of print for several years, was found in the possession of any striker or strike leader. A reprint, which was a facsimile in everything except the price mark and the union label, was widely circulated from the middle of September on by officials of the steel companies. The absence of the union label indicated that the reprint was not in behalf of any labor organization. What organization bore this expense of reproducing the book was not investigated. There was no need to investigate who distributed it. Steel company officials openly supplied it to newspapers, to preachers and investigators. In McKeesport, for example, it was mailed to all the pastors in the city who were then summoned to a meeting with the Mayor, attended also by representatives of the Sheriff, the State Constabulary and the Steel Corporation. The representative of the Steel Corporation, who was the Superintendent of the local corporation plant came well supplied with the "Red Book" and read extracts . . . In cities like New York and Boston, far from the strike areas, newspapers carried extracts from the book as the principal news of the beginning of the strike. The book's relation to the strike, therefore, was in no sense causative: it was injected as a means of breaking the strike.

U.S. Steel used the "Red Book" and other "proofs" to brand the strike as Red. Judge Gary's men, however, attempted to create the illusion that the strike was not only Red but led by Bolsheviks willing and ready to resort to violence and terror. Some violence was initiated by strikers. Most of the violence, however, was initiated or provoked by public authorities and what amounted to a small private army of mercenaries employed by U.S. Steel. Robert Murray describes this aspect of the strike.

From the very beginning the steel companies openly prepared for war and surrounded their plants with guards armed with rifles and riot guns. Also, because of their control over local politics, particularly in western Pennsylvania, the steel corporations strengthened and assumed charge of the law enforcement agencies in many local communities where citizens were sworn in by the droves as special deputies and were armed to prevent picketing and violence. It was estimated, for example, that along the Monongahela from Pittsburgh to Clairton (a distance of twenty miles), 25,000 men were under arms at the onset of the strike and that in some areas there was a deputy sheriff for almost every striker.

Such a condition merely opened the way to violence. Police officials and local deputies were often overzealous in displaying their authority. In certain areas, union meetings were summarily broken up, picket lines were dispersed, and orderly participants were clubbed. In some small mill towns the local mounted police rode over pedestrians on the sidewalks, injuring peaceful groups of men and women. When strikers attempted to defend themselves against such brutality, they were treated ruthlessly. For example, at Farrell, Pennsylvania, in a skirmish between strikers and police arising from the latter's oppressive curtailment of free speech, four strikers were killed and eleven badly wounded.[7]

The rioting and the violence were not reported by the national press as in any way provoked by the police or this private army. Quite the reverse, the violence was taken as proof of the strikers' ruthlessness and revolutionary purpose and as another bit of "evidence" to support the prophecy of an impending and apocalyptic confrontation between American civilization and international Bolshevism. *The Wall Street Journal* was quite certain that Judge Gary was "fighting the battle of the American constitution." One newspaper referred to the strike as "another experiment in Bolshevizing industry." *The Boston Evening Transcript* wrote that the strike ". . . shows the extraordinary hold which Red principles have upon the foreign born populations in the steel districts."

In a most perverse way radicals and the radical press contributed to Judge Gary's cause and to the mounting national fear of revolution by claiming credit for a major role in the strike and that it was part of a grand Bolshevik plan. A few radicals urged striking steelworkers to kill policemen and soldiers. Mother Jones did tell strikers that "We're going to take over the steel mills and run them for Uncle Sam." A communist party newspaper in Chicago urged the workers to greater heights:

Armed force must not prevail . . . Workers act! Out of your mass strikes will come . . . a state of the workers, proletarian dictatorship, which will crush the capitalist as the capitalist state now crushes the workers.

The counterpoint between the small number of American radicals and the antiradical Division of the Justice Department, could not have been more perfect from the viewpoint of its recently appointed chief, J. Edgar Hoover, who again dispatched quotes from radical publications to the press as "proof" of the Red conspiracy.

With fewer than one hundred thousand men still out in January of 1920, the strike committee voted to terminate the strike. At the strike's end, the steelworkers had lost $112,000,000 in wages and had won not a single major demand.

On November 1, 1919, while the steel strike was beginning to wane, 349,000 coal miners left the mines in defiance of a federal restraining order and the national press, mine operators, government officials, and superpatriotic societies joined in a successful effort to identify the strike as another manifestation of imminent revolution and Bolshevik conspiracy.

Coal profits had increased during the war while, as a result of a wage agreement made in September of 1917, wages remained fairly stationary. Although the United Mine Workers, in convention, had officially rejected a proposal to nationalize the mines, there was much sentiment in favor of it. The United Mine Workers convention did endorse a number of demands, which, for 1919, were well beyond traditional and accepted practice. These included a nationwide contract, a sixty percent wage increase, a six hour day, and a five day week. The demands were anathema to the operators who attempted to utilize their novelty as "proof" of the radicalism of the union and the strike. Aware of the tactics utilized by U.S. Steel, John L. Lewis, president of the union and a militant anticommunist, announced the call for a strike:

The United Mine Workers of America are now embarking upon the greatest enterprise ever undertaken in the history of the trades union movement . . . In calling this strike the United Mine Workers have but one object in view, and that is to obtain just recognition of their right to a fair wage and proper working conditions. No other issue is involved and there must be no attempt on the part of anyone to inject into the strike any extraneous purpose.

By the time Lewis made this announcement, however, the issue of American politics, indeed the issue of American life, was Bolshevik conspiracy. The mine operators knew this and attempted, successfully to repeat Judge Gary's strategy. Utilizing the support of some miners for nationalization and the relatively few radical pamphlets distributed at the mines which declared "Miners! Remember! In this Republic of sharks and pimps nothing can be obtained without violence"—the mine operators and superpatriotic societies transformed the strike into a "Bolshevik Revolution," which was the term used by the American Defense Society to describe what the strike would lead to. The leading spokesman for the operators released reports to the press that the strike was ordered by Lenin and Trotsky and financed by Moscow.

As they did in the steel strike, dozens of congressmen and senators took up the cry of Bolshevism. Predictions were made that unless the government acted, America would revert "to a state of barbarism." Once again, President Wilson lent credibility to these claims by describing the strike as "one of the gravest steps ever proposed in this country" and "a grave moral and legal wrong."

The American identification with nineteenth century laissez faire was so powerful that some of the miners' demands which went somewhat beyond what was traditionally acceptable, lent complete credibility to the superpatriots' warnings.

The press, with the usual exceptions, behaved as it had during the steel strike. It reiterated conservative opinion and claimed that the unions were led by communists. *The New York Tribune* described the miners as "thirsting for a strike . . . thousands of them, red-soaked in the doctrines of Bolshevism, clamoring for the strike as a means of syndicalizing the coal mines . . . and even as starting a general revolution in America." Typical headlines read: "Revolution is Stake Radicals Play for in Strike of Miners" and "Apathy of Members, it is Said, Allows Reds to Control Labor Unions."

The portrait of another Red-infested union preparing the way for a Bolshevik revolution was successfully painted. And it was created, more or less, by the same interlocking interests which had converted the steel strike into an incipient revolution—the mine owners, labor spies, private spies and detectives, goons encouraged by the police, military intelligence, Justice Department agents, local police guided by coal operators, editors of local newspapers owned by coal operators, superpatriotic vigilantes, soldiers, congressmen, and the president.

About five weeks after the strike began, President Wilson authorized the Fuel Administration to offer the miners a fourteen percent wage increase and the promise of an investigation by and arbitration by a commission. A few days prior to this offer, Lewis and eighty-three United Mine Workers officials were cited for contempt of an injunction. On December 10, the president's plan was accepted and the strike ended.

By this time, the major issue in American public life had been clearly drawn. The issue was Americanism versus Bolshevism. And Americanism was primarily defined as nineteenth century free enterprise, the open shop, law and order, antiradicalism, anti-Sovietism and the belief that America's representative government and popular sovereignty were about to be undermined by a vicious and secret Red conspiracy. The temper of the times was beautifully illustrated in the Massachusetts gubernatorial election of November, 1919. National attention was focused on the bid for reelection of Calvin Coolidge, who had become a national hero during the police strike. Coolidge's stand on "the Bolshevik issue" was so significant to the nation that *The Los Angeles Times* whose coverage of Bay State politics was, we may assume, slight or nonexistent, ran an eight column headline: "Red Run Election Issues . . . Battle in Bay State" under which it raised what had become a prime question in 1919, "Shall the State of Massachusetts Be Governed By Law Or Mob Rule?"

Conservative groups supporting Coolidge campaigned on the theme that he had saved Boston from Bolshevism. A subsidiary theme was "Law and Order." Coolidge was elected with a large plurality. His victory was hailed as a major defeat for Bolshevism and a smashing victory for Americanism, law, and order. *The*

Los Angeles Times thought the election "A Defeat For the Soviets." President Wilson, a good Democrat, sent Republican Coolidge a congratulatory telegram: "I congratulate you upon your election as a victory for law and order. When this is the issue, all Americans stand together."

Liberal Democrats and Progressives were as deeply involved in the antiradical hysteria as were conservative Republicans. The hysteria was thoroughly bipartisan. In fact, the leading advocate of antiradical extremism was Attorney General Palmer, a Wilson appointee, a leading Democrat, a Progressive, a Quaker, and a leading contender for the Democratic presidential nomination in 1920.

The efforts to create the impression that labor was Red were, in fact, successful. The steel and coal strikes were settled to the disadvantage of the employees. By mid-1920, many of the 250,-000 steel workers who were organized in 1918–1919 left the union. The number of strikes in November dropped to 145 and in December only ninety-four strikes occurred. The charge of radicalism was so effective that working men became leery about joining unions at all. The open shop became fully identified with Americanism, and unionism became associated with un-Americanism. This, of course, was precisely what conservative business interests wanted. For the public, the issue was Americanism versus Bolshevism. For many sophisticated businessmen the issue was unionism versus nonunionism. Political hysteria, as we shall see, has some relation to profit and loss as well as to patriotism.

A predecessor of Norman Vincent Peale at the Marble Collegiate Church used the Good Book to prove that the closed shop was "unpatriotic to the last degree" and "un-Christian." Former President Taft stated that advocates of the closed shop were "embracing Soviet methods." A particularly brutal and dramatic event, known as the Centralia massacre, brought the antiradical hysteria to fever pitch. On Armistice Day of November, 1919, the American Legion of Centralia, Washington joined the Elks and Boy Scouts for a parade. The parade was scheduled to pass the local IWW hall and the radicals, some armed, posted themselves across the street from the hall and about 400 yards away on high ground. The facts are still not entirely clear, but some Legionnaires apparently moved in the direction of the hall and shots were fired. Three Legionnaires were killed. Some Wobblies were apprehended and jailed. One, Wesley Everest, escaped, was overtaken while fording a stream, and fired into the posse, killing one Legionnaire. Everest was seized, badly beaten, had his teeth knocked out by a rifle butt, and was later thrown in jail.

That night a mob broke into the jail and took Everest outside where he was again brutally beaten. He was then taken into the Chekanlis River and castrated. He screamed "Shoot me, for God's sake, shoot me!" He was hung by a short rope from a railroad bridge, then, hauled up, he was hung again from a longer rope. He was then riddled with bullets and left dangling.

Days later, Everest's corpse was cut down and displayed for the edification of other Wobblies in Centralia. The cause of death remained officially indeterminate for no inquest was held. One story circulated that the coroner attributed his death to suicide.

Representative Albert Johnson of Washington was roundly applauded on the floor of the House when he read telegrams condemning the IWW, one of which eulogized the dead Legionnaires as "victims of a long premeditated conspiracy to bring an armed revolution to the United States." Senator Jones of Washington was also applauded when he said "the shots that killed these boys were really aimed at the heart of the Nation by those who oppose law and seek the overthrow of the government." Senator Poindexter of Washington joined his colleague: "This detestable outrage is the fearful penalty which Centralia has paid for the overlenient policy of the National government toward anarchists and murderous communities."

The New York Times described Centralia as "Radicalism Ran

Mad." *The Boston Evening Transcript* referred to Centralia as, "An Act of War against the United States."

Centralia served as the catalyst to set off antiradical police actions and vigilantism on the West Coast. On November 12, local, state, and federal officers commenced a series of raids to eliminate the "Bolshevik Menace" from the West Coast. Raids in Tacoma, Seattle, Oakland, and Spokane netted 146 alleged Reds. The publication of a Seattle labor newspaper was suspended and three staff members were arrested for suggesting in an editorial that the IWW be allowed to present its version of the Centralia affair.

After eleven months of mounting antiradicalism, many congressmen and newspapers began to demand an organized federal nationwide effort to rid the country of radicals. *The Pittsburgh Post*, more vociferous than most major newspapers, suggested that "the sooner the firing squad is got into action the better." *The United Presbyterian*, a church publication, proclaimed that the Bolshevik should be made to "change his course or swing at the end of a rope." Less militant congressmen and newspapers suggested that since many radicals were aliens, deportation might be a practical solution.

By late fall of 1919, the public was completely preoccupied with the Bolshevik menace. The national mood became truly hysterical. The Justice Department, directed by Attorney General A. Mitchell Palmer, had decided to concentrate its efforts on three projects: actively inventing Bolshevik revolutionaries and conspiracies in America, finding conspirators, and incarcerating or deporting such conspirators. With $500,000 which Congress appropriated to the Justice Department, Palmer established a General Intelligence or antiradical division of August 1, 1919, with J. Edgar Hoover as its appointed chief. Hoover's prime responsibility was the collection and coordination of all information relating to domestic radicalism. By January of 1920, the division had become the central nervous system of the department and antiradicalism the Department's prime task. Hoover established a crude card index system of information processing and retrieval. More than two hundred thousand cards containing detailed information, city by city, on radical organizations and individuals were assembled and case histories of sixty thousand men and women, deemed dangerous radicals, were prepared.

By late fall of 1919, the Justice Department had fully entered the antiradical public relations business. Palmer regularly supplied the press with copies of radical documents—some of which were "captured" in raids conducted by the department and some of which could be purchased at newspaper stands. The attorney general was also obliging enough to supply editorial comments which invariably concluded that the presence of radical literature was proof of a radical conspiracy.

In an effort perhaps to ease the burden of the press and insure full compliance with the attorney general's desired portrait of reality, the department went beyond merely supplying the press with radical documents and editorial comment. It supplied newspapers and magazines with a specimen page of stories and cartoons and plates free of charge. A notation above the top of the page informed the publisher—but not the reader—that "plates of material shown below are furnished to you without charge, carriage prepaid, on the order of the U.S. Department of Justice, Washington, D.C. The metal remains our property to be returned in the usual manner."

One headline stated, "Warns Nation of Red Peril: U.S. Department of Justice Urges Americans to Guard Against Bolshevism Menace: Calls Red Plans Criminal." Another headline read, "Overthrow World Order! Cry Communists: Manifesto of Communist Internation Seized in U.S. Department of Justice Raids, Tells Reds' Own Story of Their Plans for World Wide Plunder." Extracts from the manifesto then followed.

A third headline read: "To Conquer and Destroy State, U.S. Communists Call For Labor Revolt. Revolutionary Pamphlet,

Found in U.S. Department of Justice Investigations, Gives Message of Communists in Chicago to Russian Headquarters." Extracts from this captured document followed.

Under the headline, "What Reds Would Have Us Sing," the lyrics of an IWW song were printed.

One day as I sat pining
A message of cheer came to me,
A light of revolt was shining
On a country far over the sea.
The forces of rulers to sever
And the flag of the earth to unfold
To secure our freedom forever
And a world of beauty untold.
We have lived in meek submission

Through ages of toil and despair,
To comply with the plutes' ambition
With never a thought nor a care.
An echo from Russia is sounding
'Tis the chimes of a True Liberty,
It's a message for millions re-sounding
To throw off your chains and be free.

CHORUS

All hail to the Bolsheviki!
We will fight for our class and be free
A Kaiser, King or Czar, no matter
which you are
You're nothing of interest to me;
If you don't like the red flag of Russia
If you don't like the spirit so true,
Then just be like the cur in the story
And lick the hand that's robbing you.

While the attorney general was fanning antiradical flames, petitions from state legislatures, superpatriotic societies, and business organizations, asking the government to deport radical aliens, were received in large numbers by the Congress. On October 19, 1919, the Senate unanimously adopted a resolution requesting the attorney general

". . . to advise and inform the Senate whether or not the Department of Justice has taken legal proceedings, and if not, why not, and if so, to what extent, for the arrest and punishment/or deportation . . . of the various persons within the United States who . . . have attempted to bring about the forcible overthrow of the government."[8]

Reporting radical aliens was an expeditious way of handling the problem because the General Intelligence Division estimated that ninety percent of all domestic radicals were aliens and subject to deportation provisions of the Alien Law of 1918. In a country where radicalism is regarded as a foreign import, deportation of radicals appears to be a natural solution.

On November 7, 1919, the Department conducted raids in twelve cities against the Union of Russian Workers, an alleged communist-anarchist organization. About two hundred members were arrested in New York City and approximately fifty in other cities. Truckloads of radical literature were confiscated. According to *The New York Times,* some members were "badly beaten." Thirty nine of the "captives" were ultimately held. A few were incarcerated as long as five months before receiving a hearing.

State and local officials all over the country immediately followed suit. Hundreds of alleged radicals were seized and, ultimately, 246 were judged to be deportable aliens. The raids were front page copy all over the country and the attorney general became an instant national hero. Newspapers deemed Palmer to be "a lion-hearted man [who] brought order out of chaos," "a Strong Man of Peace," and "a tower of strength to his countrymen." The Senate complimented Palmer and listened carefully on November 14, 1919, when the attorney general testified to the vastness of the radical conspiracy in America and then requested a peacetime sedition law.

American radicals responded to the raids by crying for revenge against what they called the "White Terror" and by demanding the overthrow of "the American plutocracy." Their cliche-ridden response and escalating rhetoric provided a beautiful counterpoint for the Red baiting of the Justice Department, which promptly cited radical publications to prove the existence of the radical conspiracy. The interplay of radical and antiradical had the quality of a self-fulfilling prophecy.

Despite the fact that some members of the cabinet objected to Palmer's techniques, Woodrow Wilson, on numerous occasions, lent some of his prestige to Palmer's aims and practices. The president frequently hinted that Bolshevik agents were probably operating in America. In his annual message he referred to Bolshevism as "poison." The president requested a peacetime sedition bill. He frequently sugguested that opposition to the League of Nations was in line with Bolshevik strategy. He even implied that opponents of the League were, in fact, unwitting dupes of Bolshevism.

Wilson, however, was also concerned about the respressive possibilities of an attack on radicals. He remarked in his annual message that "the seed of revolution is repression" and he cautioned that restrictions on radicals be administered with care. The president, according to Robert Murray, warned the attorney general, "Do not let this country see Red."[8] However, he talked one way and acted another. Partially perhaps as a result of his illness, the president did nothing to curb his chief law enforcement officer, and Palmer ignored Wilson's mild warnings.

On November 25, 1919, federal and state agents raided the Russian People's House in New York City and found, according to their reports, a cache of "material for 100 bombs." The press, utilizing the exaggerations that had now become standard operating procedure, transformed the contents of several bottles that were found into a "RED BOMB LABORATORY". One paper reported, in headlines, "FIND REDS' BOMB SHOPS". An inspector from the Bureau of Combustibles described the cache as "the most deadly and most dangerous assortment of explosives and bomb ingredients seen in many a year."

Congress was soon deluged by petitions and pressure to deport alien radicals and on December 21, 1919, 249 alleged alien radicals were deported. A few of the deportees were notorious and confirmed revolutionaries. The overwhelming majority, however, had neither criminal records nor had they participated in acts of terror. They were deported on the basis of political beliefs—not actions.

The manner in which the press dealt with the deportation indicates the passion to which the political hysteria had escalated. If the reportage were sincere, it would also indicate how genuine was the fear of radical conspiracy and the sense of relief felt now that radicals were being deported. Surveying the press, Robert Murray reports:

The general press made the most of the whole deportation situation by announcing it with screaming headlines, while editorial columns bulged with favorable comment. Describing the group as "the unholiest cargo that ever left our shores," editors hailed the sailing of convicted radicals. Most agreed that the departure of these men and women was "none too soon" and "timely and just." *The New York Evening Mail* declared that "Just as the sailing of the Ark that Noah built was a pledge for the preservation of the human race, so the sailing of the Ark of the Soviet is a pledge for the preservation of America." *The Boston Evening Transcript* maintained that sailing was "as epoch-making as the immortal voyage of Columbus," while *The Saturday Evening Post* drew yet another nautical comparison by declaring, "the Mayflower brought the first of the builders to this country; the Buford has taken away the first destroyers." Quipped *The New York Tribune*, "The ultrared faction is feeling a trifle ultramarine."[9]

The Cleveland Plain Dealer editorialized, "It is hoped and expected that other vessels, larger and more commodious, carrying similar cargoes, will follow in her wake."

By late 1919, hundreds of newspapers were demanding more antiradical action by the federal government. The attorney general complied.

On the evening of January 2, 1920, federal agents rounded up more than 4,000 alleged radicals in raids in thirty-three cities in twenty-three states. Almost every known communist organization was raided and almost every known local and national communist leader was arrested. The motive behind the Palmer

raids was to break the back of the Communist Party by ultimately deporting all alien members. Deportation of alien radicals rather than arrest and conviction of citizen radicals was
selected because deportation of aliens required no criminal proceedings, no indictments, and no judge or jury. Deportation was
an administrative matter handled by the Department of Labor.

There is no doubt that the raids involved the violation of the
civil rights of a few thousand people. Many arrests were made
without warrants. Many prisoners were held incommunicado
and denied the right to counsel. Some prisoners were forced to
march in chains. The conditions in some places of detention
were deplorable—freezing cold with no decent sanitation facilities. In Boston, one captive committed suicide by jumping out
of a five story window. Another went insane. Two of the arrested
died of pneumonia. Many of the men and women were American citizens. Many were not radicals. Of 800 incarcerated in
Detroit, 300 were released after six days when it was obvious
they had no connection whatsoever with radical causes. Federal
agents and the police in several cities beat prisoners. Thirty-nine
bakers in Lynn, Massachusetts, were arrested on suspicion of
holding a revolutionary meeting when, in fact, they had met
to organize a cooperative bakery. In Newark, a man was arrested
because he "looked like a radical."[10]

The extent of the violation of civil liberties and the extent of
police brutality were carefully documented in May of 1920 by
twelve eminent lawyers, including Dean Pound of Harvard Law
School, future Supreme Court Justice Felix Frankfurter, and
Professor Zachariah Chaffee of the Harvard Law School, the
country's leading authority on free speech. They published a
scathing attack on Palmer entitled "A Report Upon the Illegal
Practices of the United States Department of Justice" which was
largely based on the testimony of men and women incarcerated
after the raids. Bits of the testimony are worth quoting because
they illustrate the degree to which the alleged radicals were
denied their humanity and the extraordinary passion which was

generated for their extermination. The report describes the situation in the Hartford jail.

In the Hartford Jail there exist four punishment rooms, all alike, unventilated and utterly dark, size 4 feet 3 inches by 8 feet 10 inches, with solid concrete floors, no furniture of any kind, and placed over the pump room of the boiler so that the temperature in them becomes unbearably high. A number of the supposed anarchist or Communist prisoners, probably ten to fifteen, were confined in these rooms for periods of 36 to 60 hours. During their imprisonment in the suffocating heat without air, they were given one glass of water and one slice of bread every 12 hours. Some of them on being released had to be revived before they could be carried to their cells; one man who was in only 36 hours was unable to get to his cell unaided.

These Hartford prisoners were practically buried alive for five months, being even denied the privilege of seeing their relatives or friends.[11]

Peter Musek, who went to the U.S. Post Office in Hartford to request a pass to visit a detained friend, testified to the following under sworn affadavit:

PETER MUSEK, being duly sworn, says:
I reside at No. 437 Helen Street, Bridgeport, Conn. I am 33 years of age and am working as a tailor in Bridgeport. On the 24th day of December, 1919, I left Bridgeport for Hartford and applied for a pass to see a friend, Mike Lozuk, who was arrested on the 8th day of November, 1919, at a meeting place of Russians in Bridgeport. I heard that Lozuk was confined in the Hartford Jail and wanted to see me. As soon as I appeared in the U.S. Post Office Building at Hartford, Conn., where I asked for a pass to see Lozuk, I was searched and immediately put under arrest and questioned by an agent of the Department of Justice. Six men, I presume agents of the Department of Justice, questioned me and threatened to hang me if I do not tell them the truth. In one instance, an agent of the Department of Justice, whose name I do not know, brought a rope and tied it around my neck, stating that he will hang me immediately if I do not tell him who conducts the meetings and who are the main workers in an organization called the Union of Russian Workers. This inquisition lasted fully three hours, after

which I was again threatened to be put into a gas-room and suffo-
cated unless I gave more particulars about other men in the Union
of Russian Workers. This was all done in the U.S. Post Office
Building in the presence of six agents of the Department of
Justice.[12]

Mitchell Lavrowsky, a teacher of Russian, was seized at gun
point during the November 7 raid. Under oath he testified:

I wear eye-glasses and the agent of the Department of Justice
ordered me to take them off. Then without any provocation, struck
me on the head and simultaneously two others struck and beat me
brutally. After I was beaten and without strength to stand on my
feet, I was thrown down stairs and while I rolled down, other
men, I presume also agents of the Department of Justice, beat me
with pieces of wood which I later found out were obtained by
breaking the banisters. I sustained a fracture of my head, left
shoulder, left foot, and right side. Then I was ordered to wash
myself and was taken, as I now understand, to 13 Park Row,
Borough of Manhattan, City of New York, where I was examined
by various people and released about 12:00 midnight.

The Communist Party and the Communist Labor Party had
been heavily infiltrated by federal agents. These agents arranged
many macabre self-fulfilling prophecies by urging their radical
"colleagues" to commit some act and then reporting it to nonradical colleagues who then made arrests. The settings of many
of the raids of January 2 were even arranged by federal agents.
The Department of Justice, in its Confidential Instructions of
December 27, 1919, instructed its agents on procedures for the
forthcoming raids.

For your own personal information, I have to advise you that the
tentative date fixed for the arrests of the COMMUNISTS is Friday
evening, January 2, 1920. This date may be changed, due to the
fact that all of the immigration warrants may not be issued by that
time. You will, however, be advised by telegraph as to the exact
date and hour when the arrests are to be made.

If possible you should arrange with your under-cover informants
to have meetings of the COMMUNIST PARTY and the COM-
MUNIST LABOR PARTY held on the night set. I have been

informed by some of the bureau officers that such arrangements will be made. This, of course, would facilitate the making of the arrests.

On the evening of the arrests, this office will be open the entire night and I desire that you communicate by long distance to Mr. Hoover any matters of vital importance or interest which may arise during the course of the arrests.[13]

Hysteria appears to be insatiable. The high drama of the raids bred an increased demand for more antiradicalism, more raids, and more deportations. Attacks on the free speech of radicals increased. *The Washington Post* editorialized: "There is no time to waste on hairsplitting over infringement of liberty."

Despite the fact that by this time a few major newspapers had vigorously attacked his procedures, Palmer continued to feed the hysteria. He assured the nation that information secured in the raids proved, without doubt, that aliens dominated the radical movement and were, therefore, a threat to America's security. He stated that most of the alien radicals were controlled by Moscow and received orders from Lenin and Trotsky. Describing the prisoners caught in the raids, he remarked:

Out of the sly and crafty eyes of many of them leap cupidity, cruelty, insanity, and crime; from their lopsided faces, sloping brows, and misshapen features may be recognized the unmistakable criminal type.[14]

For about three months, from November of 1919, through January of 1920, public opinion on the radical issue was so virulent that the Congress and almost every state legislature proceeded to consider numerous laws aimed at curbing the Bolshevik menace. The issue was not partisan. Democrats and Progressives were as militantly antiradical as were Republicans. Votes in favor of curbing freedom of speech and expelling socialist members of the legislature often had near unanimous support.

The fate of socialist Congressman Victor Berger of Wisconsin is a case in point. He was found guilty of violating the Espionage Act by his pacifist statements and sentenced to

twenty years in jail. The issue of seating Berger arose in April
of 1919. A special committee labelled Berger "traitorous" and
"Bolshevistic" and recommended his expulsion 8 to 1. With one
dissenting vote, the House expelled him. Various representatives during the debate cried out "hun," "Dutchman," "un-
American," "traitor," and "Bolshevik."

The national press, again with a few exceptions, applauded
the action taken by the House. *The Washington Post* opined
that the House could not have given a "finer or more impressive demonstration of Americanism." *The Baltimore Sun* was
indignant that even one vote was cast for Berger.

In a special election to fill the seat, Berger was re-elected.
This time a handful of representatives expressed concern for the
principle of representative government but Berger was still
refused his seat by a vote of 330 to 6.

Berger's expulsion was symbolic. Congress, however, turned
to the crux of the matter—freedom of speech and press for
the dissenters—and approximately seventy peacetime sedition
bills were introduced in the late fall and early winter of 1919–
1920. Many of these proposals were amalgamated and introduced on January 5, 1920, as the so-called Graham Bill which
provided for twenty years imprisonment and/or a $10,000 fine
for anyone who sought to overthrow or destroy the federal
government, or prevent or delay the execution of a federal law,
or harm or terrorize any officer or employee of the federal
government. The terms of this proposed law were vague and
sweeping. According to it a picket who blocked the entrance to
an army base, a crowd that prevented a federal officer from
speaking, or a young man who refused to attend a preinduction
physical examination might be guilty.

While the House was debating the Graham Bill, numerous
bills were being proposed in the Senate which provided for
strict control of the press through suspension of mailing
privileges, fines up to $50,000 and lengthy jail sentences for
seditious utterances. On January 10 the Senate passed a bill

which was similar to the Graham Bill. Substantial opposition to these proposed bills was raised by the press, not primarily because of any abstract commitment to freedom of speech, but because of possible censorship. The AF of L, through Gompers, also opposed the bill because of the possible effect it might have on strikes and picketing. Congress, for a variety of reasons, failed to pass a peacetime sedition bill. Although it was not clear at the time, opposition to these bills marked the beginning of the termination of the hysteria.

There were, however, two Red scares being waged—federal and state. In many instances, the states were substantially more repressive than the Federal government. The major weapon used by the states to suppress nonconformity was legislation directed against criminal anarchy, syndicalism, sedition, and Red flag laws. During the war several states had enacted criminal anarchy laws which were directed against the IWW. Criminal anarchy was customarily defined as "the doctrine that organized government should be overthrown by force or violence or by assassination . . . or by any unlawful means." In several states, a person convicted of criminal anarchy was subject to a fine of $5,000 or ten years in jail or both.

In 1919, twenty state governments enacted criminal anarchy laws. In several state legislatures the vote was unanimous. Many of these laws were directed against the expression of opinion regardless of the probability of criminal acts. Severe penalties were often provided for petty offenses and, according to Murray, in many states "a practical censorship of speech and press was established post facto."[15] In 1920, several states passed criminal anarchy laws and sedition laws which made the speaking or printing of abusive language directed against public officials or the republican form of government a major offense. By 1920, thirty-five states and Alaska and Hawaii had passed peacetime sedition laws or criminal syndicalist laws which permitted ". . . the rapid crackdown on speech that might by its expression produce unlawful actions geared to

stimulating improper political or economic change."[16] The
Connecticut law provided punishment for "disloyal, scurrilous
or abusive language about the form of government of the
United States." The Colorado law dealt with ". . . advocacy
by word or in print of forcible resistance to constituted government either as a general principle or in particular instances as
a means of affecting governmental, industrial, social or economic conditions."

Perhaps the best indication of the intense feeling that lay
behind the super-Americanism of the Red scare was the passage
of laws by thirty-two states, and several cities, which forbade the
display of the Red flag, symbol of communism. In most states,
conviction could involve a fine not in excess of $500 and a jail
sentence of up to six months. Approximately 1,400 persons—
citizens as well as aliens—were arrested under these laws and
about 300 were convicted and imprisoned.

In the state of New York three duly elected Socialist assemblymen were expelled by a vote of 116 to 28 and two were expelled
by a vote of 104 to 40. The vote did not follow party lines.
One assemblyman, looking at two of the Socialist members,
remarked "These two men who sit there with a smile and a
smirk on their faces are just as much representatives of the
Russian Soviet Government as if they were Lenin and Trotsky
themselves. They are little Lenins, little Trotskys in our midst."
The day after the expulsion *The New York Times* commented,
"It was an American vote altogether, a patriotic and conservative vote. An immense majority of the American people will
approve and sanction the assembly's action."

On September 6, 1920, the five Socialists were re-elected and
the Assembly expelled three of them. The other two resigned.
Numerous assemblymen concurred that the Socialist Party
was precisely what it was not—revolutionary, unpatriotic, disloyal, and under direct orders from the Third International.

In April of 1920, the New York Assembly passed two bills

which made the Socialist Party an illegal organization and which barred its candidates from the ballot. Two other bills which were passed required a loyalty oath from all teachers and gave the Board of Regents power to license all nonreligious private schools. The Assembly passed another law which appropriated $100,000 for the establishment of a State Bureau of Investigation to investigate and prosecute sedition, disloyalty, and criminal anarchy.

As antiradical sentiment mounted and public opinion became more unanimous in its fear of the Bolshevik conspiracy, it was inevitable that politicians at various levels would attempt to exploit it. Businessmen and special pleaders for dozens of interests discovered that patriotism, like motherhood, was not only beyond reproach, but also that it was profitable. One could not lose by depicting one's opponents as part of the international Bolshevik menace. Tagging one's opponents as Red, or Red "dupes," or an agent of Lenin, became standard operating procedure for hundreds of organized interests.

Red baiting was not restricted to individual businessmen or firms or pressure groups or "causes." Dozens of new groups —superpatriotic societies—were suddenly organized and the pursuit of radicals and the elimination of the Bolshevik conspiracy became their avowed public purpose. But the principle object of attack by the largest and most well financed superpatriotic societies was organized labor. The heaviest fire was reserved for the demands made by organized labor which management considered to be unusual and illegitimate and therefore un-American. The open shop became "The American Plan." The closed shop became "sovietism in disguise." Many of these societies were headed by America's most prestigious and wealthiest businessmen and prominent ex-public officials.

The American Legion, founded in May of 1919, though not formally a superpatriotic society, was, in fact, one of the most militant purveyors of super-Americanism. By December of 1919, the American Legion had more than 1,000,000 members. The Legion's first commander ordered his men to be "ready for action at any time . . . against the extremists who are seeking to overturn a government for which thousands of brave young Americans laid down their lives." *The American Legion Weekly*, a leading repository of superpatriotic literature, in literally every issue, warned of imminent radical revolution in America, pleaded for quick government action, deportations, extended jail sentences for radicals, text book purgings, sedition laws, and "one hundred percent Americanism."

The legion officially denounced violence and vigilantism as antiradical tactics—apparently to little avail. Robert Murray has described the extralegal activities of some Legionnaires as follows:

In some areas, legionnaires assumed the responsibility of running all suspected radicals out of town after holding drumhead trials to ascertain their loyalty. In other areas legionnaires tarred and feathered aliens who were thought to be a particular menace to the community. Indeed, everywhere in the country members of the legion were inclined to take hasty action and brawled with socialists whenever the opportunity arose. In Detroit, one local post prided itself on consisting of "one thousand Bolshevik bouncers," while in Denver, legionnaires had a pact that they would reply with their fists to any malcontent who talked of revolution or anarchy. Under such circumstances, it was not strange that "Leave the Reds to the legion" soon became a national cry.[17]

The most prestigious and affluent of the societies, however, concentrated on defaming the labor movement, the closed shop, the Plumb Plan for nationalizing the railroads, and the idea of "one big union." The great bulk of the money contributed to superpatriotic societies was used for this purpose, not surprisingly, since four of the major societies—The National Civic Federation, the National Security League, The Better America Federation, and the American Constitutional Association—received almost all their funds from leading businessmen, large corporations, and public utilities.

An example of the current issues in American politics that were regarded with suspicion by superpatriots is contained in this questionnaire which the American Defense Society sent to schools and colleges to discover "the extent to which socialistic and communistic principles are advocated by members of the faculty or entertained by such student organizations as may exist in the form of liberal clubs, forums, alliances, etc."

In any of the above courses are any of the following principles advocated or recommended? _____
a. Referendum to the people? _____ b. The recall of judges and judicial decisions? _____ c. The initiative or direct legislation by the people? _____ d. The right of the people as a whole to the earnings of the individual? _____
Is there active propaganda among the students or faculty for further reduction of the size of the Army or Navy? _____
If so, is such propaganda based on the idea that military preparedness tends to produce war and that disarmament by this country is the first step toward permanent peace?
Are any of the above principles or theories offered as a subject for debates between the students and, if so, to what extent?[18]

On February 4, 1919, the Senate unanimously resolved to permit a judiciary subcommittee which was investigating German propaganda, to also investigate Russian propaganda. Meeting from February 11 to March 10, the so-called Overman Committee produced a 1,200 page report which concluded that Bolshevism was the prime danger confronting the United States. Most of the witnesses were militantly anti-Bolshevik and told tales of the horrors of the Russian Revolution and the Leninist regime. Ambassador Francis testified that Lenin was a tool of the Germans and that the Bolsheviki were killing everybody "who wears a white collar or who is educated and who is not a Bolshevik." Other witnesses stated that the revolutionary army was composed primarily of Jews who formerly resided in New York's Lower East Side.

The press, again with few exceptions, responded in predictable fashion. Robert Murray summarizes reportage of the Overman hearings.

Anti-Bolshevik testimony was played up in the columns of the nation's newspapers and once again the reading public was fed on highly colored tales of free love, nationalization of women, bloody massacres, and brutal atrocities. Stories were circulated that the victims of the Bolshevik madmen customarily had been roasted to death in furnaces, scalded with live steam, torn to pieces on racks, or hacked to bits with axes. Newspaper editors never tired of referring to the Russian Reds as "assassins and madmen," "human scum," "crime mad," and "beasts." Russia was a place, some said, where maniacs stalked raving through the streets, and the populace fought with the dogs for carrion. Then, when the final report of the investigating committee was released, newspapers climaxed this sensational reporting with gigantic headlines: "RED PERIL HERE," "PLAN BLOODY REVOLUTION," and "WANT WASHINGTON GOVERNMENT OVERTURNED."[19]

The most notorious investigation of radicalism was initiated by the legislature of the state of New York in June of 1919. The so-called Lusk Committee, in April of 1920, published a massive four volume report containing 4,456 pages and entitled "Revolutionary Radicalism, Its History, Purpose, and Tactics: With an Exposition and Discussion of the Steps Being Taken and Required to Curb It." The Report, which is a master cut-and-paste job, cost about $100,000, and was made up of thousands of "captured" radical documents, and hundreds of footnotes, histories of socialism in dozens of countries, maps, charts, tables, lengthy bibliographies, and testimony from so-called expert witnesses, comes to the predictable conclusion that radical movements in the United States are financed and directed by European communists and that they comprise a serious threat to the United States.

The sheer bulk of the Overman and Lusk reports—the thousands of pages of testimony from alleged experts, the reprinting of large numbers of socialist, anarchist, and communist documents, many of which were "captured" by government agents in raids on secret meetings, the barrage of alleged facts and figures concerning the size, financial resources, and secret plans of radical sects—created the impression that the reports were works of serious scholarship and impeccable research, and legitimized the claims of Overman and Lusk. The nature and function of such pseudoscholarship is of considerable importance and will be discussed further.

Both committees recommended the passage of more stringent sedition legislation, careful oversight of immigration, the rigid enforcement of provisions for the deportation of undesirable aliens, and nationwide programs of Americanization, which included loyalty oaths for teachers, and censorship of textbooks.

These last two proposals reflect the fact that superpatriots correctly understood that the grammar and high schools have always been training grounds for Americanism. Attempts to purify textbooks and screen the loyalty of teachers multiplied during the hysteria. In some areas, teachers were suspended or arbitrarily dismissed for discussing Marxism and comparing it with Liberalism. The definition of what constituted loyalty became so restrictive that a Radcliffe graduate was suspended from teaching in Cambridge, Massachusetts, when the fact was made public that she had formerly been a member of the Radcliffe Liberal Club which advocated an impartial analysis of Bolshevism. Several school teachers were dismissed in New York City, the overwhelming majority of whom were not radicals. However, a few of the teachers in New York City —seven to be exact—were members of the Communist Party and a handful in other cities either belonged to the party or made statements that were obviously in support of the Russian revolution. In Boston, one teacher was dismissed for attending Communist Party meetings and for stating, "Give us one generation of small children to train to manhood and womanhood and we will set up a Bolshevist form of Soviet government." The few genuine communist teachers who were dismissed were used by superpatriotic societies and the press as proof of their contention that radical penetration of universities and public schools was widespread. The superintendent of schools in New York City, a superpatriot in his own right, ultimately admitted that the percentage of radical teachers probably was negligible.

The situation with respect to churchmen was similar to that of teachers. The overwhelming majority of ministers, priests, and rabbis were antiradical, as were the overwhelming majority of church publications. Loyalty to country, the virtues of America, and godliness were common religious themes throughout the war and the hysteria. Virulent attacks on Marxism and the Russian revolution were common fare during sermons.

Several churchmen and groups, however, were interested in social and economic problems. Some advocated public work proposals to reduce unemployment. Some advocated social welfare schemes in the areas of accident, health insurance and unemployment compensation. Some strongly supported labor's demand for a closed shop. For these reasons, the suspicion of radicalism in the churches spread.

In their attack on the church, superpatriots invented a new criterion—"leaning towards Bolshevism." This label was pinned upon the National Welfare Council, the Federation for Social Service of the Methodist Church, the Commission on the Church and Social Service of the Federal Council of Churches of Christ in America, because they opposed a variety of attempts by management to curb or destroy unionism. The church group that analyzed the great steel strike and concluded that it was not a Bolshevik effort was itself attacked as communist. Dozens of America's most prominent clergymen were typed as parlor pinks. Dr. Harry Ward, professor of Christian Ethics at the Union Theological Seminary, was bitterly attacked for an article in which he argued that a state composed entirely of producers and controlled by producers was "manifestly a Scriptural aim." After the publication of the article, the Publisher's Section of the Interdenominational Graded Sunday

School Syndicate refused to reprint teacher's manuals and textbooks written by Dr. Ward.

The attack mounted against organized labor, universities and public schools, and the church spread to liberal public officials; Senators Borah, La Follette, and Norris were attacked for their liberal views and for their defense of the constitutional rights of radicals and other minorities. The secretary of labor was attacked by numerous conservatives because, as a union man, he was an "unconcious ally of Bolshevism." The assistant secretary of labor was attacked because he had formerly published a liberal journal. On December 23, 1919, *The Wall Street Journal* queried "We talk of parlor Bolshevists, but what of those other Bolshevists in the Cabinet, or at any rate, near the throne?" Inevitably, a few superpatriots branded President Wilson as a parlor pink.

The web of suspicion spread quickly from individuals, to institutions, to particular religious groups, and then to races. In June, in its report on "Revolution Radicalism," the Lusk committee reported much radical activity among Negroes and predicted more. The press, according to Murray "met such claims with fear and trembling and had agreed that of all the reprehensible actions of radicals none surpass this attempt 'to undermine the loyalty of Negroes'."[20] For a variety of very complex reasons, of which radicalism was a very minor one, a series of bloody race riots occurred in the summer of 1919. At least forty persons were killed in Washington, D.C., and Chicago. Despite the fact that a hard core of newspapers and journals of opinion denied that radicalism was a significant factor and argued that the prime causes of the riots were Negro migration into white neighborhoods, inadequate housing, high rents and competition for good jobs, some newspapers, like *The New York Times*, made the radical charge, and others, more cautious, conceded that radicalism may have been a cause. *The Cincinnati Enquirer*, on October 6, 1919, noted that "there may be, as is intimated, insidious and sinister agitation of a revolutionary character back of these phenomena."

A few Negro newspapers fed the suspicion by taking a positive position toward the ideas of Marx and the Russian revolution.

From its onset in January of 1919, the antiradical hysteria continued to escalate for about twelve months. In retrospect, the Palmer raids, in January of 1920, can be seen as the apex of the Red scare. By that time antiradicalism had become the national preoccupation—actually the national compulsion and passion. Other issues faded into insignificance. Robert Murray describes the American mood as "national insanity."

By the fall of 1920, however, antiradical rhetoric had become such a bore that when a bomb exploded across the street from the House of Morgan on September 16, killing thirty-three persons, and injuring more than two hundred, statements by Palmer to the effect that the bombing was part of a gigantic plot to destroy the United States evoked ridicule and indifference. *The Cleveland Plain Dealer* responded with remarkable calm.

. . . Capitalism is untouched. The federal government is not shaken in the slightest degree. The public is merely shocked, not terrorized, much less converted to the merits of anarchism. Business and life as usual. Society, government, industry functioning precisely as if nothing happened.

Palmer, who had presidential aspirations, failed to receive the Democratic nomination in 1920. And Warren Harding reiterated during the campaign that "too much has been said about radicalism in America." The country turned its attention to fads, fashions, mah jong, bathtub gin, radio, bathing beauties, crime, women, smoking, sex, and Babe Ruth.

The Red scare was dead, and its death was almost as sudden as its birth. It came to maturity in twelve months. Its demise took about eight months.

Improved reality testing and the reduction of stress had something to do with its demise. By mid-1920 neither Germany, Italy, nor France had succumbed to Bolshevism. The domino prediction had failed. Predictions of imminent and castastrophic revolution in America—endless predictions—had also not materialized. No massive conspiracy had been discovered. Relatively few radicals had been convicted. The great coal and steel strike ended. The number of strikes sharply declined. Twenty-five race riots occured in 1919. No significant riots were reported in 1920. Only one major bombing was reported in 1920. Domestic food prices declined to prewar levels with a bumper crop. Price controls on wheat were discontinued. Peacetime conversion proceeded with no more than the anticipated degree of disruption to the economy. Despite Palmer's warnings, the Republic was very much intact.

The decline in the aggressivity of organized labor also had something to do with the decline of the Red scare. Many militants had been discredited. Union membership began to decline. Grandiose plans for nationalization and "one big union" were little publicized. The IWW was in disarray. Big business was beginning to succeed in its drive to identify the closed shop as the American plan. Gompers and the AF of L fully realized the need to advance the cause of labor with great caution.

The decline of the Red scare had something to do with the fact that the ranks of American radicalism were decimated, and the radicals intimidated. The cumulative effect of hundreds of antiradical raids, deportations, destruction of radical headquarters and schools, preventive detentions, and convictions was great. The IWW, the Communist Party and the Communist Labor Party were effectively dismantled.

American liberals and Progressives suffered as well. The attack on "parlor pinks" and "intellectuals" largely succeeded. Much of the liberal community was intimidated by the charge that liberals were really Red sympathizers. The successful "chilling" of the expression of liberal and progressive opinion had something to do with the decline of the Red scare.

If many of the big businessmen who promoted the Red scare intended to use the hysteria to smash strikes, to weaken and conservatize the labor movement, to dismantle radical parties, and to intimidate liberals, they had reason to rejoice. The Red scare may have declined, in part, because it succeeded.

But the hysteria also declined because its promoters evoked some opposition. One significant and very public violation of due process, to wit, the expulsion of five Socialists from the New York Legislature, set off a wave of protest. For the first time since the Red scare began, newspapers throughout the country—conservative as well as liberal—condemned an antiradical action.

For the first time since the Red Scare began, a small but prominent number of men and women—many of whom had been vociferous superpatriots—defended the rights of radicals. Senator Warren Harding, in a freakish coalition, joined Fiorello La Guardia and Al Smith in opposing the ouster. The Little Flower declaimed, "If we keep on at this rate, we shall build up a radical party in this country." The likelihood that the attack on radicalism will create more radicalism was common liberal coin. Al Smith noted, with untypical pomposity, "To discard the methods of representative government leads to misdeeds of the very extremists we denounced and serves to increase the enemies of orderly free government." "Denial of lawful free speech," former Senator Beveridge remarked, "is the noxious culture in which crazy radicalism is propagated most rapidly." The concern was not for radicals, but for free speech and due process. The Delphic Oracle of Kansas, William Allen White, said that the action of the New York Legislature "merely martyrizes the advocates of a stupid cause."

The liberal counterattack was led by Charles Evans Hughes —former Justice of the Supreme Court and hallmark of eastern Republican Establishmentarianism. He denounced the expulsions as a fundamental violation of representative government and offered the services of the New York Bar Association to the five Socialists. The Association, the most powerful and prestigious in the country, adopted a resolution condemning the expulsion.

Justice Holmes attacked the expulsion in a well publicized speech before the Harvard Club and Judge Anderson of the United District Court remarked:

Many of the same people and newspapers that for two years were faking pro-German plots are now promoting "The Red Terror." It is time that we had freedom of speech for the just contempt that every wholesome-minded citizen should have for the pretentious, noisy heresy-hunter of these hysterical times.

This nationwide explosive burst of opposition by some prestigious figures apparently provided a cue for a rapid escalation of opposition. It was as if flood gates had been opened.

While the issue of the five Socialists was raised, Congress, as we noted, was considering a peace time sedition bill—the Graham-Sterling Bill. Two major supporters of the Red scare —organized labor and several major newspapers defected on this issue.

The press was concerned with the possibility of widespread censorship which might have been available to the postmaster general. Freedom of the press, which had not been an issue in 1919 when some radical publications were harassed or closed, suddenly became the American birthright again. *The New York Times*, which saw nothing un-American in the expulsion of five duly elected Socialist legislators, did perceive a danger to American freedoms when it was reminded that *The Times* might have become a target of superpatriots.

Organized labor, led by Gompers, had been a major ally of the antiradical crusade, in part, to prevent left wing and IWW infiltration into the AF of L. The AF of L took the position that the sedition bill would infringe labor's right to strike, thus causing more harm to the labor movement than would the suppression of radicals. Gompers testified against the section of the bill prohibiting organizations to seek social change by force. This section, he said, would make strikes illegal, enforce involuntary servitude of labor, and disproportionately hurt the reform efforts of the working class. "Strikes," he argued, "are nothing more or less than an aspiration of the working people for a better life."

After Gomper's testimony the alliance of the AF of L with militant antiradical groups was never quite the same and organized labor's participation in the Red scare waned.

The NAACP, which had remained silent during 1919, suddenly became an opponent of Palmer. Leaders of the association testified that the section of the Graham-Sterling Bill which prohibited appeal to racial prejudice would, in a bizarre way, adversely affect the Negro's right to work for social and economic change for Negroes.

Opposition to the proposed sedition bill *per se*, lead to attacks upon Palmer's motives and methods and those of the Justice Department. Prominent attorneys testified before the House Rules Committee that Palmer and the Justice Department had willfully exaggerated the extent and danger of radicalism in America. Palmer and his agents were accused of police brutality, illegal incarceration, refusal to grant the right to counsel, and failure to use search warrants. A prominent Wall Street attorney and former captain in military intelligence testified that the Justice Department had actually provoked several alleged crimes through the use of agents provocateur. This former intelligence agent urged Congress to investigate "just how Russian" Palmer was.

Dozens of prominent conservatives who were committed civil libertarians continued the attack on Palmer and the proposed bill. Their prestige and conservatism made it difficult for Palmer's supporters to brand them successfully as biased radicals. By early March of 1920, a survey of newspaper editors revealed that about one third favored the bill, one third were opposed to its passage, and one third were uncertain. And this was only about sixty days after almost every major newspaper in the country hailed the Palmer raids as a major victory for Americanism. The attack on Palmer and the sedition bill was so sharp, so sudden, and so national in scope that the attorney general, for the first time since the onset of the hysteria, went on the defensive. He testified that the Graham Bill might adversely affect freedom of the press and the right to peaceful picketing. He attacked postal censorship and said that the Graham Bill made him "shudder." The Rules Committee reported the bill out unfavorably, and the matter was dropped.

Palmer's prime strategy had been the raid on radical head-quarters followed by arrests of aliens, detentions, hearings before the commissioner of immigration of the Labor Department and culminating in deportations. Commissioner Caminetti, a superpatriot, acted as a willing tool of the Justice Department and cooperated in the denial of the rights of hundreds of aliens. Thirteen months after the onset of the hysteria a few federal judges and administrative officials began to question the procedures of the Justice Department and the commissioner. Justice Holmes, speaking for the majority in January of 1920, declared that information gathered through illegal search could not be used to incriminate. A federal judge two weeks later applied this dictum to an alien who was "captured" in one of Palmer's raids. The Assistant Secretary of Labor, Lewis Post, who believed that hundreds of aliens had been illegally arrested, illegally searched, and denied the right to counsel, applied the Holmes rule, and by April, ordered the dismissal of about 3,000 pending alien deportation cases. The secretary of labor had, in the interim, ruled that membership in the Communist Labor Party was not a deportable offense and 300 additional aliens were released.

Opposition to Palmer stimulated a brief but sharp outburst of Red-baiting. Post was attacked by dozens of newspapers and many Congressmen. He was charged with "coddling the Reds" and described as a "moon-struck parlor radical." The rumor was widely circulated in Washington that the Labor Department was "honeycombed with Bolshevism." In mid-April, a resolution of impeachment was introduced in the House. The Rules Committee decided that the evidence was insufficient but offered a resolution of censure. Post demanded the right to testify and did so on May 7, 1920. He was charged with overruling the commissioner of immigration for political reasons.

Post first clarified his authority by making the point that the authority to deport aliens rested ultimately with the secretary of labor and not the commissioner. He then attacked—in specific not general terms—the actions of the commissioner, the attorney general, the House Immigration Committee, and the press. He presented numerous specific examples of the violation of due process—illegal searches and seizures, arrests without warrants, police brutality, illegal detention, and refusal to grant the right to counsel. He demonstrated the disparity between the claims of imminent conspiracy advanced by Palmer and the press and the facts of the case. He noted that only three pistols capable of being fired were found in the January 2 raids, and that two of these were only .22 caliber. He noted that almost all the arrests were based only on alleged membership in radical groups and parties—not on the acts or convictions of the arrested. He demonstrated that only about fifty of the arrested aliens were, in fact, committed to violent methods of social change. He charged the press with wild distortion for the precise purpose of building up circulation. Post's testimony was so incisive and factual that the Rules Committee suspended the investigation and many newspapers hailed his testimony. The House, in a dramatic reversal, decided to investigate the attorney general and called hearings for the first of June.

For weeks prior to Post's testimony, the General Intelligence Division of the Justice Department, on Palmer's instruction, warned the country of an impending May Day radical insurrection and terror. The division warned of plots to kill high government officials, the bombing of government buildings, and a general strike. Palmer's men claimed that these plots were part of a master Bolshevik conspiracy to overthrow the American government and force the recognition of the Soviet Union. The division assured America that every available agent would be on the alert and urged local officials to supplement their police forces.

The press transmitted the division's warning in banner headlines. Robert Murray describes the effect:

Local police officers immediately alerted their forces to be in a state of complete readiness. Public buildings, churches, and the homes of prominent citizens were placed under guard. State militias were called up in certain states in order to thwart any riots which might occur. In New York City, the entire police force of 11,000 men was put on twenty-four-hour duty and the public library, Pennsylvania Station, and the general post office were heavily guarded. In Boston, trucks with mounted machine guns were parked at various strategic locations while special protection was provided for the state house and the city jail. In Pittsburgh, the bomb squad was placed on a twenty-four-hour alert; in Washington, all public buildings and the homes of certain federal officials were protected; in Chicago, 360 suspected radicals were put under lock and key for the day "just in case."[21]

On May Day, 1920, a few radical meetings were held but absolutely no violence occurred. The press, with very few exceptions, denounced Palmer. He was described as "a national menace," "full of hot air," "Little Red Riding Hood with a cry of Wolf," and the Red scare was described as "a mare's nest hatched in the attorney general's brain." The full range of radical, liberal, and conservative newspapers—urban and rural —joined the attack. The Justice Department claimed that the impending revolution did not occur because of the preparations taken at the attorney general's behest.

But the greatest blow to Palmer was yet to come. Three weeks after May Day, when the country had warm weather but not revolution, the pamphlet quoted previously entitled "Report Upon the Illegal Practices of the United States Department of Justice," was published. The authors, as noted, were unimpeachable dignitaries of the law. Their sixty-seven page pamphlet contained sworn testimony, analysis, and nineteen exhibits. Now Palmer and the department stood publicly accused of wholesale illegal arrests of both aliens and citizens, arrests without proper warrants, illegal detention, illegal search and illegal seizure of papers and property without warrant, illegal treatment of prisoners, the use of agents of provocateur and entrapment, police brutality and illegal expenditures of federal funds, activities outside the legal scope of the Department's power and purpose, and violation of the right of self-incrimination. Palmer was openly accused of promoting the Red menace to advance his own political ambitions.

The evidence to support these accusations went far beyond that of any previous testimony presented to the Congress—sworn testimony from aliens and citizens who were arrested, detailed descriptions of the arrests, of police brutality in jail, and of forced testimony. There were instructions from the department to agents in the field urging provocative acts.

Violation of law and due process was the issue they posed, not freedom of speech. Not only was free speech for dissenters not raised but some of the authors were militant antiradicals; witness the remark of Judge Miles which he made after describing his anger at violation of due process:

seemed to me . . . that if any Reds were in jail it was a good thing and that there were probably a great many more of them out of jail who ought to be in . . .

On June 1, Palmer appeared before the House Rules Committee. He denied both the charges of Assistant Secretary Post and the claims of the twelve attorneys. He defended his actions and referred to the attorneys as "friends of anarchists" and their evidence as "half-facts from public enemies." "We find several of them," Palmer remarked, "appearing as counsel . . . at deportation hearings . . . I have difficulty reconciling their attitude with that of men who have sworn to uphold the constitution of the United States."

On June 23, the attack shifted to the judiciary when Judge Anderson in *Coyler et al v. Skeffington* declared that membership in the Communist Party was not necessarily grounds for deportation of aliens. Judge Anderson, who had been served by Professor Chaffee as *amicus curiae* in the Skeffington case, repeated the charges which were published in the report of the twelve attorneys, many of which, in turn, were extracted from the proceedings in the Skeffington case. An organized community of conservatives and liberals opposed to Palmer had been formed. Judge Anderson also accused Palmer of manufacturing a fictitious Bolshevik conspiracy to advance his personal ambitions. "This case seems to have been constructed under the modern theory of statesmanship that you hang first and try afterwards," he wrote in the decision. "A more lawless proceeding it is hard for anyone to conceive. . . . I can hardly sit on the bench as an American citizen and restrain my indignation. I view with horror such proceedings as this." He thought it evident that the "Government owns and operates some part of the Communist party."

A small but influential community of conservatives and liberals thus did form in the spring of 1920 to oppose Palmer and the antiradical hysteria. As in the case of McCarthyism, however, the counter-attack did not organize itself until the hysteria had already become a national phenomenon and the prime issue in American politics. The liberals and those conservatives allegedly committed to due process were so intimidated by Palmer and the antiradical impulse that for the first twelve or thirteen months of the hysteria they remained silent or supported the drive against un-Americanism.

Unofficially led by Former Chief Justice Charles Evans Hughes, the core of this counter-community consisted of about

twenty activists who could count on about another fifty for
contributions and sustained work. These men were concentrated in New York City, Washington, D.C., and Cambridge
—with a handful in Middle and Far West. Some of these men
were prominent and sophisticated upper middle class partners
in America's most prestigious law firms. Those who were not
prominent conservative attorneys were distinguished liberal
professors at prestigious law schools. A few were former judges
and prominent ex-politicians and a few, like LaGuardia and
Post, were liberal office holders. The members of the counter-
community, as we have seen, were staunch antiradicals but
they were outraged by Palmer's methods and those of the New
York State legislature. Their commitment to due process, not
any sympathy for radicalism, caused them to organize an opposition. Many of these men had highly placed contacts in
the government and the judiciary. They also had the skills
and prestige that made it possible for them to be heard and
have an effect—technical legal knowledge, the capacity to
raise money, high professional status, political skills, political
visibility and access to the major means of communication.
One member, the Assistant Secretary of Labor, Louis Post,
happened to be in an administrative position which permitted
him to block off a major means used to promote the hysteria
—the deportation of alien radicals.

This counter-elite—and it was an intellectual and professional
elite—formed a legal defense committee and defended a few
of Palmer's "victims." They published their report attacking
Palmer and the Justice Department which we discussed, and
they continued to publicly attack Palmer, exposing numerous
violations of laws and administrative procedure which the
Justice Department and the commissioner on immigration had
committed. They acted as friends of the court in the Skeffington
case. They testified against the sedition bill, and they prepared
extensive memos for Gompers when he testified against the

bill. They gave dozens of speeches and wrote articles. Their function was to alert and arouse public opinion—not by defending radicals—but by illuminating violations of the law.

These activities helped to discredit Palmer by destroying the illusion of his objectivity, his role as defender of justice and the law, and his integrity. The counter-community hurt Palmer by attacking his selflessness and patriotism when they suggested he was using the Red scare to promote his own aspirations for the presidency. In so doing, they exposed a latent function of the hysteria and made it appear less than an honest and pure defense of America. The counter-community also broke the unanimity of prohysteria cues which had been emanating from prestigious political and business sources. The success of the antiradical crusade undoubtedly had something to do with the fact that dozens of America's most prominent figures supported the myth of the Bolshevik conspiracy and literally no one publicly opposed it until it had begun to run wild. Some of the men who played a prominent role in the attack on Palmer were impeccable establishmentarians whose credibility would be difficult to question. When they attacked Palmer they must have created substantial cognitive dissonance, doubt, confusion, and questioning among the public.

In a sense the counter-community broke the momentum of the hysteria and forced Palmer to retreat. Political hysteria, we shall see, depends upon elites sustaining high levels of anxiety among the masses—anxiety based upon the anticipation of great conspiratorial danger. To sustain such high levels of anxiety for months or years probably requires total control of the apparatus of terror and the means of communication, and a unanimity of cues which supports and escalates the anxiety. The hysteria has, among other qualities, the quality of a trance and a panic, and these require momentum and continuous reinforcement. The counter-community introduced discord, helped to break the unanimity of cues, and thus halted the effective momentum and reinforcement. The counter-community by attacking Palmer, interrupted the hypnotist and the hypnosis.

These facts seem to confirm the idea that American democracy contains elites which rise to the defense of democratic values and processes when they are threatened—elites committed to the rights of minorities and the democratic way. But this is questionable. The counter-community did not effectively form and act until the political hysteria and the repression was in an advanced stage. Conservatives and liberals, allegedly committed to due process stood by quietly—with occasional exceptions—for more than one year while business elites and politicians and the press created and successfully sold the Bolshevik conspiracy, smashed the steel and the coal strikes, defamed the labor movement, deported alleged alien radicals, reaffirmed the Americanism of business values and the open shop, and created an atmosphere of fear and intimidation which stifled critical thought. The counter-community did not organize until the New York Legislature committed a gross and public act which obviously violated a fundamental rule of the political game. It took a violation of the very heart of liberalism—the election—to mobilize a counter-hysteria group. While impotent and dehumanized minorities of aliens and radicals and alleged radicals were being repressed, allegedly democratic elites did essentially nothing in an organized and effective way. In fact, it was pluralist elites which promoted the hysteria.

We noted that organized labor and the press—major promoters of the hysteria—did not turn against it until Gompers and many publishers decided that their self-interest might be adversely affected by the proposed sedition bill. The press was little concerned with freedom of the press for radical publications. Freedom of the press became an issue only when *The New York Times* and *The Washington Post* concluded that they were potential victims themselves. One is reminded of the fact that organized and forceful opposition to Joseph Mc-Carthy did not really begin until he attacked one of the elites central to modern America—the United States Army. When Gompers and the publishers, for reasons of self-interest, joined the small number of those committed to due process, the counter-community came to represent a confluence of political philosophy and self-interest. The elites allegedly committed to democracy not only failed to expose the latent function of the hysteria, to wit, the promotion of self-interest of dozens of interest groups, but those very elites—mostly business elites —promoted the mass and antipluralist politics that was the Red scare.

The hysteria terminated, in part, because the very elites who promoted the hysteria succeeded in getting most of what they wanted. They succeeded in using the hysteria as a technique to manage tensions and maintain their power. When they resolved these tensions they no longer found it useful to promote antiradical crusades.

This alleged commitment of group leaders to democracy is a very pragmatic thing. John Higham, the historian of nativism in America, has commented on the role which group self-interest played in the termination of the Red scare:

First of all, the seething labor unrest of 1919, which formed the social basis of the antiradical spirit, faded early in 1920. The great steel strike collapsed in January amid the wreckage of labor's post war dreams, and the unions passed to the defensive. The return of industrial peace dissipated the fear of imminent revolution. Especially among industrialists, many of whom had joined in the cry of alarm, the easing of class tensions produced a deep reaction. Now that the immigrant seemed docile again, his bosses recalled his economic value. In purely business terms, a rampant antiradical nativism cut off industry's best source of manpower. A number of business leaders began actively defending the foreign-born from the charge of radicalism. The Inter-Racial Council, which was a mouthpiece for some of America's biggest tycoons—men like Cleveland H. Dodge, E. G. Grace, Thomas W. Lamont, and Daniel Willard—came out flatly in April 1920 against the common association of immigrants with unrest, demanded a reform of deportation proceedings, and urged the public to take a friendly attitude toward ethnic minorities. Its chairman, T. Coleman Du Pont, asserted that native Americans created most of the industrial disturbances and that the immigrant's critics were suffering from pure Red Hysteria, nothing more. The head of the National Founders Association took the same view. The American Constitutional Association, an organization of a thousand West Virginia business leaders formed in 1920 to defend the interest of the coal operators and to promote the open shop, said "Bolshevism was conceived in America by Americans."[22]

When the self-interest of major business groups which depended upon immigrant labor appeared to be at issue, businessmen began to oppose the repression of immigrants. Prior to this time, many business leaders promoted the hysteria to defame organized labor. Newspapers like *The New York Times,* which had applauded the Palmer raids, soon took their cue from the more sophisticated and powerful businessmen and began to publish articles on the value of immigrants to American industry.[23] The pragmatic and self-serving nature of the support and opposition to the hysteria and the repression is clear in the sudden reversal of business attitudes. Charles Schwab, of Bethlehem Steel, a major employer of immigrant labor and a supporter of the hysteria, came to call the radical menace a "bogey" and predicted that the Palmer raids would create more Reds than they eliminated.

While Palmer's crusade concentrated on those groups at the fringes of American life, no significant or organized opposition developed. When the unrest of 1919 was muchly resolved in favor of the status quo, then opposition developed.

In late June, Palmer not only failed to receive the presidential nomination of the Democratic convention but also became the object of considerable scorn and ridicule. The "Fighting

Quaker," the national hero of January, 1920, had become, by the summer of 1920, the "Fighting Faker," and the "Quaking Quitter." The ensuing presidential campaign was noticeably free of antiradical rhetoric. Except for occasional antiradical outbursts from the Justice Department, other superpatriotic societies, and open shop proponents, the hysteria had run its course.

The Red Scare was dead. But the effects of the political hysteria—perhaps reverberations is a better word—continued for decades. One can measure a few of these with some precision: the increase in membership in the K.K.K. and superpatriotic societies, the growth of the open shop movement, the dramatically rapid decline in union membership and union influence, the growing conservatism and red-baiting of labor, the rash of antistrike legislation, the passage in 1924 of restrictive immigration laws, the dissolution of radical parties, the purging of textbooks, and the passage of state legislation dealing with sedition, criminal anarchy and loyalty oaths for teachers.

We know with some certainty that suspicion of the labor movement was so great that more than one million men left their unions by 1923. We know that membership in the Communist Party dropped from about 70,000 to 16,000 in 1920. We can even document a move to the right by Socialist parties. We know that more than 240 open shop groups sprung up in more than forty-four states and that the open shop became identified as the American Plan. We know that four states required loyalty oaths for teachers in 1921 and that fifteen states followed suit in the decade following the Red scare. We know that many bar associations—in the twenties—supported purification of textbooks and urged that the criterion for expurgation be whether or not a passage tended to lessen the greatness of the nation and its leaders. We can document the process by which public schools—to a greater extent than before—became institutions for socialization into Americanism.

We can document Supreme Court decisions in the twenties which upheld state legislation that made the advocacy of certain revolutionary ideas a crime. We can demonstrate a fairly sharp rise in nativism, anti-Catholicism and anti-Semitism in the twenties. If not direct effects of the antiradical hysteria, these events were certainly influenced by it.

But the most significant effects of the antiradical hysteria are not so easy to measure, because they have to do with the distribution of power and the way Americans look at themselves and the non-American world. The critical effect of the Red scare was its effect on the American mind-set. The Red scare was promoted, in large part, by major business groups which feared their power was threatened by a leftward trend in the labor movement. They developed mass support for the anti-radical hysteria by stimulating many deep-seated forces and fears which often lie dormant below the surface of American thought—nativism, antiintellectualism, a deep and abiding popular indentification with capitalist cliches, a disturbing sense of rootlessness and fear of status loss, xenophobia, and a shallow commitment to variety and dissent. Power elites also stimulated the American perception of America as the em-bodiment of self-evident truth and the consequent belief that nonliberal values are the embodiment of antitruth. The hys-teria was also nourished by the paranoid style in American politics and our proclivity for conspiratorial thinking. The deeper significance of the hysteria lay in the nourishment that it provided for those very American perspectives, fears, and values which nourished it. The hysteria renewed its source, and, in so doing, nourished the most repressive, antidemocratic, and regressive face of America.

The Red scare further demarcated what is American and un-American. It heightened the already powerful identification with Horatio Alger and Adam Smith. Free enterprise, the Protestant Ethic, and capitalism were again defined as Amer-ican truth and the embodiment of loyalty. Socialism was again typed as evil and Russia as the embodiment of that evil. To be radical was to be disloyal. Red-baiting became a legitimated technique for politicans and business and labor leaders—an integral element of pluralist politics. Fear of radicalism was stimulated. Militant anticommunism became a core American idea. If one pushed the origins of the domino theory and the Cold War mentality back to the creation of a profound anti-Russianism, one could with much justification, trace this complex of attitudes to the hysteria of 1919. The conspiratorial theory of history—always appealing to an American fringe—became more appealing to the center. The conspiratorial perspective fed the American need to deny the possibility of genuine grass roots revolutionary movements. Socialist revolutions were hatched and provoked by Bolshevik conspiracy—against the peoples' will.

The idea that the ultimate aim of the U.S.S.R. was, and always would be, the violent overthrow of the American government took root at this time. Intervention to prevent the spread of communism became "more logical." Of course, isolation from the un-American world—an ancient American technique for purifying America from foreign contamination—was also fed by Red scare perspectives.

The hysteria nudged the paranoid style in American politics from the periphery of American political culture to a more central position. The paranoid style and the conspiratorial perspective also made it easier for Americans to satisfy their need to attribute America's political and economic troubles to malevolent and conspiratorial bosses and machines, or to administrative inefficiencies, or to trusts and business cabals rather than to American political institutions or capitalism.

The Lockian political system with its emphasis on private property, the unlimited right of acquisition, majority rule, minority rights, periodic elections, and limited state power remains thereby pure and guiltless.

Thus the hysteria which is nourished by our passionate

identification with American values and experiences, our eleva-
tion of Locke and Smith to universal truth, in turn nourishes
that America. America, in American eyes, becomes ever more a
redeemer nation, ever more, that special place which found
ultimate truth in philosophy and perfect freedom in fact, that
purity and equality which left the contamination and hierarchy
of Europe behind. The superpatriot teaches America once again
that she is a City Upon a Hill with a mission to spread the
American truth. The hysteria is a desperate reaffirmation of
ancient American political institutions and capitalist values. The
hysteria is a product of America's irrational liberal immobility—
and further secures that immobility.

The hysteria was an attempt—largely successful—to freeze
and preserve nineteenth century economic liberalism and eighteenth century political institutions. This was its cause, and its
effect. The hysteria was an attempt—largely successful—to
ieaffirm the legitimacy of the power elites of capitalism and to
further weaken workers' class consciousness. The hysteria was
an attempt—again successful—to defuse progressivism, smash
radicalism, and hinder transcendent speculations. Hysteria is one
of many American purification rites—a reaffirmation of one
hundred percent Americanism. The hysteria taught us that we
were blessed and free and that the idea of a noncapitalist world
was cursed and dangerous. The hysteria taught us that Americans are susceptible to a repression promoted by legitimated
business and political leaders, a pluralist and nonviolent repression, which primarily utilizes the law as its medium. Democratic
repression can be very seductive.

We turn now to examine how the myth of Bolshevik conspiracy was made credible to the American people by appeals to
the semblance of reason.

3

THE CREDIBILITY
OF CONSPIRACY

THE Red scare was phantasmagorical. It was a dream. It was magic. It was an orgy of superpatriotism. It was a ferocious burst of supernationalism. It was nativism and anti-Semitism. It was anti-Catholicism and racism. It was a purification rite—a reaffirmation of ancient American values. It was hysteria.

The fundamental quality of the Red scare is the enormous imbalance between the nationwide anxiety and the objective danger. The anxiety was massive. The danger was miniscule. This is poor reality testing on a truly grand scale. And it had profound political implications.

The problem is to explain how and why the fantasy of imminent Bolshevik conspiracy was taken for reality. Part of the answer has to do with the way in which events like the Bolshevik revolution, the growth of socalism in America, and the postwar dislocation—bits and pieces of reality—were woven together to create a portrait of conspiracy whose appeal made it not only plausible, but very believable—though nonexistent. The maneuverings of mythmakers that we deal with in this chapter were designed to appeal to reason. In a later chapter we will analyze appeals to the irrational and the unconscious. Here we will show how an aura of plausibility that a rational man could take for reality was created. The promoters of the Red scare succeeded in creating that aura. To analyze how they did this is to develop a theory of social and political myths and mythmaking.

Here is how Stanley Coben, the biographer of A. Mitchell Palmer, appraised the revolutionary capability of American radicals in 1919.

Actually, there was not even a remote possibility of a serious uprising in 1919–20. Most of the evidence which convinced Justice Department officials that the government was in danger, consisted of printed matter collected by the GID. After the Bolshevik triumph in Russia, American radicals became unduly optimistic; scores of new foreign-language communist and anarchist journals began publication.

However, such calls to revolt, as a recent historian of American Communism pointed out, "belonged to the realm of literary make-believe. No preparations accompanied them; no consequences followed them. The Communist factions were talking to themselves." During an investigation of the Palmer raids, Senator Thomas J. Walsh remarked caustically: "Nothing, so far as the evidence here has described, has evinced anything in the nature of preparation for a military uprising. No guns, no munitions of war were accumulated; there was no drilling of soldiers or anything of that kind. . . ." Furthermore, American workers were indifferent if not hostile to communist or any other kind of radical propaganda, and the Communists had practically no contacts in 1919–20 with the trade unions. Even the new Bolshevik regime in Russia was not yet in a position to offer leadership or funds to the disorganized American Communists.

Nor did any other radical organizations provide a serious threat to national institutions. American anarchists were capable of isolated bomb atrocities, but a more ambitious organized attempt was far beyond them.[1]

The problem is also how and why and by whom was this perceived danger to America engineered. To understand this is to understand something important about America.

The Red scare commenced almost immediately after the war ended. The connection is more than temporal. In some ways the Red scare is a symbolic continuation of the Hun scare, for the war nourished a way of looking at the world and activated many satisfying feelings which later fed the Red scare and which, in turn, were satisfied by the hysteria. The Committee on Public

Information, which was designed to produce fervent and unified support for the war, fed Americans stories of sinister German agents and international plots and conspiracies directed toward America's destruction. The Committee nourished superpatriotic instincts and American nationalism and spread the doctrine that the Reds were not only in league with the Huns, but also that the Russian revolution was a German creation. One hundred percent Americanism was the committee's credo. Intellectuals and radicals who opposed the war were portrayed as traitors. All Germans were stereotyped as wreckers of Western civilization.

The portrait of America was beautiful—freedom loving and democratic—and was contrasted daily with that of murderous, totalitarian and conspiratorial Germany. The task of converting Europe to America's version of self-evident truth was depicted as a holy crusade. America, again became a "Redeemer nation." Disloyalty became a prime category of thought and loyalty the prime virtue. Opposition to the war became anathema and particular uses of freedom of speech to advocate the pacifist cause became illegal. Nativist sentiments deepened. Foreigners became suspect. Pacifist words were perceived as the equivalent of anti-American deeds. The country was in a state of high excitation, and belligerent nationalism was the national model.

After the war, George Creel, the chairman of the committee, described what had been the goal of his group:

What we had to have was no mere surface unity, but a passionate belief in the justice of America's cause that should weld the people of the United States into one white-hot mass of instinct with fraternity, devotion, courage and deathless determination . . . every task (was) a common task for a single purpose.[2]

He succeeded so well that America, the nation of competition and separateness, experienced one of its most rare and elusive pleasures—fraternity and cooperation—a common unity of purpose. It was, however, an artifacted and not an organic unity, for it necessitated the presence of an enemy and a great sense

of danger. Nevertheless, it was a pleasure and a marvelous
catharsis for aggressive impulses. The latent psychic pleasures of
war are many. The identity of the nation and thus, the self, are
revitalized and well defined. Values are revivified. Contrast with
the image of the enemy sharpens the sense of self. Inner rage
may be legitimately projected. One may hate and enjoy the
simple dichotomies of the conspiratorial perspective. Cues become unanimous. Cognitive dissonance is minimal. These are
gratifications not customarily experienced. Why should they be
easily surrendered just because the war is over?

During the war, the drive for 100 percent Americanism became institutionalized and bureaucratized. Superpatriotism became a big business and the Committee on Public Information
was aided by superpatriotic societies for whom loyalty and disloyalty were the staff of life, indeed, dollars and cents. Societies
like the American Protective League, according to John Higham,
the historian of nativism in America,

. . . had no intention of dissolving. It looked forward to a happy
career ferreting out new disloyalties, sharpened its surveillance of
radical meetings, and tried to work out with the United States
Naturalization Service an arrangement for investigating every ap-
plicant for citizenship.[3]

The establishment of the American Legion in January of 1919
assured that the drive for loyalty would continue. The constitution pledged the Legion "to foster and perpetuate a one hundred
percent Americanism," which it attempted to do by continually
warning the American people of endless treasons in their midst.
A careful reading of the *American Legion Weekly* for 1919 and
1920 reveals that as memories of the war faded and became less
serviceable as a binding force for the organization, ferocious
antiradicalism served as a more than adequate substitute.

And then the war ended. And the fraternity and cooperation
were shattered by postwar dislocation and bitter labor struggles.
It must have been difficult to relinquish a pleasurable belligerent nationalism and the excitation of hatred and the gratification

of *communitas*. It must have been difficult to give up simple conspiratorial explanations which left no doubt about good and evil. To some degree, the antiradical hysteria was a symbolic transformation—a continuity of wartime perspectives and pleasures. The "Red" provided many services for the American people which had been performed by the Hun. The character of the hunted seems to be far less significant than the pleasures of the hunt. It was not by chance that the radical movement in America was portrayed as part of a vast world conspiracy financed by German Junkers.

Psychological interpretations undoubtedly deepen understanding of politics, but great outbursts of emotion, particularly in America, where politics is customarily passionless, must first be traced to some stress in the world of conscious experience. It may be postwar dislocation, or status loss, or the disappearance of a familiar world, or an attack on treasured values, or a threat to the power of elites. The stress may be dealt with in terms of psychic needs but the particular stress will effect the particular response. The two years following the war were years of stress and change, for both the American people and for big business. And many of these changes could be dealt with in ways that had become familiar and effective during the war.

The plausibility of a secret and apocalyptic Bolshevik conspiracy in America was nourished by the high drama of the Russian revolution and the shock it produced in America. The revolution frightened American conservatives. Lenin's rhetoric concerning the inevitability of a world-wide Communist revolution fed this fright. Newspapers, with rare exception, portrayed the revolution as an orgy of mass murder, individual assassination, rape, pillage, and slaughter. It was commonly claimed that nuns were raped, monasteries burned, and it was reported that the Bolsheviki in Petrograd used an electrically operated guillotine to behead five hundred victims per hour. Bolshevik rule was described as a "compound of slaughter, confiscation, anarchy and universal disorder . . . the paradise of IWW's and the superlative heaven of anarchists and direct-action socialists."

The revolution was originally engineered by a conspiratorial minority of disciplined radicals. Superpatriots built the myth of an American revolution on this fact. It was possible to admit, without injuring the case, as superpatriots did, that American revolutionaries were a small and secret minority. In a bizarre way, this admission even strengthened the argument because the radical threat became all the more unknowable and therefore sinister—a few evil and brilliant men, directed by Lenin, secretly plotting the violent destruction of millions of good people. The precedent had been set. The fear of revolution and conspiracy in America mounted when communist uprisings occurred in Bavaria and Hungary in March of 1919. The Communist Party in France and Italy gained strength at this time and, for a brief time, it appeared that western Europe might follow the Russian route. Karl Radek, the executive secretary of the Third International, lent credence to an emerging domino theory when he remarked that the money sent to Germany for the Spartacist revolt was nothing compared to the funds transmitted to New York for the purpose of spreading Bolshevism in the United States. The conspiratorial case was becoming more plausible.

In 1919, the Communist Party of America and the Communist Labor Party were organized. Again, the apocalyptic pronouncements of the wildest superpatriots seemed more credible, despite the fact that total membership in the former was about 60,000 and membership in the latter about 10,000. Actually the myth of a massive conspiracy was nourished both by the shock of their founding and by the exaggerated rumors of their great strength. What made the situation appear to be particularly sinister and provocative—and therefore believable —to "loyal" Americans was the potential use of a fundamental American political institution—the political party—for such perverse anti-American purposes.

The Communist Party and the Communist Labor Party, however, were not the only radical public vehicles that proponents of a Bolshevik conspiracy could cite as proof of an imminent Red takeover. The International Workers of the World—militantly disruptive, violent, and communist-syndicalist-anarchist —was cited as unquestionable "proof". The IWW, although not substantial in numbers, was vocal, visible, and revolutionary, and it did play a significant role in a few dramatic and violent strikes. Of its anticapitalism, and thus, naturally, its un-Americanism there was no doubt. Witness the lyrics of an IWW song and imagine their impact on the America of 1919:

> Onward Christian soldiers! Drench the land with gore;
> Mercy is a weakness all other gods abhor
> Bayonet the babies, jab the mothers, too;
> Hoist the cross of Calvary to hallow all you do
> File the bullets' noses flat, poison every well;
> God decrees your enemies must all go plum to hell.

The plausibility of a Bolshevik conspiracy and the hatred of radicals upon which it fed was enhanced by the fact that large numbers of American intellectuals fell in love with the Russian revolution, which they saw as the termination of a feudal, barbaric, and exploitative historical epoch and the beginning of a reign of justice and freedom. They perceived the new Russia as a potential Arcadia, free of the cruel past, just as the founding fathers perceived America as an escape from the bonds of Europe. The revolution represented to this intelligentsia the possibility of a brave new world and they raptured in this vision while decrying the repressions of American capitalism.

The "betrayal" of American intellectuals was cited as additional proof of America's internal threat. Because this "betrayal" tapped the strain of antiintellectualism in American life, the conspiracy became more credible and the affect behind the hysteria more powerful. The hysteria is not based on facts but upon facts which connect with deep seated American prejudices or values or fears or repressed wishes. The country is prepared by its history to react in a particular way. It is the confluence of fact and fantasy and America that produces political hysteria. In some countries a left wing intelligentsia is taken for granted. In America it is often a cause for legal action.

Superpatriots now had six facts to work with—facts which evoked strong feelings in a country that hated and feared radicals: the Russian revolution, the spread of communism in Europe, the formation of the CP and the CLP in America, the operations of the IWW, and the "betrayal" of the American intellectuals.

The fact that many alleged leaders and followers of the alleged Red conspiracy were aliens, Russians, East Europeans and/or Jews served the needs of those who promoted the hysteria. The CP and the CLP were composed primarily of immigrants, many of whom were Russian, German, and Jewish and many of whom did not speak English. A very large number of those who struck against U.S. Steel were foreign born citizens or aliens. As a matter of fact, a large proportion of the working class in 1920 in several basic industries was composed of aliens. Some strike leaders were aliens—not only in the steel strike but in several other strikes. A very large number of those rounded up in the Palmer raids were aliens too, and many were Jews. Many of the newspapers considered to be radical were published in a foreign language. In fact, about fifty radical newspapers were established in 1919–1920 and published in twenty-six foreign languages.

These facts made it possible for superpatriots to mine the vein of American nativism and anti-Semitism. The conspiracy becomes ever more believable. In America it is easy to hate radicals. It is even easier to hate alien and Jewish radicals. The nativism and anti-Semitism and antiintellectualism and antiradicalism of America become resources with which superpatriots can work. America feeds the hysteria, because the facts tap deep American roots. Jewish radicals are taken for granted in Israel. In America, they often evoke a visceral rage.

The hysteria, however, was not merely a product of deeply rooted American impulses being fed by facts. It was also a reflection of the state of America at a particular time. As of the First World War, American culture had by no means fully assimilated the vast influx of immigrants. The Americanization problem was of very serious concern to millions of natives. People were very much aware of the fact that very different attitudes towards America were held by alien groups and that the loyalty and "Americanness" of new citizens was not to be taken for granted. Differences of national origin, religion, language, and length of residence are often converted, in America, into a scale of loyalty and disloyalty—into Americanism and un-Americanism. Edward Shils has succinctly noted this fact.

There is more a tendency in the United States, as compared with Great Britain, to think of differences in terms of loyalty and disloyalty, in terms of liking and disliking America. Each successive tier of the nativity scale, each successive generation of arrivals, looks askance on those who arrived later than their own. Ethnic and nativity differences are reinterpreted as attitudinal differences. The American way of life involves the affirmation of ideals.[4]

There is a sense in which the Red scare can be understood as a very crude technique designed to achieve integration as well as a response to a concern with disintegration. An America that had integrated its immigrants would be much less likely to respond with such ferocious passion to radicals qua aliens. This does not mean that political hysteria would become impossible or even more unlikely in a more integrated America or a less antiintellectual, anti-Semitic America. It does mean that the mix which produces the hysteria would be different.

For Shils has hit upon a very significant fact when he pointed out that loyalty and disloyalty are fundamental categories of American thinking. America has very special meaning to Americans. Identified for centuries with the ideas of John Locke in politics and Adam Smith in economics, to the exclusion of all others, liberalism in America has become all that there is and, as such, it has tremendous force. Locke and Smith in the form of fourth of July-ized cliche has become the American nationalism, the American essence and ethos, the American way of life. America, as the inevitable unfolding of liberalism, provides many services for its people. It provides them with an identity. They are Americans. They are political liberals and capitalists. It provides them with a way of life. It provides them with self-evident truth—certainly a beautiful thing to possess. It provides them with a self-righteous pride in the certainty of that truth. It provides them with a definition of liberal good and antiliberal evil. It defines their enemies and friends. It convinces them that their way of life is good and true and beautiful and that messianism in the pursuit of self-evident truth is justified. The identification with America becomes passionate— a grand love affair. America, therefore provides many of the roots by which Americans define who they are and are not. So one's being is very much tied up with one's America. An attack on America—real or fictional—becomes an attack on one's self. And the defense of America against its enemies— real or fictional—becomes a defense of one's self and truth. It is a reaffirmation of one's being. It depends, therefore, less upon a specific American anti-Semitism or a specific American antiradicalism than upon the strength of the identification that Americans make with America. It is a passionate America threatened by perceived enemies qua enemies, not alien enemies or Jewish enemies, that triggers the purge. Joseph McCarthy managed to convince millions of Americans that Dean Acheson and his friends—white Anglo-Saxon Protestant Groton and Yale—were enemies of the people.

But we anticipate. The fact nevertheless remains that since many alleged radicals were aliens and Jews, the conspiratorial myth was more credible because it was allegedly composed of low status out-groups upon whom native Protestants could vent their hatred and frustrations. A dehumanized victim enhances the appeals of purge and lessens or eliminates the guilt that might be aroused if one were dealing with human beings as opposed to human vermin—an adjective commonly used in 1919 to describe alien radicals.

Superpatriots who promoted the hysteria only had a few thousand radicals to "work with" but they did have millions of radical words out of which to weave conspiratorial myths. The American way of life and the American economic and political system were attacked more publicly and militantly by words in 1919 than perhaps at any time in American history. By a subtle process of symbolic transformation, judges, juries, legislators, big businessmen, and a host of superpatriots converted these words into deeds. Radical literature became the equivalent of radical action. As millions of revolutionary words were produced, circulated, captured, and reprinted, an aura of credibility began to emerge that the word—particularly the written word—was not only father to the deed, but an action in itself. On the basis of the faith which Americans customarily bestow upon written words, a structure of unreality was created. The discovery of a statement of revolutionary aims in a radical pamphlet was perceived as if it were *prima facie* proof of the actual existence of a revolutionary conspiracy.

This symbolic transformation was facilitated because the words were fighting words, disrespectful and provocative words, because there were millions of them, and because many of them were printed or spoken in a foreign tongue. Words were captured by the Justice Department in raids and then publicly exhibited, just as an enemy might be captured and exhibited.

The militant and revolutionary character of radical rhetoric helped to create the impression that a violent and apocalyptic movement of colossal proportions was underway. The Wobblies reminded their followers to "take what you need where you find it; it is yours." Opposing the war, the IWW distributed pamphlets which exhorted workers not to become "hired murderers" and not to make themselves "a target in order to fatten Rockefeller, Morgan, Carnegie . . . and the other industrial pirates." An anarchist pamphlet predicted revolution in bloody terms.

The senile fossils ruling the United States see red! . . . The storm is within and very soon will leap and crash and annihilate you in blood and fire. You have shown no pity to us! We will do likewise. . . . We will dynamite you!

Radical rhetoric was dominated by the very same Marxist jargon that was used to forge the dreaded Russian revolution. It was a lingo particularly foreign to America and dramatically provocative. Much of the rhetoric of Marxism confirmed the superpatriot's portrait of radicals. It was apocalyptic, conspiratorial, violent, vague, secretive, condemnatory, prophetic, atheistic and revolutionary. The Communist Party call to a constituent assembly in 1919 was fairly typical of the Marxist incantations.

In this the most momentous period of the world's history capitalism is tottering to its ruin. The proletariat is straining at the chains which bind it. A revolutionary spirit is spreading throughout the world. The workers are rising to answer the clarion call of the Third International. . . .

The problem of the proletariat consists in organizing and training itself for the conquest of the powers of the state. This conquest of power means the replacement of the state machinery of the bourgeoisie with a new proletarian machinery of government.

We favor international alliance of the Communist Party of the United States only with the communist groups of other countries, such as the Bolsheviki of Russia, Spartacans of Germany, etc., according to the program of Communism as above outlined.

The party shall propagandize class-consciousness industrial unionism as against the craft form of unionism, and shall carry on party activity in cooperation with industrial disputes that take on a revolutionary character.

The number of radical papers praising the Russian revolution and extolling communism did not exceed about fifty, but the call to an American revolution was printed in hundreds of thousands of leaflets and distributed by hand or thrown by the thousands from moving elevated trains. If one did not know that the pamphlets, the posters, and the newspapers were written and distributed by relatively few people, one could easily conclude that the radical movement was enormous and effective.

When the government agents raided radical headquarters, the press frequently reported the capture of "tons of literature of a subversive nature." Senatorial investigation of the Palmer techniques suggested that the prime task of the Department of Justice was, in fact, the collection of radical words.[5] The Justice Department, in its report to Congress on antiradical activities in 1920, describes no activities at all. It merely cites revolutionary propaganda captured during raids, trial records of radicals, and a variety of sedition laws. Max Lowenthal, who wrote extensively on the operations of the Justice Department during the Red scare, reports that the Bureau of Investigation "had the largest collection of radical literature in the world."[6]

The department increased the provocative power of these words by distributing "captured documents" to the press and to congressional committees. The burden of the press coverage was eased when the department helpfully collected many radical documents in one pamphlet, "Red Radicalism as Described by Its Own Leaders."

Using the abundance of this literature upon which to build its case of a vast conspiracy, the Department of Justice announced that 471 radical newspapers were being published in 1919. William Burns, the noted private detective, placed the number of American communists at 422,000, while the head of the National Security League—a major superpatriotic society—estimated the figure to be 600,000. According to the president of the Allied Patriotic Societies, communists were holding 10,000 meetings every week and publishing 350 radical newspapers.

Radical words and superpatriotic words were, in a bizarre way, mutually supportive. Radical statements provided superpatriots with a wonderfully useful self-fulfilling prophecy. Superpatriots argue that a revolutionary plot is brewing in America. Radical responses in print support the Russian revolution and call for an American version. Superpatriots then cite radical speeches and writings as proof of an American conspiracy. Radicals then cite superpatriotic rhetoric as the onset of an American repression. This heightens the bombastic quality of radical rhetoric—much like the sixties. It is as if the publicists of the Red scare ask their enemies for public confirmation and their enemies cordially supply it. The national press claims that a particular strike is "Red-directed". The radical press responds by greatly exaggerating radical participation in the strike and the patriots respond by quoting the radicals' claims as proof. If the radical press denies involvement, the Justice Department responds by arguing that secrecy and denial are part of the conspiratorial plan. The words become echoes. Denial becomes guilt. Silence becomes confirmation. Confirmation becomes guilt.

The word itself ultimately became, in the minds of Americans, not only deeds, but crimes. Aliens, allegedly radical, were deported solely on the basis of words spoken or written by them. Wobblies were convicted, with increasing regularity, not for their overt acts, but for their words. William Preston, a leading authority on the treatment of aliens and dissenters in America notes:

The "overt acts" proving conspiracies on both the industrial and war counts were mainly official statements, policy declarations, newspaper articles, and personal expressions of opinion. . . . Although "overt acts" carries with it the connotation of force and violence, in most cases the prosecution relied on the spoken and written word to convict the Wobblies.[7]

If further proof of the magical and symbolic power of words were needed one could cite the fact that literally every solution to the Red menace, other than incarceration and deportation of Reds, had to do with the power of pro-American words to counter the power of anti-American words—the elimination of anti-American words from textbooks, the elimination of German language courses from the curriculum, and the swearing of loyalty oaths.

The power of written words had become the power of the conspiracy. Since radical words seemed to be everywhere, clearly, the conspiracy was ubiquitous. The Red scare, in part, was epiphenomena.

The predisposition to believe that America was imminently threatened by a colossal Bolshevik conspiracy was not based, however, entirely upon the capacity of the mind to engage in magical thinking. The seductiveness of symbolic transformations was obviously involved. But myths as powerful as the ones we speak of are always woven out of some bits and pieces of reality. Bits of reality are "used" to construct conspiratorial fantasies. Superpatriotic mythmakers, as we have shown, "used" the reality of the Russian revolution, and the reality of the formation of the Communist Party, and the reality of bombings to construct the myth. There is a kernel of "distorted" truth behind all fantasies. That is what makes them credible. Mass reality testing of such grandiosely distorted proportion—like the breakdown of cognitive capacity in individuals—is based on the presence of some real facts which are potentially frightening, a prior disposition to perceive reality in particular ways, and the presence of stress. The fact, the predisposition, and the stress, effect the ability to see the world as it actually is. A dislocated and rapidly changing world that is threatening and stressful can induce distorted portraits of reality.

The facts, the predispositions, the dislocation, the threat, and the stress were all present in 1919—and, as we will show, so was the motivation of men of power to unite in order to promote poor reality testing in their own self interest. One problem worth examining is the uniqueness of this particular mixture and the variety of these factors that must be present for a democratic repression and political hysteria to unfold in America. On the surface it would appear that this constellation is quite unusual.

The alleged Red danger was a postwar threat, and the war and the demobilization that followed destabilized facets of the American economy and society. During the war, 9,000,000 men and women were employed in defense industries and about 4,000,000 were in uniform. Much of the economy was regulated and, despite wartime prosperity, prices continued to rise. The cost of living in 1920 was 105 percent above the prewar level. Since 1914, the cost of food rose 84 percent, clothing rose about 114 percent, and the cost of furniture 125 percent. Salaried employees, most of whose wages had not risen more than 10 percent, were forced to lower their standard of living. Robert Murray reports that ". . . the professional classes, salaried clerks, civic officials, police, and others in a similar category were worse off economically than any other time since the civil war . . . their lack of organization and their middle-class pride precluded any effective protest on their part."[8]

The lower middle class was seriously hurt by inflation as prices rose steeply in the spring of 1919 and continued to rise until the fall of 1920. Nevertheless, the war years were a period of substantial prosperity. The enormous demand for war material and the withdrawal of 4,000,000 men from the work force created a sharp increase in the demand for labor and sharp decrease in the supply. Wages rose to new highs, particularly the wages of organized labor. Profits in most major industries rose above prewar levels. Hundreds of thousands of Negroes migrated to northern and midwestern cities where they were employed in war industries at wages far in excess of what they could have earned in the South.

With the exception of lower middle class and middle class employees on relatively fixed incomes, and there were millions, most sectors of the economy did well and continued to do so throughout 1919.

The antiradical hysteria of 1919—like the McCarthyite political hysteria of the 1950's—was not primarily a response to economic difficulties. The great depression of 1929 produced FDR —not A. Mitchell Palmer or Joseph McCarthy. The Democratic capacity for repression is subtle and deeply rooted and, for it to flower in America, extreme economic hardship is not necessary. It need not come to the rampant inflation of the Weimar Republic.

Within a few weeks after the armistice, hundreds of war contracts were cancelled and, in most cases, the government made allowance for only one month's operation at current production rates. Most of American industry, however, succeeded in converting to peacetime production remarkably well. Industrial production declined slightly less than ten percent, but, by the end of 1919, the production index exceeded the wartime highs. The migration of Negroes to the North, and the fact that, in many jobs they replaced white men, did sharpen racial tensions and shake up neighborhoods. The movement of so many people from place to place, the death, in war, of so many young men, the break up of so many families, the economic difficulties of millions on fixed incomes, the rise in prices in the spring of 1919, and the intense desire to return to normalcy did create a situation in America that could be characterized as much more than irritation and concern about the economy but much less than rage and economic desperation.

Mark Sullivan deftly portrayed the ambiance of America in August 1919—the ambiance within which the hysteria grew. The motif is inconvenience, annoyance, and disappointment— not rampant inflation, or economic disaster.

As I move about the country I am impressed by the fact that there is a good deal of fretfulness and irritation in the world. There is an annoying sense of inconvenience at every turn. I call

it inconvenience because that is what it is. I started to call it discomfort, and discomfort is what most folks call it when they don't
use a harder word. But it isn't discomfort. No person in the United
States who has any capacity whatever for applying a judicial mind
to his own circumstances can say that he isn't comfortable, or
that it isn't possible for him to make himself comfortable.

What people are doing, unconsciously, is recalling a state of the
world when things ran more smoothly than they do now, and
comparing their present state with that. They think that the end
of the war ought to bring that happier prewar world back, automatically. They are irritated by inconveniences and little pin pricks
of lack of order; they don't adjust themselves to the new world; they
keep on hoping and insisting and demanding that the old world
shall come back, as of July 31, 1914; and every time an inconvenience reminds them that it hasn't come back yet, they fill the air
with grumbling.

. . . Comfort has to do with primary things like food and clothing
and shelter, and any human being in America who says he is
uncomfortable, in the sense that he can't get enough of these
primary human needs, is simply giving exaggerated expression to a
grouch. There is plenty for all, and plenty of opportunity in the
shape of work to acquire any one person's quota. The grouch has
failed to exhaust the possibilities of the employment agency and
the Help Wanted column of the newspapers.

But inconvenience there decidedly is. Every time I come back to
New York from a few days' or weeks' absence I am impressed with
an increasing sense of contrast. Each time the streets are less clean
than the last time; hotel floors are less well swept; hotel bedrooms
are less tidy; taxicabs and street cars are more shabby; and most
conspicuous of all is the deterioration of the telephone service.
About this last everybody scolds and grumbles.[9]

The fretfulness and inconvenience of the middle classes and
the inflationary squeeeze of those in fixed incomes were sources
of tension for millions, but political hysteria is not a product
of spontaneous mass combustion. It is triggered by elites who
feel their hegemony is threatened and it is promoted and guided
by elites. Elites, particularly business elites, were very worried
about the growing power and militancy of organized labor,
and the hysteria was excited largely by business leaders to curb

labor's new aggressiveness. For elites, political hysteria and democratic repression can be a technique for managing tension and sustaining power.

The American Federation of Labor, which had about 500,000 members in 1900, numbered more than 4,000,000 in 1919. During the war an effective truce had been arranged between labor and management even though wages had fallen slightly behind prices. When prices rose sharply after the war, labor broke the truce and strikes broke out all over the country. There were strikes by the building trades, coal miners, steel workers, stockyard workers, longshoremen, shipworkers, subway employees, carpenters, policemen, shoe workers, telephone operators and others. In 1919 there were 3,600 strikes involving more than 4,000,000 employees. Management, for the most part, resisted fiercely. The great strikes—coal and steel—were broken, and labor had little success.

The immediate and less troublesome issues were wages, working conditions, and hours. The more fundamental issues were industrial unionism, the closed shop, collective bargaining, and the nationalization of railroads and coal. Many employers granted modest wage increases and modest reduction of hours but refused to bargain collectively or accept a closed shop. In 1919, these demands were perceived by most businessmen as illegitimate demands which ran counter to fundamental American tradition. As big business resisted, organized labor became more militant and its demands became greater. Influenced much more by the British Labor Party's demand for nationalization of basic industries than by the Russian revolution, the railway brotherhoods, which prospered under government operation of the roads during the war, advocated nationalization of the railroads. Although Samuel Gompers, the powerful president of the American Federation of Labor, vigorously opposed the so-called Plumb Plan for the railroads, his union endorsed it. Congressional critics characterized the plan as "a bold, bald, naked attempt to sovietize the railroads of the country." One congressman thought the plan "might have been formulated by Lenin and Trotsky." The railroads' spokesmen termed the plan "the first step along the road to socialism." Numerous editorial writers reminded the country that nationalization might next be applied to banks, natural resources, and public utilities.

A bill to nationalize the railroads was introduced into the House of Representatives but was never considered seriously. Labor, however, continued to make demands than ran counter to the American business ethic. In September of 1919, the United Mine Workers not only voted to strike but also proposed the nationalization of the mines. While the mine workers struck, about 200,000 farmers in North Dakota and adjoining grain producing states, joined Townley's Non-Partisan League, a cooperative scheme, which was described by its enemies as "an agrarian soviet".

American business was beginning to fantasize a powerful socialist thrust emerging in the labor movement. That fantasy was strengthened by the fact that the IWW began advocating "One Big Union"—the idea that the entire labor movement form a grand alliance, regardless of the nature of a particular union's work, in order ultimately to confront American capital with the demand for a socialist commonwealth . . . Bits and pieces of reality were beginning to emerge in 1919 from which government officials, big business, the press, and superpatriotic societies could weave a portrait of an America threatened by a gigantic, secret, and apocalyptic Red conspiracy to utterly change America. The portrait was mythic, but labor's militancy and occasionally transcendent proposals, coupled with thousands of strikes, and the existence of Bolshevism abroad, heightened fears. The myth was not woven entirely out of whole cloth.

A minority of organized labor was rapidly developing a new sense of labor's role in the economy and a conception of socialized property—a conception which grossly violated the sense of morality and justice of American business and its profits. The postwar period was one of those rare moments in American history when organized labor was not only a major force for change, but a force that questioned the sanctity of private ownership and the process by which wages, hours, and profits were to be negotiated. The Americanization of American labor, that is, the embourgeoisment of labor, had not yet been fully completed.

The extremism and ferocious passion of the American response to the perceived threats—an enormous overreaction—suggests that, in addition to a challenge to the power of business, some very deep seated threat to the American people was also involved. A passionate attack on an alleged threat—a visceral and hysterical defense—is usually the result of a passionate attachment to the object perceived as threatened. "America the Beautiful" was portrayed as threatened with extinction. There must be some highly affective identification with American values and symbols out of which this mass hysterical defense emerges. The enormous response of the American people to the conspiratorial myths promoted by elites must be accounted for. The identification of the people with the ancient values of John Locke and Adam Smith—the classic, the venerated, and the dominant American cliches and dogma, is, of course, the issue. But more of this in the appropriate place.

Despite the fact that business prospered during the war, big business felt threatened by labor's aspirations. The wartime priority—military equipment at any cost—magnified the role of the industrial magnate. His financial acumen, his administrative talent, and his ability to manipulate the factors of production, were absolutely essential to the war effort and made the businessman appear the most loyal of Americans. The reputation of the businessman, which had been under attack since the Populist movement, was largely restored when he combined private profit with public service. When he cried Bolshevik conspiracy in 1919, Americans were more willing to listen.

When the war ended, big business wished to return to the liberalism of nineteenth century America—freedom from significant government regulation, freedom to deal with labor authoritatively within the structure of the open shop, freedom, in other words, to pursue profit with minimal interference. Frederick Lewis Allen has perceptively described the milieu which motivated business sponsorship of the Red scare:

He, too, had come out of the war with his fighting blood up, ready to lick the next thing that stood in his way. He wanted to get back to business and enjoy his profits. Labor stood in his way and threatened his profits. He had come out of the war with a militant patriotism; and mingling his idealistic with his selfish motives, after the manner of all men at all times, he developed a fervent belief that 100 percent Americanism and the Welfare of God's Own Country and Loyalty to the Teachings of the Founding Fathers implied the right of the businessman to kick the union organizer out of his workshop. He had come to distrust anything and everything that was foreign, and this radicalism he saw as the spawn of long-haired Slavs and unwashed East-Side Jews. And, finally, he had been nourished during the war years upon stories of spies and plotters and international intrigue. . . . His credulity had thus been stretched until he was quite ready to believe that a struggle of American laboringmen for better wages was the beginning of an armed rebellion directed by Lenin and Trotsky, and that behind every innocent professor who taught that there were arguments for as well as against socialism there was a bearded rascal from eastern Europe with a money bag in one hand and a smoking bomb in the other.[10]

A class conscious and very sophisticated national business elite had been developing and consolidating its power since the 1880's. As these elites pushed America toward modernity, they confronted the problem that emerging industrial elites throughout the world face when undermining agrarian cultures with rural and fundamentalist and populist values. To wit, they were forced to insulate themselves from attacks sponsored by the adherents of the old order who were losing power, status, and identity. They had also to defend themselves against the possible proletarianization of the working class. The Red scare must be placed in this context of modernization, although deep forces in America can make political hysteria an American potential in other contexts.

Motivated by both sincere and by pretended fears of a growing radicalism and by a shrewd, pragmatic, sense of how they could escalate the Red threat far beyond objective fact and thus exploit it for conservative purpose, American businessmen played a major role in the creation of the political hysteria of 1919. The Red scare, in part, was one of several techniques utilized by big business to defend its hegemony against destabilizing threats from a potential Left during the period of modernization. The Red scare even had a solid interest group basis. We shall observe that repression can be a pluralist phenomenon and can provide numerous and differentiated payoffs for numerous and varied interest groups.

This transformation from a basically rural, agrarian, Protestant, traditionalist America to an industrial, urban, somewhat Catholic America in which traditional status arrangements were giving way to the uncertainties of mobility not only created the elites problem of insulating itself from attack, but also created an identity crisis of major proportions for those millions whose being was rooted in preindustrial values and ways. The erosion of their America was tremendously frightening and upsetting. In defending their world, they sought an explanation of its demise. They found one explanation which was, oddly enough, being propounded by the very business elites who were threatening their way of life. That explanation, of course, was rooted in the alien, Jewish, Catholic, intellectual radical conspiracy to destroy America. The explanation was particularly appealing to the threatened tribal-mind nativist, rural Protestant, and antiintellectual. The explanation was particularly ap-

pealing to business elites who could mask the pursuit of
self-interest behind a facade of patriotic rhetoric and thus exploit the prejudices and unsophistication of the tribal mentality. The Red scare was so many things—a death rattle of
the nineteenth century mind, a response to disintegration, and
an effort to create a new unity which would safely take America
into the twentieth century.

Political hysteria as a phenomenon raises many interesting
problems of political analysis. One of the most significant is
the problem of mythmaking and reality testing. A fundamental
quality of the Red scare was poor reality testing on a truly grand
scale—millions of people believing in, and taking drastic actions
to counter, a massive conspiratorial threat when no such threat
existed. The myth was so powerful that for about fourteen
months the fantasy of Bolshevik conspiracy became the prime
and very real issue—a fright at the center of American life.
We can now suggest some reasons why the myth appeared to
be quite credible. In so doing we create what might be termed
a sociology of myth-making.

Political mythmakers are rarely, if ever, completely free to
weave myths out of whole cloth. Such myths, to be credible,
must link up at some point with aspects of reality—external
or intrapsychic—even if the link is symbolic or paleological.
The credibility of myths is probably enhanced if the myth can
draw upon deep seated prejudice, fear or repressed desire
and offer the believer an opportunity to experience the pleasure
of acting out the prejudice or repressed wish or give him the
chance to project the fear upon an object in the external world,
rather than upon the self. The credibility of myths is probably
enhanced if mythmakers utilize perspectives and ways of cate-
gorizing experience which exist prior to the creation of the myth.
The myth of the Bolshevik conspiracy drew upon all of these
sources.

Perspectives and categories of thought nourished during the
war were tapped by conspiratorial mythmakers. The conspira-

torial mode of thought was legitimated and fostered by the government. Superpatriotism, a ferocious and belligerent nationalism, and xenophobia were standard wartime rhetoric. America as a redeemer nation and America the Beautiful, were constantly contrasted with the Hun as vermin and villain—good and evil, truth and falsehood, friend and enemy, were clearly delineated. Dichotomous thinking nourished the appeals of the conspiratorial perspective and the conspiratorial perspective greatly simplified the world. The common enemy created a common bond and thus the many pleasures of *communitas*. One could publicly hate Germans and love America even more as the United States became a truly united nation.

The myth of apocalyptic Bolshevik conspiracy dwelt on this "prefabricated" base. As a continuity of prior perspectives and pleasures the Bolshevik myth required little alteration of mind or feeling. Precisely how mythmakers may break with the past and still succeed is uncertain.

How much reality must lie behind the myth for the myth to be believed? No one can say with certainty. Referring to conspiratorial interpretations of history heavily laden with mythic content, Franz Neumann has written that ". . . this view of history is never completely false, but always contains a kernel of truth and, indeed, must contain it, if it is to have a convincing effect."[11] This was certainly true of the myth of a Bolshevik conspiracy in America.

A usable fact—or a bit of reality—is one which produces a ring of plausability bordering on certainty. Such facts have many characteristics. I have no idea of how many or what combination of these characteristics is necessary for a fact to be useable so my idea is tentative and and far from sufficient. But useable facts do seem to have certain characteristics. A useable fact is not obviously and publically and repeatedly and easily disconfirmed by legitimated sources. A useable fact is supported and repeatedly reconfirmed by esteemed providers of cues. A fact to be "useable" does not grossly violate widely accepted values and

prejudices or ways of acting; indeed, it prospers precisely because it connects with old and deep seated values and prejudices
and because the actions it leads to fit traditional forms of
behavior. We will see that political hysteria in America is
seductive to Americans because it is a product of democratic
pluralism and because the repression it demands unfolds
primarily through laws, judges, juries, and administrative officials—not through concentration camps. A pluralist, legal, and
nonviolent repression does not grossly violate widely accepted
values or practices.

A useable fact creates minimal cognitive dissonance and substantial cognitive confirmation. It links with one's experience
and world view and the link may be logical, tautalogical, or
paleological. A useable fact evokes anxiety and pleasure-fear of
Bolshevik conspirators but spit on them and deport them. A
useable fact provides a dehumanized enemy which may be
eliminated or cruelly treated, with pleasure and without guilt.

Useable facts become more useable when many of them exist
simultaneously. One nourishes the other particularly when one
is followed quickly upon another. One may then be perceived as
the cause of the other and all of them can be seen as the consequences of a common cause. A most useable fact is a bit of
reality—like a bombing—that outrages and creates a demand
for a quick, simple, and anxiety reducing explanation. And
finally the utility of a bit of reality is facilitated if it is subsumed
in an aura of some uncertainty—not fully bounded, as it were,
by stark and evident realities. Useable facts as building blocks
for fantasy need this unboundedness. It strengthens them and
it leaves a little room for symbolic maneuvers and confirmation.
Vagueness is important.

The number of bits of reality that became facts supporting
the case for a Bolshevik conspiracy were many, and they came to
public attention within a few months of each other. Among
them were the Russian revolution, press treatment of the Russian revolution, communist uprisings in Europe, Lenin's rhetoric

of world revolution, the founding of the CP and the CLP, the operation and rhetoric of the IWW, the unusual and radical demands of labor, the "defection" of intellectuals, the efflorescence of foreign language radical newspapers, millions of radical words, provocative words, apocalyptic radical rhetoric, bombings, threats, 3,600 strikes in 1919, alien radicals, Jewish radicals, Palmer raids, violence in the steel strike and the coal strike, some radical strike leaders, police on strike, race riots, doubt cast on America by Negro newspapers, May Day parades, ousted socialists, Red flags, labor spies gathering "facts," Justice Department agents provocateur gathering "facts" and provoking radical action, and military intelligence reports, all of which were transformed from secret memo into very visible and shocking testimony before the Congress and very visible headlines day after day, month after month. Each bit and piece of reality reinforces the power and meaning of the other bits until a massive symphony, a crescendo, is reached and one overpowering and repetitive theme is heard, although in fact only disconnected and random fragments without thematic unity are being played. The bits add up. The whole becomes more than the sum of its parts. The larger the number of bits, the closer together they occur, the more compelling the "reality" and the more credible the conspiracy. When superpatriots turned to pseudoscholarship they operated on the assumption that so many events could not possibly occur in so brief a period of time without a common cause.

In their efforts to brand the steel and coal strikes as the product of Red conspiracy, proponents of the Red scare built their case, in large part, on the fact that a few strike leaders were radicals, anarchosyndicalists, and/or members of the Communist Party or the IWW. A few did urge violence as a strike tactic and some urged violent overthrow of the government. Much radical literature was distributed to strikers. Many strikers were aliens.

Dozens of facts and partial truths were available, on the basis of which one could argue that many strikes were either "Red" promulgated, or "Red" financed, "Red" led, "Red" infiltrated, or "Red" inspired. Dozens of major newspapers drew this conclusion. The conclusion, though false in its totality, did contain these germs of truth, and when the press and a variety of public figures emphasized these truths to the exclusion of others which were contradictory, the conspiracy became quite real.

Although the overwhelming majority of the strikers were American citizens, many newspapers built their reportage around those few who were aliens. Newspapers concentrated on the activities of William Z. Foster to the exclusion of more representative reporting. What radical literature was distributed, was widely reported and given prominent coverage. Although some violence was instigated by the strikers themselves, some violence was instigated by labor spies, Army intelligence agents, local police, and Pinkertons. The national press concentrated on the strikers and ignored the questionable contributions of spies and agents.

The usability of a bit of reality is enhanced when contrary facts and interpretations and counter-conspiratorial cues are rare or absent. A near unanimity of proconspiratorial communications may be a necessary precondition for the successful creation of the myth. The absence of counter-cues eliminates cognitive dissonance and enhances believability. This is precisely why would-be totalitarian mythmakers seek total control of the means of communication.

The myth of a Bolshevik conspiracy was enormously boosted because it was supported not only by a near unanimity of proconspiratorial cues emanating from dozens of highly legitimate sources led by the president of the United States. Labor, of course, is the target of a hysteria largely fostered by businessmen. The line up against labor on strike was impressive. Hundreds of newspaper and magazine publishers, several cabinet officials, the attorney general, the secretary of labor, judges, labor spies, senators, army intelligence agents, college presidents, corporate management, private detectives, congressmen, Justice Department agents, ex-President Taft, vigilantes, and superpatriots. Both federal and state lent testimony that labor unrest in the United States was primarily due to outside communist agitators, Red trade union members, and disloyal aliens, some of whom were members of a "Red" conspiracy. Secretary of Labor Wilson declared in 1919 that major strikes in Seattle, Butte, and Lawrence, Massachusetts, had been fomented by Bolsheviks and the IWW, not to benefit workers, but to initiate a nationwide socialist revolution. In April of 1920, the secretary agreed with Attorney General Palmer in a cabinet meeting that the railroad strike had also been caused by the IWW and assorted radicals.

In the midst of the steel strike, a Senate investigating committee reported that "behind this strike there is massed a considerable element of IWW's, anarchists, revolutionists, and Russian soviets . . ."[12] According to J. Edgar Hoover, perhaps one half of the influence behind the rash of strikes could be traced directly to communist agents.[13]

The conspiratorial myth becomes irresistible when the leaders of both political parties support it and particularly when liberals and progressives like A. Mitchell Palmer lead the crusade. We are not speaking of a Democratic or Republican phenomenon but wholly bipartisan American potential. And we are speaking of an American potential that was excited, in part, because the most authoritative and legitimated figures in the country lent their prestige to the undertaking. Their weight contributed to the credibility of conspiracy.

The opinion makers and the educated public also looked to "authority" for guidance. One of the unquestionable sources of authority in early twentieth century America was "scholarship." Anything vaguely Germanic, pedantic, annotated, footnoted, and above all voluminous was presumed by the educated public to contain truth.

The myth of Bolshevik conspiracy was made credible, in part, by an outpouring of what purported to be scholarship, but what was, in fact, pseudoscholarship. Pseudoscholarship was one of the techniques which conspiratorial mythmakers utilized to rationalize the myth by appealing to a semblance of reason. The most massive and "scholarly" example of this pseudoscholarship was produced by an investigating committee of the New York State Legislature.

MYTHMAKING AND
PSEUDOSCHOLARSHIP

In April of 1920, the Joint Legislative Committee Investigating Seditious Activities of the New York State Legislature published a massive 4,456 page four-volume report entitled "Revolutionary Radicalism, Its History, Purpose, and Tactics With an Exposition and Discussion of the Steps Being Taken and Required to Curb It."[14] The report, prepared under the chairmanship of Senator Clayton R. Lusk, concluded that revolutionary radicalism in the form of a gigantic international conspiracy does imminently threaten the safety of the United States. The frontispiece contains a quote from *The Labor Defender*, an IWW paper, which catches the committee's main theme: "Every Strike is a Small Revolution and A Dress Rehearsal For the Big One." The first paragraph of the first chapter forewarns the reader:

The most important questions of the day are socialism and labor. The men who are leading in both these fields of thought and action are quite aware of their international character. The American public is not. It must be educated to see that every big movement on the other side has its parallel in the United States, and that they are so closely interlocked and so governed by the same group of men that we cannot ignore the European situation. Otherwise our people cannot understand the centralized strategy behind the action. It cannot realize the tremendous forces at work nor the crises present and impending.

These four volumes, which became the bible of superpatriotism, were assembled—manufactured is a more accurate word—by a large staff of "experts" at a cost of approximately $100,000 during a period of several months. The documentation and size of the report is staggering. The thoroughness of the report, on the surface, appears to be beyond question. The attention to detail appears to be impressive. The report contains appendices, extensive notes, thousands of documents reprinted verbatim, lengthy bibliographies, an addendum of 123 pages, maps, tables and hundreds of "opinions" submitted by "experts," witnesses from many disciplines including high government officials, eminent scholars, presidents of prestigious universities, men of the cloth, repentant radicals, and leading businessmen. The impression conveyed by a superficial reading is that the report is encyclopaedic, exhaustive, and definitive.

The comprehensiveness of the report is almost beyond belief. The first section of the first volume (177 pages) contains separate chapters—about fourteen pages per country—on the development of socialism in Germany, Italy, France, Belgium, Holland, Scandinavia, Finland, Switzerland, Spain, Austria, Czechoslovakia, the Balkans, and Great Britain. Original documents pertaining to "The Russian Soviet Regime," "Revolutionary Socialist Activities in Europe Since 1919," and "The Third Socialist International" are reprinted for 290 pages. Three entire pages are devoted to a comprehensive survey entitled "Socialism in Mexico, Central and South America."

A historical sketch of the socialist movement in America is presented in nine pages. American socialist and communist documents occupy 258 pages. The first volume also deals with radical activities of nine unions. The IWW and the ILGMU are analyzed in the same section. Radical activities in the academic world and American churches occupy the last twenty-eight pages of Volume 1.

Volume 2 opens with a 382 page section on radical propaganda in newspapers and periodicals and agitation in churches, schools, and among Negroes. Volume 2 also deals with "Subversive Movements Abroad and at Home," and includes dozens of documents pertaining to Russia, the Socialist Party of America, the Communist Party, Revolutionary Industrial Unionism, and the IWW. Anarchism in America is exhaustively treated in four pages.

Volumes 3 and 4 deal with "Constructive Movements and Measures" designed to counteract radicalism. The number of subjects dealt with is bewildering—freedom of speech, the closed shop, guild socialism, British plans to combat radicalism, labor arbitration, Americanization programs in all states of the union, state by state, major cities of New York State, state normal schools and public schools in New York City. Americanization programs in churches—Presbyterian, Methodist, Episcopalian, Baptist, Congregational, Catholic, Lutheran, Dutch Reformed, and the Society of Friends—are also examined. A review of all the legislation on radical activities (818 pages) in every state of the union is presented as is a review of legislation on naturalization.

The Lusk Committee also published testimony on radicalism and Americanization from representatives of 47 organizations, 21 colleges, universities and institutions, and 6 trade schools—all of which were published in 205 additional pages. In size, documentation, and scholarly paraphernalia, the Lusk Report rivals the most pretentious works of nineteenth-century German historical scholarship. But serious scholarship is, in fact, totally absent. The data is presented without any effort—serious or otherwise—to evaluate its validity or relevance. Generalizations and conclusions, unsupported by data, are sprinkled throughout. Hundreds of irrelevant documents are reprinted. Subjects that could be treated seriously only in several volumes are treated in a few pages. No effort is made to evaluate testimony. It is merely reprinted. The authors of the various parts of the report cite each other's analysis as authoritative. Documents are taken at face value, regardless of their source or the context within which they originally were presented.

The works of unknown pamphleteers—some of them obviously psychotic ravings—are given equal weight with the works of reputable historians. What is supposed to pass for exhaustive scholarship is, in fact, a collection of unrelated and unverified opinions, reports, etc., in which indiscriminate compilation passes for in-depth research. Bulk is taken for substance.

The Lusk report's treatment of the radical press in New York State is a good example of its method. The report[15] lists sixty-five publications under the title "Revolutionary and Subversive Periodicals Published in New York City" with a total circulation of 841,600. Under the title "Liberal Papers Published in New York City having Endorsement of Revolutionary Groups," the Lusk Report lists seven periodicals with a combined circulation of 168,000. Another fifteen periodicals with a combined circulation of 117,500 are listed as "Discontinued Within the Past Year." The report also lists thirty-two publications with a combined circulation of 1,072,700 under the title "Revolutionary and Subversive Publications Printed Outside of New York City, but Circulating Freely in This City." The population of New York City in 1920 was 5,620,048 so the unstated but implied conclusion to be drawn is that one-fifth of the population of New York City was reading radical literature and was on the verge of bloody riots.

The data on newspapers as presented in the Lusk Committee Report appeared to be impressive and to have the ring of authentic scholarship. It seemed to be the product of exhaustive "research"—long and allegedly complete listings with exact circulation figures. The source of all these figures, however, was not cited. No effort was made to evaluate overlapping readership, which must have been large. Radicals, like other highly political people, tend to read several publications of similar persuasion.

The criteria for defining what constitutes a subversive publication is nowhere presented. The list entitled "Liberal Papers Published in New York City Having Endorsement of Revolutionary Groups" is neither preceded nor followed by a definition of a "liberal paper" or a "revolutionary group." *The Nation* and *The New Republic* are included in this group. The endorsement of the revolutionary groups is nowhere presented. It is, like hundreds of other bits of data, merely cited. The report also specializes in capsule one paragraph presentations of enormously complex historical situations. The following passage, which is drawn from a section entitled "American Conditions— An Historical Sketch" illustrates these characteristics of the Lusk Report.

Conditions in Europe inevitably have a reflex action upon the people of the United States. So long as the communist elements are in control of the masses of Russia and remain a force to be reckoned with in the other countries of Europe, so long will they continue a menace to the institutions of the United States.

As an illustration of the effect of European movements upon the United States, we may make reference to the influence which the Jacobin Clubs of the French Revolution had upon the malcontents in the United States in the latter part of the eighteenth century.

The Whiskey Rebellion of Western Pennsylvania was the outgrowth of agitation carried on by so-called democratic societies acting under the guise of protectors of civil liberties, which received their inspiration from the French revolutionary societies.

The power of these agitators continued to grow until Robespierre was brought to the guillotine, and the political power of the revolutionary clubs of France was destroyed.

In referring to this condition, John Marshall, in his "Life of Washington," published in Philadelphia in 1832, says on page 353: "Not more certain is it that the boldest streams must disappear, if the fountains which feed them be emptied than was the dissolution of the democratic societies of America, when the Jacobin Clubs were denounced by France". . . .

The Socialist, Communist, and Anarchist movements in this country, as well as the industrial organizations which are the outgrowth of their propaganda, are not spontaneous expressions of unrest brought about by critical economic conditions in this country, but are the result of systematic and energetic propaganda, spread by representatives of European revolutionary bodies. The agitation was begun many years ago largely among the elements of foreign workmen who had come to this country, and was carried on almost exclusively by alien agitators. But with the increasing number of aliens and the renewed activity of agitators the propaganda has spread from alien groups, so that today it permeates all classes of society in this country.[16]

The inevitability of the effects on the United States of European conditions is not demonstrated. It is merely stated. The example of the impact of Jacobin Clubs is not demonstrated. It is merely stated. No proof of the French origin of the Whiskey Rebellion is offered. In pseudoscholarly fashion, an authority—John Marshall—is cited, page and verse, but again no argument or analysis, merely a citation. The same is the case with respect to radical agitation in America. But in each case, an alleged connection between Europe and America is posited, apparently on the theory that if enough such cases are presented, the ultimate point will emerge; that is, a Red conspiracy in America ultimately directed by Lenin. We have here argument by bulk—but argument designed to appeal to a semblance of reason and not to the irrational or the unconscious.

The Lusk Report was the crowning achievement of the Red scare "documentation" and pseudoscholarship, but there were dozens of lesser works in the period. All of these were repeatedly cited as "scholarly" and "irrefutable" proof of the presence of a secret Red conspiracy in America.

The essence of pseudoscholarship,[17] like that of other devices used to substantiate the reality of the alleged threat, lies in the fact that it begins with a vague assumption, supported by odds and ends of reality fitted together to prove a mad hypothesis. The pseudoscholar proceeds to laboriously accumulate vast numbers of "details" and documents which allegedly support his case. Some of the details and documents refer to facts. Some of the details are fiction. Nothing remains unexplained.

No ambiguities remain. All contingencies and qualifications are "adequately" dealt with. Possibilities are converted into certainties. Following the presentation of endless details, the conclusion is "inevitable." The data itself is neither collected in a systematic nor discriminating manner, nor verified. It is simply collected, collated, and printed. So much "data" is collected that, symbolically speaking, a critical mass is formed. An explosion of imagination—a great fantasy leap forward—then occurs, and conclusions emerge.

The analysis in the Lusk Report is neither structural nor systemic as scholars use these terms, though, in a bizarre way, the authors do continuously refer to a worldwide system of Communism and a structure that they assume underlies the system. Simultaneity is taken as proof of cause and effect. Strikes in Europe and America that occur simultaneously are obviously related. Spatial coexistence is taken as proof of cause. Similarity of ethnic or religious or racial background is taken as proof of common purpose. They utilized the logic of guilt by common characteristic, condemning all Jews, all aliens, all radicals. Isolated facts are introduced as explanations of enormously complex historical forces when they have no conceivable or logical connection.

It is a peculiar fact that there exists not a single system of Anglo-Saxon socialism, nor a single system of Latin race socialism. In fact, the only scientific, concrete, and perfectly systematic scheme is of German-Jewish origin—the scheme of Karl Marx. This is the basis for the materialism inherent in present-day socialism, for its antagonism to religion, to ethics, and to all idealism based on principles, on sentiments and intellectual concepts that do not relate to purely material life and wealth interests.[18]

Behind the logic of conspiratorial pseudoscholarship lies the assumption that vast historical forces are set in motion by the mere will of a few monstrously evil but brilliant men. They pull puppet strings and duped and compliant millions act out their will. Despite the "fact" that these supermen operate in secret and utilize arcane powers, the pseudoscholar is able to pierce the unknown and identify the entire conspiratorial operation.

The traffic in simplism and dichotomies—worlds in collision —and unquestioned causes and effects, encased in a pseudo-scholarly format can be very appealing, particularly when it has the imprimatur and legitimacy of the legislature of the Empire State.

Another major component of the mythmaking apparatus was the national press. Publishers implemented and refined super-patriotic pseudoscholarship. But their effect was much greater than that of the pseudoscholars. The latter published pamphlets from time to time, but publishers supplied conspiratorial cues, day after day and month after month. And there was no other media with access to millions that supplied counter-cues. The press, more than any other bit of the mythmaking apparatus, defined the situation as one of imminent catastrophe. In so doing, the press presented thousands of "useable" facts, rumors, exaggerations etc., in an effort to appeal primarily, though not exclusively, to a semblance of reason. Reportage was constructed to appeal primarily to the reason of Americans.

MYTHMAKING AND THE PRESS

The behavior of the press during the hysteria was more complex than might be expected, but patterns emerge. The same news-paper supported and opposed the Red conspiracy and the hysteria at different times and with respect to different issues. Antihysterical, realistic, and sober reportage occasionally char-acterized some newspapers in relatively small towns—towns which are customarily regarded as strongholds of super-Ameri-canism. However, almost every great metropolitan daily—*The San Francisco Examiner, The Chicago Tribune, The Philadel-phia Inquirer, The New York Times, The Washington Post, The St. Louis Post Dispatch* and *The Boston Evening Tran-*

script, for example, supported, with occasional exception, the wildest claims of Attorney General Palmer, the large corporations, and the superpatriots in Congress.

A small circle of staunchly liberal journals like *The Nation* and *The New Republic*, consistently opposed Palmer and frequently warned their readers of the dangers of an American repression. These warnings and exposes of superpatriots were occasionally supported by carefully researched and documented articles. The circulation of such journals, however, was small and their influence minimal. The socialist press, substantially more strident than liberal journals, consistently opposed Palmer and his confreres. Communist newspapers, many of which were published in a foreign language, militantly opposed the hysteria with articles characterized by Marxist cliches and headlines warning their readers of an American absolutism, indistinguishable from the reign of the Czars.

Nevertheless, with all these exceptions and qualifications, support for the conspiratorial myth among newspapers and with large circulation was consistent until the closing months of the Red scare when publishers became concerned with the possible effects on them of the proposed sedition bill then before Congress. Relatively few counter-conspiratorial cues were supplied by the mass circulation press. Respectable newspapers repeatedly exaggerated and distorted facts, manufactured "facts" that did not exist, published rumors, failed to check the sources of rumors, interviewed proponents of the conspiracy, did not interview liberals or radicals, failed to comment on the biased source of stories, and introduced editorial comment in news columns. In hundreds of instances, newspapers—reputable newspapers—acted as conduits for the Department of Justice or big business interests and superpatriots, by printing their press releases without citation of the source.

The myth of an American Bolshevik conspiracy was made more plausible by the press's portrait of what occurred in Russia during the revolution. The apocalyptic and terroristic quality of an impending American revolution was predicted primarily upon analogies based on the atrocities attributed to Lenin's followers.

The Russian revolution did—as civil wars do—involve substantial violence. Land, factories, and mines were confiscated. People were killed. The government was deposed. A massive reign of terror, however, did not occur. The American press, however, almost without exception, portrayed the revolution as an orgy of mass terror and violence. The Bolsheviks were depicted as brutal, sadistic, violent, despoilers of civilization who raped hundreds of nuns, murdered priests, burned monasteries, and slaughtered thousands of people indiscriminately. American press reports concentrated on the violence that occurred, invented innumerable and grotesque exaggerations, and failed to report contradictory facts. One press report claimed that in Petrograd the revolutionaries used an electrically driven guillotine to behead five hundred people per hour. Lenin's rule was described, not untypically, as a "compound of slaughter, confiscation, anarchy, and universal disorder." The Bolshevik was invariably portrayed as a master bearded criminal brandishing a gun, a bomb, or a whip. The reportage lent credence to the characteristics attributed to Reds in general and, by implication, to Reds in America. The dehumanization of American Reds— their depiction as vermin and lice—and the portrait of the Red conspiracy in America as monstrous and apocalyptic became more plausible in view of the unanimity of the "evidence" of what conspiring Reds had done in Russia.

The prime contribution of the press to the hysteria, however, was the role it played in defining the situation as apocalyptic and thus in creating an apocalyptic expectation. This was done by converting numerous actions which were neither radical nor revolutionary into confrontation which threatened the foundations of American civilization. A definition of the situation was also made by converting radical talk or writing into the equivalent of radical deeds. The situation was defined into reality by the publishers' repeated predictions of impending doom or by reporting the predictions of prominent public figures. Strikes, radical statements, and bombings were converted into conspiracies and interpreted as part of an impending American revolution.

The Wall Street Journal, referring to the Boston Police strike commented, "Lenin and Trotsky are on their way." The New York Times, in an editorial, perceived the police strike, as "not merely a glimpse, but a long look at the fires of anarchy and crime that smoulder asleep under civilization."[19] One newspaper, referring to the police strike, congratulated public officials for the stand they had "so stoutly taken against the Bolshevists in their city." The paper credited Governor Calvin Coolidge with having prevented "the beginnings of Soviet governments."[20] It would be difficult to imagine a police force in 1919, less addicted to Bolshevism and more staunchly Roman Catholic than the Boston police force.

Robert Murray has commented on the manner in which the national press transformed the Seattle strike into a precursor of a Bolshevik revolution.

For almost a week the nation's eyes had been focused on Seattle. Caught in the tremendous excitement emanating from the general strike situation, the nation's press reprinted the exaggerated assertions of the Seattle newspapers and wildly elaborated on the indications of radicalism present. On the day the strike began, newspaper headlines throughout the country notified readers, "REDS DIRECTING SEATTLE STRIKE—TO TEST CHANCE FOR REVOLUTION." Thereafter, editorials consistently blasted labor's action in Seattle and fed their subscribers on a constant diet of "The Seattle strike is Marxian," "a revolutionary movement aimed at existing government," and "the stepping stone to a bolshevized America." The Cleveland Plain Dealer claimed that in Seattle "the (Bolshevik) beast comes into the open," while The Chicago Tribune warned, "it is only a middling step from Petrograd to Seattle."[21]

Palmer and the superpatriots handled the fact that the predicted disaster of revolution did not materialize by arguing, post hoc, that preparations taken at their behest to stave off the revolution did in fact succeed. Most of the major newspapers went along with this interpretation most of the time. *The New York Times*, for example, reprinted, as a headline, the following unsupported statement of Mayor Hanson, "Anarchists Tried Revolution in Seattle, but Never Got to First Base."[22] This unverified quote was a favorite of *The New York Times*. Without comment, and without making an effort to check the facts of the Seattle strike, the *Times* quoted Hanson, "The sympathetic revolution was called in the exact manner as was the revolution in Petrograd. Labor tried to run everything. This was an attempted revolution which they expected to spread all over the United States."[23] On January 4, 1920, *The New York Times* reported, again without substantiation, the view of government officials that the Palmer raids nipped the revolution in the bud.

Radical leaders planned to develop the recent steel and coal strike into a general strike and ultimately into a revolution to overthrow the government, according to information gathered by federal agents in Friday night's wholesale round-up of members of the Communist parties. These data, officials said, tended to prove that the nationwide raids had blasted the most menacing revolutionary ploy yet unearthed.

Referring to Judge Gary's statements that the steel strike was led by revolutionaries, *The Wall Street Journal* concurred and portrayed the strike not as a conflict involving wages, hours, and working conditions, but as "the battle of the American Constitution."[24] Although very few radicals had positions of leadership in the strike, *The New York Times* warned Samuel Gompers against the "Red element" and declared that the strike was called, not for better wages and hours but "for power, for control of the industry."[25] The strike was described by another newspaper as "another experiment in the way of Bolshevizing American industry."[26] *The Boston Transcript* editorialized that the strike "shows the extraordinary hold which 'Red' principles have upon the foreign born population in steel districts."[27]

The national press also treated the coal strike as a Red insurrection although, like the steel strike, it was neither led nor supported by many radicals. *The New York Tribune* falsely characterized the miners as "thirsting for a strike . . . thousands of them, red-soaked in the doctrines of Bolshevism, clamor for the strike as a means of syndicalizing the coal mines . . . and even as starting a general revolution in America."[28] These interpretations in addition to being patently false, drew attention away from the real causes of the strikes and focused attention upon alleged revolutionary plots; thus, the press greatly aided the cause of capital.

Dozens of newspapers repeatedly cited senators, corporate officials, and federal agents as if their statements were undoubtedly true. There is no evidence that these papers made any serious effort to check the facts before they converted nonradical and nonrevolutionary events into radical acts and revolutions. On the day that the bomb plot was discovered *The New York Times* reported, without documentation, and thus helped to legitimate, the government's version of the situation.

A Nationwide bomb conspiracy which police authorities say has every earmark of the IWW—Bolshevik origin . . . has been discovered. . . .

IWW—Bolsheviki suspicion entertained by the federal and local authorities is strengthened because of the past activities of some of the men to whom the bombs were mailed.[29]

On the following day, when absolutely no evidence had been found concerning who had sent the bombs, *The Times* editorialized that, "Bolsheviki, anarchists and IWW's were obviously implicated."

In failing to note the possible or actual basis of their sources, and in failing to check the facts, many newspapers did exactly what the Justice Department and other advocates of the hysteria wanted and needed them to do—i.e. they acted as conduits and promoters for conspiratorial propaganda.

In many cases, newspapers consciously and willfully lied to the public, or failed to report facts that ran counter to the conspiratorial myth-facts that were often common knowledge. For example, wage rates of steel workers were widely publicized. Nevertheless, some newspapers reported that steel workers received seventy dollars per day. Robert Murray noted that some newspapers reported "that the more luxurious New York hotels expected an influx of striking steel workers who would use the occasion to take a vacation and spend their high wages."[30] During the period when the steel strike was about ninety percent effective, Los Angeles and Pittsburgh newspapers reported in headlines that the strike was terminating: "Conditions Almost Normal in all Steel Plants;" "Workers Flock Back to Jobs;" "Strike Crumbling."

It was well known that U.S. Steel had surrounded their plants with armed guards and that the corporation employed large numbers of strike breakers who often provoked violence. Murray commented on reportage of these events.

The ruthless methods employed by the Steel companies were not described to any extent in the press. Instead, reports of riot disorders were written in such a manner as to make it appear that steel officials were always on the defensive against those who were attacking law and order. Newspapers dwelt mostly on the evidence of radicalism involved and related all other factors to it. The public, therefore, received a completely biased picture of the strike situation. Actually, the vast majority of the riot disturbances contained no traces of radicalism whatsoever.[31]

Radicals were rarely interviewed and rarely quoted, and when they were, the statements quoted were invariably extravagant and false claims to the effect that particular events were inspired and organized by radicals. Statements from the radical press were repeatelly quoted to prove the conspiracy and quoted without efforts to validate their contents.

During the Seattle strike, the press concentrated on the antics and statements of superpatriotic Mayor Hanson and not on alleged radical actions. During the steel strike the press concentrated on the activities and statements of Judge Gary. During the Boston police strike, the press concentrated on the actions and statements of Governor Coolidge and the actions of a few looters. Policemen were not interviewed, and the press, with rare exception, made no serious effort to investigate police grievances.

When radicals were quoted it was rarely in the form of an interview which would permit the radical to explain and defend his views. Radical quotations were invariably taken from radical literature and presented, not with analytic commentary or with some explanation of the context of the document, but with a bold statement to the effect that the written word was fantastically dangerous and the equivalent of revolution. A very telling example of this symbolic transformation was reported in *The New York Times* on October 15, 1919. A local intelligence agent commented on a captured communist pamphlet which urged violent revolution.

This is the most dangerous piece of literature that has come to my attention. . . . It is a most dangerous situation to deal with, and it will be dealt with accordingly. Before we leave, we intend to clean Gary (Indiana) of Red agitators.

The captured documents become evidence not only of conspiracy but of the "unrestrained spread" of the conspiracy. It is as if the documents have a magical power of their own to infect all who read them and even those who do not. Written words are both the germ of radical epidemic and the epidemic itself.

Many newspapers shared the assumption that the spoken

word was as dangerous as the written word. The escalation of the demand for repression was due, in part, to the demands of newspapers, most of which were no more concerned with the rights of dehumanized "deviants" than they were with the American people. Robert Murray has commented on the intolerance of some newspapers.

Indeed, stirred by the Red threat which May Day seemed to reveal, most papers expressed the belief that "the time for tolerance is past," yet evidenced by their own attitudes that tolerance, in fact, did not exist. Even free speech was put on the auction block. "Free speech has been carried to the point where it is an unrestrained menace," said *The Salt Lake Tribune*, and from the shadow of the nation's Capitol came the voice of *The Washington Post*: "Silence the incendiary advocates of force . . . Bring the law's hand down upon the violent and the inciter of violence. Do it Now."[32]

Referring to the illegal incarceration of several thousand alleged Reds "captured" in the Palmer raids, the respected *Washington Post* commented, "there is no time to waste on hairsplitting over infringement of liberty."[33]

Although several important newspapers vehemently opposed the ousting of five duly elected socialist members of the New York Assembly, several applauded the action. The position of *The New York Times* and other newspapers was summarized in *The Literary Digest's* review of press opinion.

But many newspapers will oppose such a course, if we may judge from the editorials which reach us. "These Socialists were declared unfit by a large majority of the Assembly a few months ago." *The Buffalo Commercial* reminds us: "have they changed their views regarding their obligations and duties as representatives of the American people? Shall traitors who defy the law be allowed to participate in the making of the law?" Moreover, asserts *The Albany Journal*, "these Socialists do not represent American people; they represent an anti-American group whose members are misusing the rights and privileges of citizenship, which they are unfit to possess." Dr. John Brooks Leavitt, writing in *The New York Times*, charges the ousted Socialists with "aiming to upset the republican form of government in our State and substitute a communistic one." And he continues:

"As private citizens they are free to advocate such a change, even as some of our misguided ones would like to have a king. So long as they do not advocate the change by violent means, no one will deny their right to hold in private and urge in public such a substitution. But how can they qualify for membership in a law-making body under a republican form of government by taking a false oath to support the Federal Constitution, which contains that guaranty for the preservation of the republican form?"

Editorially, the *Times* declares that the housecleaning of the Socialist party meant "a change of words, not of heart." Therefore, thinks this paper:

"The Socialist party and its members ought not to stand there. The voters in the districts from which these men were sent to Albany should take account of public sentiment, which we believe to be much stronger even than it was last winter against allowing enemies of the State and of the Constitution to take a part in the business of law-making."[34]

Throughout the hysteria, very few newspapers cited the sources of their information. Very few newspapers attempted to verify the "facts" given to them by corporate officials or government agents. Very few newspapers informed their readers that a particular story was, in fact, a press release written by Mr. Palmer or the public relations men in the employ of corporations. This failure to examine the sources is important to the mythmakers because many were highly biased, many paid for their information, many were untrained in the collection of information, etc. When *The New York Times* or *The Washington Post,* or any other authoritative source publishes a rumor or a blatant lie, that rumor or lie may be perceived as an authoritative statement of fact. Its authority is nourished by its legitimated source.

Throughout the hysteria one aspect of the behavior of the press remained constant and fundamental and that was its deep and abiding commitment to the principles of capitalism and the protection of private enterprise and private property. Like the rest of America, the press rallied to the defense of one aspect of the Americanist identification—capitalism—and not to the other—the defense of minority rights and the right to advocate social change. Almost without exception, newspapers, as well as the government, condemned strikers and defended corporations. The Interchurch Report commented on the behavior of the Pittsburgh press during the great steel strike. The behavior of the national press was not dissimilar.

Finally the press in most communities, and particularly in Pittsburgh, led the workers there to the belief that the press lends itself instantly and persistently to strike-breaking. They believed that the press immediately took sides, printed only the news favoring that side, suppressed or colored its records, printed advertisements and editorials urging the strikers to go back, denounced the strikers and incessantly misrepresented the facts. All this was found to be true in the case of the Pittsburgh papers (as analyzed in a subreport). Foreign language papers largely followed the lead of the English papers. The average American-born discriminating citizen of Pittsburgh could not have obtained from his papers sufficient information to get a true conception of the strike; basic information was not in these papers . . . In the minds of workingmen outside steel states the newspapers' handling of the steel strike added weight to the conviction that the press of the country is not the workingman's press.[35]

Not unexpectedly, many newspapers took a strong stand in favor of the open shop and provided its advocates extensive coverage. The press provided the near unanimity of proconspiratorial cues that is probably necessary for successful conspiratorial mythmaking. The support of the hysteria further legitimated the claims of leading businessmen, government officials, and a large variety of superpatriots. The press reshaped "facts" into the conspiratorial mold.

Several bombings occurred in 1919. The targets, in many cases, were some of the most prominent men in American politics and business. And some of these men—like Palmer—

were leading conspiratorial mythmakers. Bombing, as a means of political protest, is obviously directly counter to the American political experience. It is a particularly ferocious and violent and frightening action likely to evoke an extreme reaction and perfectly fits stereotypes of "Bolshevik behavior."

Despite accusations by the attorney general and the police and dozens of other government sources to the effect that the bombers were Bolsheviks engaged in conspiracy, no conspirators were ever captured, indicted, or convicted. Newspapers throughout the country and many public officials, however, drew Palmerian conclusions. *The New York Times,* for example, editorialized on May 2, that "Bolshevik anarchists and IWW's were implicated." The bombings and events surrounding them were eminently "useable" for conspiratorial mythmaking.

The fact that some of the men selected as targets of the bombings included prominent government officials was used by proponents of the myth to "prove" that the bombers were part of a conspiracy to overthrow the state. The fact that the targets include some leading antiradicals was used to prove that the bombers were radicals. The fact that Wall Street was a target, led superpatriots to the conclusion that the bombers were anticapitalistic radicals of the left. The fact that the pamphlets found near the Wall Street bombings were written in badly broken English and contained anarchist rhetoric was taken as "proof" that the bombers were foreigners and anarchists. The fact that the bombers were not caught eliminated the possibility of disproof. The fact that some of the men selected as targets were in no meaningful sense antiradical was simply ignored.

The "evidence" in this case of the bombings, like almost every other bit of evidence, of course, was both circumstantial and imaginary. It would not stand up in a court presided over by a judge committed to strict standards of judicial procedure. But the point is that the "evidence" was presented to the bar of public opinion—not to a court of law. And it was not at all implausible. A reasonable man could accept a conclusion drawn from so much "evidence" based on so many bombings. It is at least plausible to assume that a man who attempted to kill Palmer was a radical. Of course, given the lack of solid "evidence," it would have been possible to accept the conclusion that the bomber might have been essentially an apolitical psychotic, a very angry but deranged liberal committed to due process, or a frustrated patronage seeker. There is, however, a discernible pattern to these bombings. Many of the targets do have common characteristics, and, what is more "useful" to mythmakers, is the fact that several bombings in widely scattered cities occurred on the same day or within a few days of each other. Simultaneous bombings in widely scattered locations, the targets of which have some common characteristics, can be presented as "proof" of an organized and centrally directed conspiracy—and plausibly so. This was precisely the conclusion drawn by newspapers throughout the country.

But the bombers were never caught, so no one really knew. It was, therefore, not merely just as easy to assume that a would-be killer of Palmer was a radical rather than a deranged liberal, it was, in fact, "more logical" to assume it. In fact, it was probably irresistible, since dozens of highly legitimated authorities said radicals were behind the bombs and none said that they were not. We return to our point involving the unanimity of cues and the legitimacy of cue givers. Who can really resist a message that is endlessly repeated by dozens of highly respected authorities and newspapers, and not opposed by other venerated figures?

We have then, in this chapter, indicated the great variety of appeals to reason or a semblance of reason. All of them contributed to the credibility, and the plausibility, of a nonexistent phenomenon. In form, they range all the way from appeals to what must fairly be called sensible rational logic to travesties on and paradoxes of the process of rational thoughts.

We have documented the process by which poor reality testing on a national scale was induced by mythmakers. The

Bolshevik conspiracy, if one existed at all, consisted of a handful of radicals and anarchists with no capacity whatsoever to overthrow the government of the United States. Yet tens of millions believed that America was imminently threatened. How such grandiosely poor reality testing was engineered is surely germane to an understanding of American political culture.

Our argument is not merely that quite normal and rational men found the conspiracy plausible, but that they found it irresistible. And the irresistible quality of the myth was built, in large part, on appeals to reason and to the semblance of reason. It was largely the use of cognitive process resembling reason that led to unreason.

The essential elements of successful mythmaking appear to be: the presence of elites who find the myth to be self-serving; a myth, many facets of which exploit old and deep seated mass beliefs; the presence of a stressful situation; and a unanimity of cues emanating from highly legitimated sources. Other elements would include a national press devoted to the myth, a large scale bureaucratic apparatus devoted to mythmaking, positive confirmation of actions of the state and both political parties— or, at least, the neutrality of the state and the minority party.

But mythmakers supplemented appeals to a semblance of reason with undisguised appeals to the unconscious and irrational parts of the American psyche. We consider these next.

4

VERMIN, FECES, AND SECRETS: ANXIETY AND APPEALS TO THE IRRATIONAL

NONE of the many appeals to reason or to the appearance of rational thought which took place during the Red scare could have succeeded as thoroughly as did they had they not been reinforced by powerful appeals to deeper layers of unconscious and irrational fears shared by a large portion of the American populace.

The hysteria escalated quickly from its base of anxiety. People became frightened of the Bolshevik threat. Their fright and desire to alleviate it helped them identify with political leaders who sponsored the hysteria. Their anxiety approached the dimension of a national panic and their panic further impaired their ability to test reality.

The Red conspiracy to overthrow the United States was portrayed as a small part of a worldwide conspiratorial network whose ultimate purpose was to transform the world into a brutalized Bolshevik satellite. Part of a larger whole, it was, nevertheless, the most colossal conspiracy in American history. By comparison, Papish plots, Masonic maneuverings, and operations of international Jewish bankers were petty and inept.

The radicals' goal was not merely the elimination and replacement of the American government, but the total subversion of the entire American way of life—the end of Christianity, the destruction of the family, the elimination of private property. It was godless atheism. It was anti-Christ. It was free love. It was the separation of children from parents. It was sexual license. It was state property. It was the destruction of free speech, and press, and freely chosen religion. It was slavery. The perspective was catastrophic and apocalyptic.

The Bolsheviks had the will, the ambition, and the determination to succeed. The conspirator was completely dedicated to a demonic ideology which assured him of ultimate victory, convinced him of the righteousness of his cause, and directed him on each step of the way. A combination of sincere belief, personal ambition, and greed made him willing to sacrifice for the cause, willing to resort to any means, and capable of enormous patience. The Communist had been trained to lie in wait—like a snake in the grass—for the right moment. Patience unlimited would permit him to outlast the petulant American. The fact that the leaders of the conspiracy had followers who were equally patient and dedicated—dupes, willing blindly to follow—merely enhanced their power, and chance for success.

At times the conspirator was portrayed as if he were almost outside the flow of history. It was as if he had transcended the normal limits on humanness. The superpatriot suggested that the directors of the conspiracy were able to will what happened. The conspirators not only had the will, but the means. No one really knew for certain how many actively participated in or were sympathetic to the Red cause, but the number must certainly have been vast—unknown millions in America, in Russia, and in Europe. After all, the radical press itself freely supported the superpatriotic contention that the number of radicals in America was in the millions. *The Cleveland Socialist News* characterized the steel strike in a headline: "Half Million Workers in Open Class War."

The conspiracy, superpatriots reminded Americans, did not draw its strength merely from America. Lenin, Russia, and particularly German socialists lent aid, succor, and provided infiltrators. When bombings occurred in nine cities in June of 1919, the director of the Justice Department's Bureau of Investigation announced that the bombers were "connected with Russian Bolshevism, aided by Hun money." A few months later *The Saturday Evening Post* warned its readers of "the Russo-German movement that is now trying to dominate America."[1]

Hun money plus parlor pink money and Lenin's money add up to a lot of money. Neither the professional superpatriots nor the Justice Department ever claimed to be absolutely certain how much money was being shipped into the United States for the conspirators or contributed by Park Avenue socialists, but it was never less than millions. According to Red-scare folklore, even part of the profits from the Soviet sale of the Russian crown jewels went to American Reds.

Vast amounts of money and vast numbers of conspirators and sympathizers might be dissipated without brilliant leadership, but the leaders of the conspiracy, though depraved and mongrel, were credited with an uncanny appreciation of the psychology of Americans which permitted them to understand the most subtle nuances and weaknesses of the American mind. And this permitted them to poison minds and brainwash the innocent and unsuspecting. It was to be an insidious rape of the mind, more terrifying than armed revolution. Armed revolution may be smashed by counter-military power but the rape of the mind cannot be prevented by armies and navies.

The rape was all the more monstrous and obscene because the first victims were to be America's most helpless and susceptible —unprotected children, uneducated adults, blacks, and untutored aliens.

Superpatriots and government officials did not entirely agree on exactly when the Reds would strike. Some argued that it would take the conspiracy five or ten years to complete its preparations. The message here was to be constantly prepared. Others set no specific date but suggested that time was running out. True believers would therefore remain in a state of constant uneasiness. Many senior government officials predicted imminent revolution. Senator Miles Poindexter announced that "there is real danger that the government will fall."[2] The attorney general testified before the House Appropriations Committee that "on a certain day, which we have been advised of," radicals planned to "rise up and destroy the government in one fell swoop."[3] Senator Thomas of Colorado warned his colleagues that "the country is on the verge of volcanic upheaval." The imminence of the revolution demanded immediate action, sacrifice, and obedience to political leaders who knew the conspiracy and knew what to do about it.

Earlier, we have examined the usefulness of half-truths, selected "facts," and other devices appealing to what appears to be rational thought. But facts are not invariably the prime basis of belief—emotions frequently are. The conspiracy is believed in and acted upon for two reasons. The first—which I deal with in a later chapter—has to do with the fact that the conspiracy is portrayed as a fundamental attack on America and, therefore, an attack and threat to all the identifications that Americans make with America. Since these identifications are highly affective, the defense mechanisms created to protect them are powerful. The second reason the conspiracy is believed in and acted upon is that the alleged characteristics of the conspirators, and the nature of the arguments used to "prove" the conspiracy, excite deep unconscious wishes and anxieties and tap primitive and infantile ways of thinking.

Superpatriots appeal to every man's wish to escape the psychological controls each man places upon himself. Superpatriots also appeal to each man's desire to abandon the controls imposed upon him by society. The superpatriot not only says that it is perfectly all right to hate, rage, spit, scream, swear, deport, jail one's enemies and demand immediate and total satisfaction, but that it is necessary and patriotic to do so. The superpatriotic appeal is an invitation to surrender to the id, to discard a part of the conscience and some controls of the ego, and to act out entirely, without restraint.

The appeal is actually an attempted seduction, an effort to induce surrender, an effort to induce abandonment, an effort to induce feeling and only feeling. To be caught in the sweep of political hysteria is to be, in a very real sense, hypnotized and seduced. But not everyone can be hypnotized and seduced— Freud and Don Giovanni notwithstanding. So the problem is two-fold: to explicate the nature of the seduction and the susceptibility of the seduced.

The conspiracy is portrayed as apocalyptic—a portent of catastrophe and doom. A successful world conspiracy means the destruction of America. It is anxiety—the fear of anticipated danger, in fact, actual annihilation—which binds the superpatriot to the true believer. The catastrophic prediction, however, also plays upon unconscious regressive tendencies. In their classic study of the techniques of the agitator, Lowenthal and Guterman note that,

the exploration of everyday mischances in terms of uncanny world catastrophes revitalizes and reinforces a heritage of infantile anxieties. The unconscious finds in the agitator's interpretations a replica of its own primitive reactions to the outside world: the listener plays the role of the little child responding to the warning that bogeys may come for him.[4]

To the infant, the world often is an awesome and forboding place. Potential catastrophes are everywhere. The superpatriot recreates this childhood world of imminent doom and reduces the man to the child—helpless in the face of gigantic and evil forces that threaten his very existence.

The helplessness and anxiety of the child-man bind him either to political leaders who claim they can prevent the impending catastrophe or to powerful political symbols like the flag or the nation from which the threatened child-man can draw symbolic safety. This is the essential element by which the child-man surrenders his sense of self and refinds it by identifying with the power of the nation or the leader. The child-man, faced with imminent catastrophe, is relieved of responsibility for a civilized and nonviolent response to those who allegedly threaten him. "As a result," Lowenthal comments, "everything goes. A man involved in catastrophe feels justified in departing from established moral codes if it means saving his life. The idea of catastrophe contains a welcome stimulus to the listeners' destructive instinctual urges."[5] Thus, political leaders can mount a ferocious attack on the conspiracy and not evoke the vigorous opposition one might expect from Americans allegedly committed to liberal principles.

The fury of political hysteria unfolds when the sense of catastrophe releases and legitimates acting out in socially approved ways. The appeal is to the child-man's dependence, helplessness, anxiety, and rage, in the face of catastrophe. The political leaders' demand is for immediate and unfiltered acceptance of their actions. It is not a demand for action by the masses but for passive acceptance. The role of the masses in political hysteria is fundamentally that of not opposing the elites which actually administer the repression. The masses become very frightened of imminent catastrophe. The masses seek relief. The masses approve, and applaud, and occasionally demand. But they neither originate the conspiratorial myth nor fill in its details. They occasionally take action to eliminate and control the danger. They occasionally form vigilante bands. They occasionally attack alleged conspirators—but only occasionally. The hysteria is originated, promoted, sustained, and administrated by elites, not masses. Like almost every political action, small groups act and large numbers react.

The function of defining the conspiracy and the conspirators in particular ways is to provoke emotional and cognitive responses which prepare the people to accept the myths and actions of the elites who make the hysteria. The fact that the people can "enjoy" the pursuit of deviants and project repressed wishes and fears upon alleged conspirators—without participating other than psychologically—makes the hysteria all the more seductive to them.

We are beginning to develop the argument not only that elites act and the masses react during political hysteria, but that elites act largely for reasons of economic or political self-interest while the involvement of the masses is largely psychological and, in a peculiar way, ideological. This is an instance of the feelings and stereotypes of the American people being maneuvered and potentiated for the concrete benefit of the elites.

Mythmakers endow the conspiracy and the conspirators with the qualities which are designed to produce the "right" kind of maneuvering and psychological involvement. The conspiracy is portrayed as monstrously evil, brilliantly directed, colossally powerful and secret. The conspirator is dehumanized—portrayed as scum or vermin, or germ, or plague.

The appeal of conspiratorial myths has much to do with the fact that the conspiracy is portrayed as secret. The clandestine and secret characters of the conspiracy is a key feature of its attraction. Americans, particularly those in the Populist tradition, tend to feel that secrecy and secrets are antidemocratic and elitist—the milieu in which the aristocratic and exploitative politics of Europe prosper. The Populist tradition in America perceives a true people's politics as unfolding in a world of open covenants openly arrived at. The People need not fear what is public.

Above and beyond any specifically American attitude that might exist toward secrecy—and one does—the secret and secrecy, intrinsically, do have very special qualities which often evoke special feelings—notably fear, fascination, and envy. The secret quality of the conspiracy, like its other attributes, taps both a universal psychological root, and a particular American root. Secrets and secrecy can evoke unconscious responses which effectively bind people to the hysteria and to its leaders. Secrecy alters human relationships—sometimes profoundly.

There is a sociology of secrets, as it were, and it is relevant to conspiratorial mythmaking.

THE CONSPIRACY AS SECRET

The anxiety upon which political hysteria is based develops in response to the portrait of a vast and powerful conspiracy which is, among other things, secret. The conspiratorial myth contains three elements: secrets, an aura of secrecy, and conspiracy.

Americans have traditionally attributed certain qualities to secrecy and those who hold secrets. American attitudes toward secrecy and publicity have frequently been institutionalized in political sects and parties and agencies of governments. Indeed, even today, an elaborate security machinery exists for the protection of national secrets and for the discovery of the secrets of alleged subversives and criminals. American history is replete with left and right wing movements and political parties that have been preoccupied with secrecy and secret conspiracies. The Bavarian illuminati, the Masons, the Catholics, the Bankers, the Communists, the Weathermen, the Panthers, and the Pentagon have been perceived as evil and conspiratorial, in part, because they operate in secret.

"Every human relation," the sociologist George Simmel wrote, "is characterized among other things, by the amount of secrecy that is in and around it."[6] To deal with someone rationally one must know with whom one is dealing and this requires knowledge of his private as well as his public aspect. The existence of secrets makes knowing who people are much more difficult, and greatly increases the likelihood that anxiety and fear will intrude in human relationships.

The secret, of course, greatly increases the richness differentiation, and individuation of social relationships. The secret, therefore, can be anathema to those who would impose homogeneity and conformity. The secret can be the enemy of authority. It can be the vehicle for social change. It can be an instrument of particularity. It can be a wellspring of dissent. It can be a bastion of aristocracy, or a vehicle of radicalism. In many of these guises, it can be an enemy of the state and those who support it, because it can be used to envision a transcendent world and it can be used to create the means to bring about that world.

"The secret," Simmel writes, "offers, so to speak, the possibility of a second world alongside the manifest world; and the latter is decisively influenced by the former."[7] It is the secret world, institutionalized in the secret society, that can become a danger to public authority. In societies with substantial ideological homogeneity, the secret political sect is likely to proliferate because dissenters are forced to resort to secrecy. Deviant public posture is prohibited by existing authority. It is not remarkable, therefore, that the public mind associates secrecy with deviance, with sinister undertakings, with subversion, with radicalism, and with antisocial forces. In the America which places high value on ideological conformity, the secret can be particularly threatening. "The fear of secrecy," Edward Shils writes, "is the fear of subversion and the proper response to the danger of subversion is relentless publicity and a degree of secrecy even greater than the subversives themselves would employ."[8]

The secret is, of course, the unknown. And the unknown can be frightening and threatening. A threat which is secret is all the more anxiety provoking than a public threat. Periods of political hysteria depend upon the production of substantial levels of anxiety and the secret aspect of the conspiracy is well suited to produce anticipations of danger. The utility of the secret as a means of producing anxiety is enhanced because the secret is associated with the magical, the sinister, the hateful, the destructive, and the apocalyptic. Simmel has asutely pointed out that ". . . although the secret has no immediate connection with evil, evil has an immediate connection with secrecy. The immoral hides itself for obvious reasons even where its content meets with no social stigma . . ."[9] In America, where the national ideology allegedly embodies self-evident truth, only men of evil need resort to secrets.

Secrets, because they are a mark of exclusiveness and the unknowable, can evoke envy, anger, and a sense of fascination and mystery. The very mystery and unknowability of the secret make the secret conspiracy a good target for the projection of fantasy.

The possesser of a secret is an exception and exclusive, and this can evoke jealousy, particularly in societies like America which place a high lip service value on equality and which are somewhat hostile to the exclusive and the aristocratic. Secrets can be hateful and fascinating, repulsive and seductive. Responses to secrets, therefore, are likely to be highly affective, irrational and laden with fantasy. This is precisely why those who propound the conspiratorial myth stress its secret quality.

The secret is like a Rorschach ink-blot—basically content-less and formless. The observer projects whatever he wishes on the ink blot and, since no one can say what the contents of the blot or the secret are, two facts follow: any qualities may be attributed to it, and no basis for refutation exists. The secret can be anything, because, by definition, its content is unknown. Therein lies its power and its utility to mythmakers. The qualities attributed to secrets noted previously—magic, power, exclusiveness, mystery, unknowability, and fear—can nourish an apocalyptic orientation toward the secret. The secret lends itself to an all or nothing orientation, and, if executed, can imply total destruction. Conversely, the secret, if quashed can imply salvation. This is the emotional frame within which political hysteria develops—projection, passion, destruction, apocalyptism, salvation, and poor reality testing.

Since no one really knows who is in possession of the secret or what the secret is, those who pursue alleged possessors of secrets must cast a very wide net. This breeds an aura of massive suspicion—the kind that breeds hysteria—and leads to the creation of extrarational and illogical criteria which are used in the pursuit of secrecy. By illogical criteria, secrecy may become an infectious disease. Contact with a holder of secrets—even in the remote past—contaminates. And anyone who has characteristics similar to those of a known secret holder may well also be diseased. People of the same religion, same university, or same ethnic background are all suspect.

At this point magical and paleological thinking comes into play. This makes the identification with the hysteria and its progenitors psychologically gratifying. The secret is frightening and potentially dangerous. This arouses anxiety. The anxiety and the desire for relief bind the masses to the leaders who promote the hysteria. Political hysteria is invariably based on the myth of the secret conspiracy composed of evil and subhuman types. A despised, deviant, and dehumanized outgroup secretly plots the destruction of the good, fully human men and women who make up the true society. The Red conspirators of 1919 were variously depicted as aliens, foreigners, Jews, vermin, lice, feces, disease, plague, epidemic, mad geniuses, scum, filth, rats, rodents, termites, snakes, criminals, idiots, anti-Christs, devils, sexually licentious, sadistic, perverse, and brutal.

These attributes arouse feelings of fear, hatred, disgust, dread, and less obviously, feelings of envy. The functions of defining the conspirators in these ways is to dehumanize them for the purpose of "legitimizing" them as future victims, to ease the guilt that might ensue upon their elimination, and to mobilize the masses in support of their extinction. The function of defining the outgroup as dangerous is to arouse anxiety. The anxiety and the wish for relief, as we noted, binds the masses with the leaders who both create the conspiratorial danger and promise relief from it. The portrait of the conspirators as sexually licentious permits the true believer to project repressed wishes and fears onto the conspirators. This also binds the projector to the proponents of the myth.

THE DEHUMANIZED CONSPIRATOR

American newspaper and magazine reports of the Russian revolution and accounts published in superpatriotic literature depict the revolution as a massive sadistic sexual orgy. The Bolsheviks, according to accounts, raped nuns, committed endless sexual perversions of a brutal and exotic kind, and planned to nationalize woman. The conspiratorial compatriots of the Bolsheviks in America were equally licentious, libertine, and sadistic. Brutality and sadism also characterized their nonsexual relations with each other and their enemies. No brutality was beyond their capacity when the revolutionary cause demanded it, and sexual freedom was their delight and cruelty.

Ole Hanson made the point that "Americanism has taught and Americans have practiced morality. Bolshevism teaches and its votaries practice immorality, indecency, cruelty, rape, murder, theft, arson."[10] The superpatriot Royal Baker raised the spectre of free love. "What has free love done for Russia? Every woman can be a legalized prostitute."[11]

The conspirator is constantly depicted as the inverse image of the ideal American type. Again, Ole Hanson:

Americanism stands for Liberty;
Bolshevism is premeditated slavery.

Americanism is a synonym of self-government;
Bolshevism believes in a dictatorship of tyrants.

Americanism means equality;
Bolshevism stands for class division and class rule.

Americanism stands for orderly, continuous, never-ending progress;
Bolshevism stands for retrograding to barbaric government.[12]

The conspirator, as the inverse image of the American ideal type, evokes both hatred and desire—simultaneously. Civilization forces the repression of precisely those impulses which the conspirator not only surrenders to but enjoys. So-called civilized men are taught to think of these impulses as unacceptable, repulsive, and filthy—infested with gross sexual appetite, avariciousness, and brutality. Although repressed, they frequently threaten to get out of control. And this is the point. They must be exorcised, deeply repressed, or projected onto others—despised conspirators, for example. The forbidden games of one's repressed inner life may thus be projected and indulged in socially acceptable and patriotic ways. The conspirator becomes the hated inner self, a purification of self ensues. The conspiracy, itself, thus becomes highly charged with affect. This affect binds the true believer to the conspiratorial myth and to the political and economic leaders who mutually create the evil conspirators but claim they have the power to eliminate them. Robert Lane, who analyzed the attitudes of some working men deeply committed to conspiratorial interpretations, put the matter as follows:

The Jews, Communists, and gangsters of social life are, in this sense, like sex and anger in personal life. Or, in reverse, sex and anger are the individual's Jews and Communists and gangsters. They need a scourge like McCarthy (whom Rapuano said "fought for people like me") or Hitler (whom Ferrera said helped solve Germany's problems of poverty by eliminating the congenitally weak). There is a fundamental relationship between one's internal experience of fighting against barely contained and inadmissible impulses, and one's external perception and reconstruction of society as threatened by some inadmissible and barely contained social force.[13]

The psychological function of the conspirator is to serve as a sounding board for what is condemned and what can be projected. Richard Hofstadter, commenting on the projections utilized by persons involved in the paranoid political style, writes:

The sexual freedom often attributed to him [the enemy], his lack of moral inhibition, his possession of especially effective techniques for fulfilling his desires, give exponents of the paranoid style an opportunity to project and freely express unacceptable aspects of their own minds. Priests and Mormon patriarchs were commonly thought to have especial attraction for women, and hence licentious privilege. Thus Catholics and Mormons—later Negroes and Jews —lent themselves to a preoccupation with illicit sex. Very often the fantasies of true believers serve as strong sadomasochistic outlets, vividly expressed, for example, in the concern of anti-Masons with the alleged cruelty of Masonic punishments.[14]

Some of the characteristics of the conspirator are characteristics of the id. The conspirator and the id have unlimited and magical power. They are lustful, aggressive, closely tied to the biological, and secret. It is the id and primal forces that are tapped by the conspiratorial myth. The major differences between the id and the conspirator, so to speak, is that the id demands immediate gratification and is not rational while the conspirator has a patience and can reason. The conspirator, most of whose characteristics represent an inverted image of the good Americans, stimulates repressed needs and desires, most of which are both frightening and fascinating. People both want and want not to "give in" to them. The appeal is to do what the conspirator allegedly has done—escape all repression.

These psychological conditions should not obscure the fact that very substantial economic and political capital was made out of the Red scare by many interest groups. The psychological dimension, however, is more relevant to understanding the behavior of "consumers" of the hysteria than its "producers." The average consumer really had little or nothing to gain economically or politically by supporting the hysteria. The average consumer was not seeking political advancement by Redbaiting. The average consumer, however, could and did derive numerous "pleasures" of a psychological kind from believing in the conspiracy.

It is obvious that during the Red Scare there was much going on which had an extrarational, mythical, symbolic, religious, and highly emotional character. The behavior of millions during the Red scare was characterized by numerous actions, notions, feelings, and thought processes which are commonly observed by psychiatrists. Among these were a profound sense of betrayal and persecution, anxiety in the extreme, rage, apocalyptic perspectives, a sense of imminent and massive danger, a demand for absolute, immediate, and total protection from threat and the use of primitive and childlike theories of cause and effect. These are responses to intrapsychic tensions which involve very poor reality testing. But we are dealing with these phenomena, *in extremis,* as manifested by millions of people and as they became central to political events. The psychologically aberrant assumes political significance when we find more or less normal people—millions of normal people—utilizing paranoid and other neurotic and even psychotic perspectives as a basis for political action.

The problem, however, with psychological interpretations of politics, is that we know very little. We must examine the motives of millions of people long dead. We cannot observe them "on the couch." We usually do not have their intimate personal correspondence or diaries. We must proceed retrospectively and at a considerable psychological distance. What we do, in fact, is observe very gross forms of mass behavior and then infer and attribute motives of a psychological kind. This does not mean that the inferences are incorrect, but that they are advanced in a speculative and tentative manner. The task is not to predict, but to postdict an immensely complex social situation with explanations of a psychological kind. Periods of political hysteria, however, are so infused with irrationalities, extreme passions, and cognitive disarrangements, obviously not connected with political issues per se, that the psychological dimension cannot be avoided.

Stripped of the convoluted language that often characterizes psychological analysis of politics, almost all observers agree that extreme passion in political responses often consists of the displacement of private affect upon public objects rationalized in terms of public interest.

In his introduction to "The Paranoid Style in American Politics" Richard Hofstadter observes that ". . . people not only seek their interests but also express and even in a measure define themselves in politics; that political life acts as a sounding board for identities, values, fears, and aspirations . . . politics can be a projective arena for feelings and impulses that are only marginally related to the manifest issues."[15]

These simple insights are about as far as the study of mass psychological political behavior has advanced.

The characteristics attributed to conspiratorial Reds probably did serve as a projective arena for repressed, deeply desired, but forbidden impulses. But this is speculative. Of course, that does not mean it is incorrect. We do know, however, that anxiety is one of the fundamental affects upon which hysteria is based and upon which it escalates. Thousands of people rushed to stores where they purchased guns and supplies to stave off the revolution. These people were frightened. We also know that rage and hate are central affects—witness Centralia, the variety of race riots in 1919, the vehemence of antiradical rhetoric, and the American Legion demand to remove dead "enemy aliens" from Arlington Cemetery. We know that as people became more frightened they demanded more antiradical action. And the hysteria escalated. We know there was tremendous passion behind this event.

To account for the mass base of political hysteria, and hopefully to illuminate the psychological approach to political studies, one must deal with the role of anxiety as the affective base of the movement. Anxiety, however, is not the sole affect that is involved. Certain attributes of the conspirators and the conspiracy evoked affective responses other than anxiety, which, if properly understood, might also help to explain why the conspiracy was so strongly believed in and acted upon. The conspirators, in addition to being enormously powerful, and sexually licentious, were portrayed as vermin, lice, germs, insects, reptiles, rodents, and feces. The response to the conspirator as microorganism, reptile, and filth was also highly affective, and bound the believer to the leader who pledged to eliminate this filthy danger.

THE CONSPIRATOR AS MICRO-ORGANISM

The analogy of disease, epidemic, and germ is used frequently to define the conspirator. The conspirator is an infection and deadly germ. The conspirator is an insect. The conspiracy is a plague which will cause untold suffering. The micro-organism combines in extreme form almost all the vicious and deadly qualities of the conspirator. Lowenthal and Guterman write, "It is ubiquitous, close, deadly, insidious. It invites the idea of extermination, and most important, it is invisible to the naked eye, the agitation-expert is required to detect its presence."[16] The contamination and destruction of the body by deadly and unseen foreign bodies raises numerous infantile fears of penetration, inundation, and extermination. And the anticipation of extermination is the ultimate and most profound signal producing anxiety. The threat of epidemic may conjure up primitive fears not only of the extermination of self, but of all loved ones.

The danger of infection is so great that immediate countermeasures are required. This also lends support to the super-patriots' cry for "action *now*." The danger is so great that time is not available for a serious and prolonged analysis of the disease. The invisible quality of the micro-organism also makes the special diagnostic gifts of the agitator indispensable. He becomes a necessary magnifier and this further legitimates his role. The invisible nature of the germ and its infectious capacity makes the would-be victim continuously fearful and suspicious of epidemic. Thus, another reason why the web of suspicion and potential suspects enlarges. The infectious danger justifies extermination by any means—and extermination without guilt.

The conspirator is also portrayed as a low animal—a bug, a louse, a rat, a snake. One can imagine the repulsion and the pleasure that might be experienced by exterminating the vermin and snake-like Reds that were described in 1919 by William Hornaday, a trustee of the *American Defense Society* and author of the superpatriotic classic, "Awake America."

The cobra is the most vicious, venomous, and deadly of all foreign snakes. The only cobras in America are those that have come to us from abroad.

The cobra is the only reptile that loves to live in the thatched roofs and under hearthstones of the habitations of man. In wet weather, when they are driven out of the fields of India by discomfort and privation, they seek the shelter of men's houses: and they do not hesitate to bite, through sheer viciousness, the people whose homes shelter them. In India, in the early days, a live cobra sometimes fell from a thatched roof, or a beam, upon the family table.

The cobra is the most dreaded of all the old-world snakes, because it is the only species that actually pursues inoffensive people, and goes out of its way to bite them. It strikes without warning, and usually in the dark, so that it can make a safe getaway. Its bite is so deadly that only the most prompt treatment, with a serum made from its own poison, can avert the death of the victim.

In comparison with the alien cobra the American rattlesnake is a gentleman. He never pursues you, nor seeks you out in order to bite you: and he always rattles a fair warning before he strikes. Thousands of lives have been saved by his warning rattle, "Don't tread on me!"

The only proper and adequate treatment for the cobra of Class Hatred is instant extermination.

I am sorry that this is true, but at this time America is thickly infested with cobras in human form that to our people are a thousand times more dangerous to peaceful people than the serpents of India are to the people of Hindustan. There are several species, and they bear various markings; but all of them are alike venomous.

It is difficult to decide which is more venomous per capita—the IWW species, the socialist-anarchist, the Non-Partisan League, the German spy species, or the Sinn Feiner. Of all these species, however, the individuals who deserve the shortest shrift are those bearing American names, and that have been bred on our own soil. But, even toward those reptiles that were hatched in the European hotbeds of class hatred and anarchy, we have been a thousand times too indifferent, too tolerant, too sleepy, and too slow with the firmly restraining hand. I think it will take a lot of blood-letting to awaken this nation of sodden sleepers to the extent of this danger.[17]

This quote contains a master catalogue of the dangers and characteristics of the conspirators. The Cobra and Rattlesnake are inverse images. American snakes are gentlemen and inoffensive. Cobra conspirators are not merely treacherous, poisonous and deadly. They are the most treacherous and deadly. There are no cobras native to America. Every one is a foreign import. Cobras not only bite the very hand that feeds them —without hesitation—but they particularly seek good people to bite. Their bite has two characteristics—it is deadly, and the effect of the bite is almost instantaneous. Thus, the antidote must be administered immediately and it must be as powerful as the venom. Nothing less potent will do. Immediate extermination is the only solution and this will necessitate the spilling of much blood. Conspirators in America are ubiquitous. America is "thickly infested" with alien cobras. Although they may have different skins, the bite of each is deadly. Particular attention should be paid to the native, white Protestant American cobra who should have known better. America had better awake before these deadly snakes strike.

The conspirator is dehumanized on several levels. He is a

snake and a germ derived from disgusting, filthy, subhuman, biological regions. He is a foreigner originating from suspect and alien regions. He is a criminal who operates in regions of unlimited immorality and cruelty. He is a threat to one's biology, ideology, and morality—slimy, repulsive, seductive, and frightening. Any sadistic impulse is justified in exterminating him. He can be isolated, incarcerated, deported, or exterminated.

The conspirator as germ, lice, scum, stench and vermin is filthy and foulsmelling. Children are taught at an early age to associate filth and smell with bad things, with untouchable and forbidden parts of the body and untouchable products of the body—excrement, urine, and gas. Toilet training and training for cleanliness is a difficult and often traumatic experience for a small child. Many children resist it fiercely and just as fiercely, many parents insist upon it and attempt to enforce it by threatening the child with punishment and sickness if he does not keep himself clean. Freud and other psychiatrists have argued that training for cleanliness can have important consequences for character. The child is both repelled by and attracted to feces which can be another forbidden fruit. The conspirator as filth and scum can tap these repulsions, repressions, and desires. The true believer can project his repulsion and hatred onto the dirty conspirator. The true believer can indict the enemy and come in contact with his filth.

The dehumanization of the conspirator on all levels transforms him into a creature that is quite incapable of human behavior. His evil is not culturally determined but rooted in his biology. He can act only in evil ways. He has no choice. His subhumanity justifies his extermination in nonhuman ways.

These perspectives are not unique to the Red scare or periods of political hysteria. The vocabulary of dehumanization and the rhetoric of filth, plague, and contamination has become the language of elite and everyday American parlance during the past three decades. Herbert Marcuse has commented on this contemporary vocabulary:

This linguistic universe, which incorporates the Enemy (as Untermensch) into the routine of everyday speech, can be transcended only in action. For violence is built into the very structure of this society: as the accumulated aggressiveness which drives the business of life in all branches of corporate capitalism, as the legal aggression on the highways, and as the national aggression abroad which seems to become more brutal the more it takes as its victims the wretched of the earth—those who have not yet been civilized by the capital of the Free World. In the mobilization of this aggressiveness, ancient physical forces are activated to serve the economic-political needs of the system: the Enemy are those who are unclean, infested; they are animals rather than humans; they are contagious (the domino theory!) and threaten the clean, anesthetized, healthy free world. They must be liquidated, smoked out, and burned out like venom; their infested jungles too must be burned out and cleared for freedom and democracy. The Enemy already has its "fifth column" inside the clean world; the Commies and the Hippies and their like with the long hair and the beards and the dirty pants—those who are promiscuous and take liberties which are denied to the clean and orderly who remain clean and orderly even when they kill and bomb and burn. Never perhaps since the Middle Ages has accumulated repression erupted on such global scale in organized aggression against those outside the repressive system—"outsiders" within and without.[18]

The political leader who utilizes and legitimates the rhetoric of vermin and lice, feces and secrets, does so to create a dehumanized victim, to frighten the people, and to psychologically involve them with the hysteria and his leadership. In so doing he utilizes some of the most ancient political myths.

THREE MYTHS AND ANXIETY

Political hysteria in America, as elsewhere, is usually founded on three classic political myths—myths which have been utilized by political leaders since antiquity, designed to arouse mass anxiety and cause people to rally behind the leader. The first is the myth of conspiracy—the invention or definition of a dehumanized outgroup which is plotting, in secret and conspiratorial fashion, to destroy and capture society. The alleged threat to society is total and apocalyptic. The threat is designed to evoke anxiety and bind the masses, in a highly affective manner, to leaders.

The second myth, invented to reassure those frightened by the first myth, is that of the political leader who is benevolent yet powerful enough to save the masses. In this myth the leader is portrayed as having performed an heroic public service in uncovering the threat. The threat must be portrayed as if it can be smashed, because, without this possibility, people would not follow the leader. If the belief developed that the leader could not control the dangers, the leader could himself become the victim and the object of attack as the bearer of evil tidings. The threat must be vulnerable but it also must be dangerous enough to provoke high levels of anxiety. The war against the enemy must alternate between "hot" and "cold" but it must never be fully won, for a total victory could end the anxiety and terminate the hysteria.

The alleged danger affectively binds the masses to their leaders. The portrait of the leader as benevolent, as aware of the secrets of the conspiracy, and as powerful enough to smash it tightens this bond. The escalating threat plays upon the powerlessness of the potential victims and increases their dependence upon the leader's wisdom and power. Only the leader can crush the threat and resolve the anxiety attack. The identification of the masses with the leaders can become so effective and powerful that it is built upon, what Franz Neuman calls, "a nearly total ego-shrinkage." The member of the mass loses his sense of individual identity and recaptures it by identifying with the benevolent and powerful leader. Neuman denotes such regressive identifications as Caesaristic. It is a combination of the conspiratorial myth and the myth of the benevolent and powerful leader that evokes Caesaristic identifications. Neuman writes,

It is my thesis, that wherever affective (i.e., caesaristic) leader-identifications occur in politics, masses and leader have this view of history: that the distress which has befallen the masses has been brought about exclusively by a conspiracy of certain persons or groups against the people.

With this view of history true anxiety, which has been produced by war, want, hunger, anarchy, is to be transformed into neurotic anxiety and is to be overcome by means of identification with the leader—demogogue through total ego-renunciation, to the advantage of the leader and his clique, whose true interests do not necessarily have to correspond to those of the masses.[19]

The interest of the leader and his clique is advanced by a third myth—the myth that the nation can triumph over its enemies if it sacrifices, disciplines itself, and follows the leader. Murray Edelman, who has written on the symbolic functions of political myths, has commented on the myth of sacrifice.

In the context of a sense of crisis, which is always present for many, this appeal evokes a strong and enthusiastic response even—perhaps especially—when the exact nature of the work, the sacrifice and the obedience is left unspecified . . . Anxious populations seem to want fervently to be exposed to this appeal and so it is predictably offered to them.[20]

The function of predicting victory if the masses will sacrifice, work, and obey is to create a sense of participation and efficacy on the part of the masses, to mobilize the masses for action, to create a public opinion favorable to whatever means the leader and the government adopt to stop the danger, and to heighten the identification of the masses with the leadership.

These three myths, plus several others, were offered to the American people during the Red scare. The threat was portrayed as enormously dangerous and powerful but conquerable by a combination of public power, the leadership of Palmer and the Justice Department, and public militance, obedience and sacrifice. The exact nature of the work, the sacrifice, and the obedience were never quite spelled out beyond the rather vague idea of being patriotic, being American, learning all one could about Reds, and being alert to the danger. A typical description of the sacrifice was spelled out by a prominent labor leader in a virulent anti-Bolshevik pamphlet.

Every American who measures his responsibility to his country must realize that his Americanism will be put to the test in this fight against the enemies of his country, and he must meet the test like a man. He must stand up squarely as an American and fight determinedly, courageously, and intelligently until Bolshevism and all that it stands for are wiped out.[21]

It is important to keep the nature of the work to be done quite vague because the alleged conspiracy itself must be kept quite vague so as to make it a proper vehicle for fantasy. A definite and concrete plan of action to combat the conspiracy would necessitate concretizing more aspects of the conspiracy; thus making it less usable as a vehicle of fantasy and exposing the mythmaker to the possible charge that the conspiracy does not exist in fact.

The Red scare was built, in large part, out of these three classic myths. The critical myth was that of a secret and powerful conspiracy. And one of the most significant aspects of that myth was that it had little basis in reality. Political hysterias are based on anticipations of future danger—not reality. The essence of the Red scare was the anticipation of apocalyptic destruction. We are dealing here not primarily with a world of objective reality but of vague and foreboding fantasies, illusions, expectation, portents, and anticipations.

The hysteria is constructed by creating myths which evoke, on an unconscious level, remembrance of past fears and wishes, and, on a conscious level, anticipation of future dangers. The state, for a variety of reasons, is the prime mover of the anxiety. Government is, after all, a struggle over the definition of reality. Various groups compete to define what is fact, what is legitimate behavior, what are proper goals, what threatens society, and what may be expected of the future. Particularly with respect to future expectations, the cues emanating from the government, are confronted with few counter-cues that reach wide audiences. Political hysteria is based on numerous cues that have to do primarily with expectations of future danger. The ability to monopolize cues relating to future expectations, particularly future dangers, is one of the most significant powers of the state because man largely defines his world through such anticipations.

The anticipated future accounts for much of man's motivation. Recent studies of motivation suggest that anticipation is of equal or even greater importance than deprivation in accounting for motivated behavior.

Berkowitz, for example, commenting on aggression, writes:

Contrary to traditional motivational thinking and motivational concepts of Freud and Lorenz, many psychologists now insist that deprivations alone are inadequate to account for most motivated behavior. According to this newer theorizing, much greater weight must be given to anticipations of the goal than merely to the duration of the magnitude of deprivation per se. The stimulus arising from these anticipations—from anticipatory goal responses —is now held to be a major determinant of the vigor and persistence of goal-seeking activity.[22]

The characteristics attributed to the conspirators, and the goals attributed to the conspiracy (which provoked the anticipation of extreme danger and shaped its content) were major determinants of the vigor and persistence with which the American masses committed themselves to the Red scare. Equally critical were the anticipation of danger and the anticipation that the danger could be eliminated.

Expectations can fundamentally influence perceptions and interpretations of current facts, particularly when the facts are ambiguous. These perceptions and interpretations, shaped, in part, by anticipations, create a cognitive map by which man

misperceives objective reality and creates his own version of
it in accordance with his anticipations. Government plays the
key role in creating the cognitive map upon which political
hysteria is founded. Widespread political hysteria probably
cannot be produced by private groups unless they have substantial support—or at least neutrality—from government figures and institutions. Certainly this was true of the Red scare,
McCarthyism, and much of the Cold War so far as these events
revolved around unreal anticipations.

The conspiracy allegedly seeks the destruction of society as it
exists. The threat is total. The danger is great. The anxiety is
a response to the danger. The relationship of anxiety to politics
involves several questions above and beyond how the anxiety is
aroused by the conspiratorial theory. What kind of anxiety
leads to hysteria? How do anxious populations behave politically? How is the anxiety "used" by interest groups? How do
myths reduce anxiety as well as create it? What is it that
masses want and need when they anticipate future conspiratorial dangers? Murray Edelman has succinctly stated some
of these needs.

It is hard, in politics, to know what causes what and which group
interest has won the last battle, let alone the last war. Worse, inner
anxieties are displaced onto public objects so that overt enemies
can be blamed and social supports created. The political events
focused upon can thereby become infused with strong affect
stemming from psychic tension, from perceptions of economic,
military, or other threats, and from interactions between social
and psychological phenomena.

The political "events," however, are largely creations of the
language used to describe them. For the mass of political specta-
tors, developments occur in a remote arena where there can be no
direct observation or feedback. The bewildering political universe
needs to be ordered and given meaning. People who are anxious
and confused are eager to be supplied with an organized political
order—including simple explanations of threats they fear—and
with reassurance that the threats are being countered.[23]

The political universe is normally bewildering. Despite the arguments of democratic theorists who assume that man can, to some degree, perceive reality accurately, political events are rarely viewed first-hand, information about them is customarily sparse and frequently distorted, and the public sense of political actions and issues is not usually full or fully articulated. The normal amount of bewilderment, which is great, is compounded during periods of political hysteria because they unfold during times of some social dislocation which is again exacerbated by prediction of more dislocation. Myths of conspiratorial danger can provide a universal, rather simple, easily understood, and meaningful interpretation of a bewildering world—particularly when those myths tap unconscious proclivities and potentiate latent American perspectives. The conspirators are the cause of the difficulty. The political world is thus ordered and explained.

The anxious public, currently upset by dislocation, and anticipating future dangers, also wants reassurance that the danger will be met and defeated. The second myth—the benevolent and powerful leader, who can meet the threat—provides this assurance. The myth, however, offers even more than the mere defeat of the conspiracy. It suggests that some truly better world will arise after the conspiracy is smashed. The mythmakers encapsulate the myth with millenarian expectations.

The third classic myth—victory over the danger will be achieved if the masses will work, sacrifice, and obey their leaders—answers another need of the anxious.

The appeal of common sacrifice is probably based on the fact that the sacrifice creates a community—a togetherness of common experience—which is mutually supportive, comforting, and cathartic. We noted this when discussing the latent functions of war. The myth provides a means of establishing communication and mutual support with others. The sacrifice, common to all, helps reduce the terror of anticipated dangers by creating the feeling that something is being done—by large numbers of people—to counter the danger. The common sense of the sacrifice demanded in situations of political hysteria is anxiety-reducing in itself. The action becomes cathartic.

It is a truism of both psychoanalytic theory and functional anthropology, that identities are created, in part, as a function of accepting particular myths. The relationship is probably mutually interactive: a person with a particular identity is prone to accept certain myths and the myths reinforce the identity. There is no reason to assume that this does not occur for groups as well as for individuals. By believing in particular myths, a person or a group selects one particular identity and rejects others. The myths of Red conspiracy and apocalyptic salvation, although creating anxiety and playing upon rootlessness, also "cure" it by providing a dramatic account of who are friends, who are enemies, and what collective action is necessary to protect oneself and society. As Murray Edelman remarks concerning the functions of political myth,

It channels individual anxieties and impulses into a widely-shared set of expectations and a widely-shared scenario to guide action. It frees the individual from responsibility for his unhappy and threatened place in society and prescribes a clear and widely supported program for protecting his identity.[24]

By accepting particular myths and rejecting others, individuals or groups create a cognitive map for perceiving the world in particular ways. Those who accept the myth of Bolshevik conspiracy also accept the myth of America the Beautiful. Superpatriotic mythmakers actually create two myths which feed each other. The first, the international Bolshevik conspiracy, has a counterpart in the myth that America approximates perfection, that America has, in fact is, what it strives for in theory—democracy, popular sovereignty, liberty, equality, opportunity, fraternity, and freedom of speech, press, worship, and assembly. The superpatriot, Rome G. Brown, provides us with a typical recital of America's rhetorical goals presented as though they had all been achieved.

It means a government established by the fundamental law, constitutional and otherwise, governing the property and personal rights of individuals. It means a government which is founded upon their individual right of private property and of certain personal rights and liberties, including the right to contract and be protected in the contract made; the right of freedom of religious worship; the right of every individual to acquire, to own and to hold as his own, the fruits of his initiative, his capacity, his effort and his thrift. It is a government which holds out encouragement and incentive to individual effort and thrift because it is a government which has established an independent judicial department whose function it is to declare invalid any legislation which is repugnant to those rights.[25]

Other superpatriots play on the Horatio Alger themes:

Ours is a poorer soil for social injustices to grow in than you will find anywhere else in the world. There is a sense of the "square deal" among us and a freedom to fight for one's rights that stand guard against injustices. We wail about our 47 cent dollars, but our dollars are the best values in the world at the present time.

We are not in want; we are all employed; we are, in fact, the most fortunate people in the world with the least reason for being discontented. Here in this great open field of opportunity called America, its very soul vibrant with the largest measure of human liberty consistent with orderly government, every man carves out his own fortune, makes his own way in the world, and if he fails it is because he did not find his job and stick to it.[26]

For the anxiety ridden, the attachment of both myths—one reinforces the other—nourishes the already powerful identification with America and the Americanist national liberal faith. As patriotism becomes superpatriotism, the average American becomes not only an American but a defender of the true American faith—a very pleasurable and patriotic role. Millions of defenders of the faith—natives defending nativism against the alien enemy—are always present in America, but the mythmakers actively labor to increase their ranks. Prejudice and nativism are resources for superpatriotism, and political hysteria is, among other things, a purification rite, and cleansing

of America. Students of prejudice in America have found that
patriotism correlates more closely with prejudice than any other
factor. The nation, national traditions, national history, the
nation's way of life—all these are significant cues for identity
in most cultures. This is particularly true for Americans because America, throughout its history, has had only one dominant tradition—triumphant and unanimous liberalism elevated
to a national faith. The absence of deeply rooted traditions on
the right and left has intensified the American commitment to
Americanist liberalism. America, as national ethos, provides a
home for all Americans but, apparently it provides a particularly
meaningful home to the prejudiced—a displaced psychic
home, a symbolic mother. When the symbolic mother appears
to be threatened, the sons rise to her defense. This is particularly true for the deeply prejudiced. The psychologist, Gordon
Allport, suggests that prejudiced persons undergoing stress
seek "an island of institutional safety and security. The nation
is the island he selects. . . . It has the definiteness he needs."

Allport pointed out with respect to nativist outbursts—which
in part, the Red Scare was—that the important factor regarding
the prejudiced

is the way fear and frustration are handled. The institutionalistic
way—especially the nationalistic—seems to be the nub of the
matter. What happens is that the prejudiced person defines
"nation" to fit his needs. The nation is first of all a protection (the
chief protection) of him as an individual. It is his in-group. He sees
no contradiction in ruling out of its beneficient orbit those whom
he regards as threatening intruders and enemies (namely, American
minorities). What is more, the nation stands for the status quo.
It is a conservative agent; within it are all the devices for safe living
that he approves. His nationalism is a form of conservatism.[27]

When government leaders, the press, and highly legitimated
figures all agree that social dislocation is caused primarily by
conspiratorial intruders and dehumanized deviants, the hostility of the highly prejudiced not only intensifies, but others,

whose hostility in normal times is mild, are also provoked. The normal tensions and social stresses felt by the prejudiced, compounded by anticipation of conspiratorial danger, are modified by indentifying even more vigorously with the nation-mother and by playing out the socially approved role of destroyer of America's enemies. The truly effective myth plays upon preexistent anxieties, creates new anxieties, and then provides a "cure." It also exalts the ancient and venerated national-mother and cries for its defense.

But the appeals of the myth are by no means restricted to the prejudiced. Others may handle stress by reaffirming their ties with the nation-mother. The American historian, Stanley Coben, has suggested that the Red scare was a manifestation of what the anthropologist F. C. Wallace has termed a "revitalization movement." Apropos of this observation Coben has written:

Since the late nineteenth century, anthropologists have been studying the religious and nativistic cults of American Indian tribes and of Melanesian and Papuan groups in the South Pacific. Recently, several anthropologists have attempted to synthesize their findings and have shown striking parallels in the cultural conditions out of which these movements arose. In every case, severe societal disruption preceded the outbreak of widespread nativistic cult behavior. According to Anthony F. Wallace, who has gone farthest toward constructing a general theory of cult formation, when the disruption has proceeded so far that many members of a society find it difficult or impossible to fulfill their physical and psychological needs, or to relieve severe anxiety through the ordinary culturally approved methods, the society will be susceptible to what Wallace has termed a "revitalization movement." This is a convulsive attempt to change or revivify important cultural beliefs and values, and frequently to eliminate alien influences. Such movements promise and often provide participants with better means of dealing with their changed circumstances, thus reducing their very high level of internal stress.[28]

The Red scare was prompted, in part, by the disruption and stress which followed the First World War. The revitalization of old American values did serve as a unifying force—a reaffirmation of the national identity—and, as such, a bulwark against disintegrating forces. The *communitas* created during the war could thus be continued.

For the anxiety-ridden, then, the attachment to the myth establishes not only a socially approved identity—patriot, American, defender of the faith—but also a collective course of action to allay the anxiety—pursuer of Reds, vigilante, purifier of the American ethic. The very anxiety which is created by acceptance of these myths is also allayed by the socially approved roles of the actions the myth creates. The truly effective political myth creates both the disease and the cure. Unless the latter is present, the myth is not likely to be effective as a technique for mobilizing the type of support desired by elites.

An account of the comforting, pleasurable, and anxiety-reducing functions of these myths suggests they will be advanced frequently. And they are. It suggests they are likely to be accepted and acted upon by masses. And they are. That is precisely why they are so useful to elites. That is why they are classic political formulations. Their utility to elites has to do with their self-fulfilling quality. The myth provokes anxiety and simultaneously provides cures which permit elites to enhance their self-interest in the guise of public interest. People in trouble can, through attachment to these myths, trace the source of their problems to an identifiable and socially disapproved enemy, and thus not perceive themselves or elites as responsible for their difficulties. The myth, as Edelman writes, becomes ". . . a means of succor against severe anxiety" and ". . . it is strongly embraced and defended, and so it becomes the mold into which perceptions of political developments are organized. Once established, the myths therefore become self-perpetuating."[29]

As the anxiety mounts, something approaching an anxiety panic, or massive anxiety attack, develops; and this can have significant political effects. The cycle of panic customarily follows a fairly well defined course. The threat becomes, in the eyes of the anxious, increasingly vague, more imminent, and more dangerous. The anxiety-ridden person does not really know the source of the danger. It can therefore be anything. Those ridden with anxiety never really know if they have correctly and/or fully identified the source of the danger. In panic, one is driven to ever more frantic, irrational, and exotic searches for the source of the danger and for "cures." Since any "cause" can be perceived as a cause, the web of dangerous —i.e., subversive—activities widens, and with it, the web of suspicion. Everyone is suspicious. Nothing is accidental. Everything is planned and laden with meaning. Viewed through panic and conspiratorial eyes, isolated, and disconnected minor, and obscure acts can be perceived as laden with meaning and as part of a larger and planned conspiratorial whole. As the process unfolds, the panic can breed an intense and conservative political reaction, which is precisely what many advocates of the hysteria—particularly big business—wish for. The conspiratorial web widens. Guilt by association, guilt by common national origin, guilt by any characteristic alleged to be commonly held with an alleged conspirator becomes a common standard. The political scientist, Theodore Lowi, has described the cycle from panic to reaction.

From acts that are known to cause injury—rape, murder, robbery . . . etc.—they move to conspiracies to do injury and to conspiracies to advocate evil. Ultimately, the notion of what causes disorder spreads to very remote acts and words that are in no way evil in and of themselves, that do not connect in a provable way to known injuries, but are acts and words which might tend to do so in the long run. This expansion of what is accepted as causing personal injury and social disorder is the road from panic to reaction.[30]

As the panic breeds reaction, the anxious masses, and those who promote the hysteria come to assume some of the characteristics attributed to the conspirators. The conspirators' passionate unquestioned commitment to revolutionary ideals is matched by the superpatriots' passionate attachment to "Americanism." Conspirators use any means to attain their ends. Superpatriots talk of using any means necessary to destroy the conspiracy. The conspirators engage in perverse and brutal sexual relations. The patriot engages in sadomasochistic sexual fantasies. The conspirators' alleged intolerance of dissent within his ranks is matched by the patriots' intolerance. The conspirators' alleged secret society is matched by the semisecret undertakings of superpatriotic societies, and the secret operations of the Justice Department, Army intelligence, and labor spies. The conspirator is the inverted image of the good American. And the good American, to combat the conspirator, comes to resemble the conspirator.

The men at the Justice Department who ferret out conspirators, the professional superpatriots, and assorted conspiratorial mythmakers, even assume some of the characteristics of the men who allegedly lead the world-wide conspiracy. Like the great revolutionary leader, the superpatriot portrays himself as the possessor of profound insights who is able to see the future which lies behind and within the facade of the present. He is able to probe and see what the masses cannot see. He is predestined to play his role as an agent of historical change —an agent of higher forces upon whom history has bestowed a heavy burden and great responsibility. The superpatriot is the supreme inside dopester. He is endowed with oracular talent. He is a purveyor of revelations. He has access to more secrets than he can reveal. In fact, as Richard Hofstadter noted, he reveals the existence of secrets but not their content. Like Lenin, for example, he is a fanatic and a prophet—sanctified by his role as savior.

These roles of the savior superpatriot not only serve him by sanctifying his leadership and placing all Americans in his permanent debt, but they allay the very anxiety he originally created. The savior knows what to do. He can penetrate the secrets of the conspiracy and destroy the conspirators. The anxious masses, knowing victory is inevitable once they join the leader and sacrifice, will experience psychic relief, and witness the restoration of national values and national purity.

Mythmakers built the plausibility of the conspiratorial myth on appeals to the irrational and the unconscious as well as appeals to a semblance of reason. The former reinforced the impact of the latter and the combination made belief in the conspiracy literally irresistible.

The political hysteria was set in motion and sustained by large numbers of business and political leaders, corporations and interest groups, the attorney general, several agencies of government, superpatriotic societies, and the press. The hysteria spawned a substantial bureaucracy interested in expansion and a small army of proponents. The hysteria was largely pluralist phenomenon involving numerous pay-offs for many individuals and interest groups. We turn now to the surprisingly pluralist basis of the American repression.

5

PLURALIST REPRESSION

THE great majority of social scientists attribute the moderation and stability of the American democracy to its pluralism. The argument is advanced that America is not governed by a coherent power elite—a unified ruling class—but by a large number of interest groups, competing and jockeying for influence and balancing and moderating each other's aggressiveness. These interest groups do pursue self-interest and they do coalesce when their interest is common, but the pursuit by one coalition usually checks and balances the pursuit of self-interest by other coalitions, so that no one coalition can exert decisive influence on public power for any length of time. Customarily, the theory runs, no coalition gets all of what it wants, all of the time, and winners on one issue, sooner or later, become losers on the other issues. Compromise, bargaining, incremental change, moderation, and stability are the results.

The leaders of interest groups, allegedly, keep American politics from being apocalyptic and moralistic and extremist and hysterical by concentrating on immediate and concrete issues of economic self-interest. They train their numbers to fight for bread and butter, not justice, truth, beauty, or utopia. They eschew the ideological, the moralistic, and the eschatological. They keep American politics down to earth, pragmatic, and incremental. Pluralist politics, it is assumed, prevents the politics of mass society—the politics of hysteria and apocalypse.

Yet the reverse was true during the Red scare. The hysteria and the democratic repression it produced were promoted by pluralist interest groups, in part, to enhance economic self-interest. The repression was pluralistic, primarily legal, and nonviolent. Pluralism can be utilized to advance extremism, immoderation, ideological movements, moralistic perspectives, and collision of good and evil. Economic self-interest can so be advanced. Extremism and democratic repression can be used to provide numerous pay-offs to numerous interest groups.

Myths probably do not succeed on a truly national scale unless major power groups support them, and major power groups usually support myths when these myths function in their interests. Some big businessmen and public officials supported the superpatriotic perspective because they sincerely believed America was seriously endangered by radical cabal. Others exploited the hysteria by stereotyping their opponents as radicals knowing full well they were not. The publicly stated purpose of the hysteria—the manifest function—was the defense of the American way against its enemies. The latent or private function for many individuals and interest groups was private gain—a salary increase for a member of the staff of a superpatriotic society who met his quota of radicals, the expansion of the antiradical division of the Justice Department, a justification for an American expeditionary force in Russia, increased lecture fees for antiradical speakers, the breaking of strikes, or even the defamation of the entire labor movement. The complex mixture of selfless sincerity and crude self-interest, of manifest and latent function, of petty enhancement and class struggle, is an inextricable part of the motivation that lies behind the hysteria.

The hysteria and repression unfolded primarily through the traditional avenues of American pluralism. It was a manifestation of interest group politics and it was a product of coalitions, mutual aid, pressure, and even bargaining. Many of the alleged restraints which elites, committed to democracy, are supposed to apply to themselves were abandoned. The Red scare was not only pluralist in nature, it was, with some significant exceptions, legal and lawful. Radicals and liberals were repressed by courts of law—not concentration camps. The pluralism and lawfulness of repression can make political hysteria a very seductive political gambit in America.

Analysis of conspiratorial mythmaking and the drive for the repression of economic and political opponents is of more than esoteric interest. American political parties and sects have promoted conspiracy and the need for repression since the founding of the Republic. The myth of the international communist conspiracy of the present day is not the most prominent in a long line of conspiratorial myths going back to the conspiracy of the Bavarian Illuminati of the eighteenth century, the Masonic conspiracy, the Catholic conspiracy, the conspiracy of Eastern Bankers, of international Jewish bankers, of the Gold Ring, the McCarthyite conspiracy of leftist Eastern intellectuals, the conspiracy of the military-industrial complex, the conspiracy of those who would fluoridate the water supply, the Communist conspiracy headed by Dwight Eisenhower, and finally, the conspiracy of the Weathermen, of Panthers, and the Berrigans.[1]

The Red threat, and the demand to repress that threat, is shaped and promoted primarily by four groups: business—big and small—agencies of federal and state government, superpatriotic societies, and the press. The hysteria is originally promoted by individual superpatriots like Ole Hanson, the mayor of Seattle. When it becomes clear that the public may respond with fervor to an antiradical crusade, the advantages of such a crusade become clear to a wider circle of interest groups. Corporate officials quickly see the advantages that might be available to them if they could type labor—particularly labor on strike—as Red-infested. The conspiratorial myth and the demand that radicals be repressed is originally made into a truly national issue by big business. As the press increases its coverage of the radical issue, in response to its definition as the prime issue by superpatriots and big businessmen, the press contributes to the primacy of the issue. Each agency builds on the definition of the situation created by other agencies and thereby participates in a transformation by which the definition of the situation becomes the situation in fact.

At some point in this process, government *must* enter the process. It has no choice. The radical issue has become not merely a lively political issue, but the most significant issue in American life. Constituencies are developing around it—potential votes. The alleged danger to America must be dealt with, and the state, for obvious reasons, is the only instrument with enough power to deal with the danger. Because the state is highly legitimated and because it has investigatory apparatus, and punitive apparatus, and financial resources, etc., it makes the antiradical crusade official government policy and the very core of belligerent nationalism.

The press now has no choice. It must make the hysteria the prime story. This further defines the situation and makes its consequences more real. As the consequences become more real, and feelings more passionate, and as antiradical constituencies grow, increasingly larger numbers of interest groups see the possibility of enhancing their particular self-interest by typing their opponents as radical. The political hysteria escalates. At this juncture, professional superpatriotic societies are revitalized or established to serve—often for profit—any interest group which might wish to find radicals in their midst. Their prime client—we shall discover—is the corporation.

In the fashion by which pluralist coalitions develop in American politics—through the perception of mutual self-interest via the advancement of common cause—the coalition behind the antiradical repression grows, and its growth nourishes the hysteria. Each escalation in the group basis of the hysteria contributes to the transformation of the definition of the situation into the situation as fact. The phenomena, we will suggest, is escalatory in nature. More pay-offs become available to more groups. More groups realize this and join the antiradical crusade. The crusade gains converts and becomes more passionate. More people are predisposed to believe in the conspiratorial myth. More people are willing to believe more interest groups as they tag their opponents as Red. More pay-offs, therefore, become available. More groups attempt to take advantage of the escalating hysteria.

The basic technique used by groups and individuals who wished to advance their self-interest through the Red scare—and not all did—was to stereotype opponents, real or mythical, as Red led, Red infested, Red financed, and interested in the destruction of some fundamental American institution or of America herself. The situation is defined in terms of all or nothing. Either the Red menace is totally eradicated or it destroys America—with apocalyptic fury.

Interest groups which stereotyped their opponents as agents of the Bolshevik conspiracy did so not merely to defame opponents but also to develop support for a variety of projects. Antiradicalism may be constructive as well as destructive and condemnatory. The pluralist basis of the repression is again illustrated by noting that the conspiratorial myth was used to develop constituencies in favor of the deportation of allegedly radical aliens, the purging of "disloyal" statements in textbooks, universal military service, scrutiny of the collection of government statistics and their use, loyalty oaths for teachers, proposed legislation to prohibit teachers from advocating any change in the constitution, the open shop, the use of injunctions in labor disputes, a proposed sedition law, less power in the hands of the federal government, and the American invasion of Russia. The hysteria was not unlike an all purpose cleanser.

As the hysteria mounts and as the awareness of the manifold benefits available to a variety of interests becomes widespread, the apparatus for the production of hysteria becomes bureaucratized. The bureaucratization of this particular apparatus, like that of others, sets in motion numerous impulses and creates many needs and roles. It takes on, as it were, a life of its own.

A bureaucracy designed to find and repress radicals, finds and represses radicals. It needs victims to justify its being. It needs victims to justify the expansion of staff and salary, and nourish the popular demand for victims. Since the agencies which compose the bureaucracy fulfill a particular self-interest by promoting a common danger, they find it beneficial to cooperate in the production of that danger. They exchange information. They exchange personnel. They exchange membership lists. They occasionally finance each other's operations. They testify in behalf of each other. They quote each other in testimony. They cite each other in pamphlets. They maintain each other's secrets. The successes of one nourishes the motivation of others. All of these moves and impulses escalate the hysteria. Escalation is dialectical. The bureaucratic apparatus becomes the agency of a colossal self-fulfilling prophecy. It creates what it predicts.

The hysteria becomes a big business involving major interests, vast sums of money, and large numbers of fulltime governmental and private employees. The bureaucracy is composed of dozens of superpatriotic societies, with tens of thousands of members, the General Intelligence Division of the Justice Department, the Immigration Bureau, Army Intelligence, the office of the attorney general, detective agencies, small private armies of Pinkertons, congressional and state legislative committees and staffs, several employers associations, hundreds of police forces, the American Legion, the Ku Klux Klan, agents provocateurs, publishers, and labor spies.

The involvement of hundreds of seemingly disparate groups and individuals in the promotion of the hysteria was based in large part on the fact that numerous and differentiated pay-offs were available for different groups—pay-offs that were neither obvious to the public nor publicly stated by those who sought them. The manifest function of the Red scare was to destroy the Red threat. The latent functions were often the enhancement of vested self-interest.

Large corporations like U.S. Steel and employers associations were interested in defaming the trade union movement and breaking strikes, mobilizing public opinion in favor of the open shop, and against enforced collective bargaining. Some major corporations employed undercover agents who were paid specifically to locate radicals among the workers. While investigating the steel strike, the Interchurch Commission heard the following testimony from a Federal officer who had served the government for many years.

. . . 90 percent of all the radicals arrested and taken into custody were reported by one of the large corporations, either of the steel or coal industry. I mean by that, that those corporations are loaded up with what they call "undercover" men who must earn their salaries, and they go around and get into these organizations and report the cases to the detective for the large companies. The detectives, in turn, report to the chief of police of the city. Generally, the chiefs of police in these small cities around Pittsburgh were placed there by the corporations.

The corporation orders an organization raided by the police department, the members are taken into custody, thrown into the police station and the department of justice is notified. They send a man to examine them to see if there are any extreme radicals or anarchists among them. They usually let all but a few go. . . .[2]

U.S. Steel was one of many American corporations that used large numbers of private detectives as labor spies. The labor spy would infiltrate unions, urge laborers not to join unions, and promote antistrike activities. For many corporations, the spy was the major source of information upon which labor policies were formulated. During the Red scare, the infiltration of various left-wing parties become a major task of the spy. "It is undeniable," wrote the authors of the Interchurch report, "that labor policies in the steel industry rest in considerable part on the reports of 'undercover men' paid directly by the steel companies or hired from concerns popularly known as 'strike busters.' The 'operatives' make money by detecting 'Unionism' one day and 'Bolshevism' the next."

During the Red scare uncovering Bolsheviks in the labor

movement became a big business. The spy was under constant pressure from headquarters to demonstrate that the communist threat was real and dominant. Sidney Howard, who wrote a lengthy study entitled *The Labor Spy*, commented on the economic aspect of the profession.

The spy's job is to report trouble. When he has no more trouble to report, his job is ended. The very nature of his job requires him to do one of two things. He may falsify his reports, or, create through his own influence upon the workers, a basis upon which to report the truth.[3]

Like good businessmen who redouble their efforts when sales are down, detectives in the antiradical business created new business. On the basis of testimony from detectives formerly in the employ of U.S. Steel, the authors of the Interchurch Study concluded:

Nor was it the custom of certain strike-breaking concerns to wait for the "labor trouble." When business was slack, they made trouble. The sub-report details, from affidavits of former operatives, how certain concerns provoked strikes in peaceful shops in the past to create "business," set union to fighting unions, organized unions in order to be called in to break the unions. They bled both sides: and the Federal Government files contained their patriotic reports.[4]

Superpatriotic societies used the antiradical crusade to boost the circulation of paid membership and to increase the size of contributions from business. The American historian, Paul Murphy, has commented on the motivation of some superpatriotic societies.

Primarily propaganda organizations, and the mouthpieces of single leaders or small cabals, their purpose was to ingratiate themselves with large private or corporate donors and thereby insure their continuation. This meant showing results, not only in broad distribution of literature but in providing speakers to help in mobilizing large elements of the general public against all manner of enemies of "the American way." Thus Harry A. Jung of the powerful National Clay Products Industries Association and later the American Vigilant Intelligence Federation could write to a potential subscriber:

> We cooperate with over thirty distinctly civic and patriotic organizations . . . It would take me too long to relate how I 'put over' this part of our activities, namely, 'trailing the Reds.' Should you ever be in Chicago, drop in and see me and I will explain. That it has been a paying proposition for our organization goes without saying. . . .

And again, Fred R. Marvin, head of the Keymen of America, could for six dollars per annum supply potential private radical hunters with his *Daily Data Sheets* which conveyed the doings of the Bolsheviks and parlor pinks to nervous and apprehensive individuals. It was Marvin's aim to inspire the leadership of such a group as the DAR to draw up and enforce a national "black-list" of undesirable speakers that included such public disturbers of the peace as Jane Addams, Sherwood Eddy, James Harvey Robinson, and William Alan White.[5]

The Ku Klux Klan and the American Legion used the fear of radicalism and the virtues of 100 percent Americanism as major selling points in a campaign to increase their membership. The Klan actually had salesmen who were paid according to the number of memberships sold. Detective agencies flourished when they were able to supply radicals on demand or evidence of Bolshevik conspiracy.

Many men and institutions that produced the "evidence" of conspiracy had a financial stake in its production. Philip Graham, Jr., who wrote a very impressive undergraduate Harvard honors thesis on the Red scare, commented on the sources of much of the "evidence."

All the transmitters of evidence had a stake in the proof of revolution. The spies themselves were paid for the evidence they produced, the companies found Bolshevism a useful weapon against legitimate labor organizations, and the detective agencies depended upon continued unrest for their livelihood. The Department of Justice's motives were undoubtedly more complex. . . . The evidence which eventually reached Congress was gathered by prejudiced observers who had a personal stake in the mounting antiradical feeling and who had every reason to find proof of a Red threat everywhere.[6]

The Department of State utilized the Red scare to muster support for its Russian policy. "Governmental agencies made most of these fears," Foster Rhea Dulles wrote, "and kept up a barrage of anti-Bolshevik propaganda throughout 1919 which was at least partially inspired by the need to justify the policy of intervention in both Archangel and Siberia."[7]

The use of the hysteria to advance individual ambition as opposed to that of interest groups is more difficult to assess because private motives are rarely revealed. We know, in retrospect, that the Red scare made J. Edgar Hoover's reputation as a radical headhunter. We know that Palmer became a national figure and a contender for the Presidency because of the Palmer raids and the Red scare. We will never know precisely how many staff members of Congressional and state investigatory committees and superpatriotic societies and detective agencies and employers organizations prospered because of their success in ferreting out Reds, but the number was in the thousands. Paul Murphy has commented on this aspect of the Red scare.

But the Red Scare, . . . introduced a new permanent dimension of intolerance. This was the aspiring, self-seeking individual or special interest group which sought to exploit the hysteria and intolerance of the moment for personal advantage. But the breadth of their operations was more sweeping in the 1920s, and the ambitiousness of their calculations was greater, as was the number of Americans they sought to affect. For aggressive politicians like A. Mitchell Palmer, Leonard Wood, or Albert S. Burleson, the ability to project themselves into the role of master defender of the endangered order could mean nomination to high office, hopefully the presidency. To an Anthony Caminetti, the first person of Italian extraction to be elected to Congress and by then Commissioner of Immigration, this was an opportunity to demonstrate that he, as well as others of his national origin, were fully one hundred percent American. To an aggressive bureaucrat like William J. Flynn, head of the Bureau of Investigation, or J. Edgar Hoover, head of the

Bureau's newly created General Intelligence (antiradical) Division,
here was a chance to enhance the power of the Bureau, and his
own power and domain simultaneously. To Flynn's successor,
William J. Burns, the ability to guide public fears and even create
fears where only apprehensions had existed was also an opportunity
to stimulate a brisk private business for the Burns International
Detective Agency until an increasingly more hostile public forced a
curtailment and a housecleaning in the Department of Justice.[8]

The behavior of the press during the Red scare, though complex, is a case in point. Why the press behaved as it did is a
complex question. To deal with the motivation of the press
is to deal with the wider problem of why so many major interest
groups supported the hysteria. There is no doubt that the
press, like the corporations and the Department of Justice,
benefited in a most practical way from the hysteria. In his
book on the Red scare, Murray emphasizes the pragmatic
aspect of interest group motivation.

Employers, in turn, were brought to the realization that the issue
of radicalism could be helpful in their fight against unionism. To
certain politicians it became obvious that radicalism would make an
excellent political issue by which free publicity as well as votes could
be obtained. The general press, meanwhile, found in the issue of
radicalism an immediate substitute for waning wartime sensational-
ism and eagerly busied itself with reporting exaggerations instead of
facts. Indeed, in the remainder of the "Scare" period the general
press suffered a temporary lapse of accuracy. . . .[9]

The very pragmatic interest group involvement in the hysteria
is clear. As the hysteria expanded, more and more special interests realized that they too could exploit the antiradical
passion to serve their self-interest. As the passion mounted,
the number of pay-offs available to interest groups increased, so
an escalation clause is written into the contract between the
Justice Department, corporate executives, superpatriotic societies, newspapers, and an ever increasing number of the interest
groups who were eager to sign. The motivation of publishers
—like that of some other interest groups—was a mixture of

genuine and selfless commitment to a loved America and self-ish commitments to profits. There is no doubt that the hysteria was profitable to most newspapers. Publishers did not resist the opportunity every day for months to headline the imminent apocalypse in the United States. A steel strike that is a revolution is more sensational than a steel strike that is merely a steel strike.

This banner year of yellow journalism, 1919, was a year of profit for the press. But the self-interest in the antiradicalism of the press was also evident when they realized that the un-restrained pursuit of that passion seemed about to adversely affect them. Serious, nation-wide opposition to the hysteria from major newspapers did not occur until the Congress seriously considered a peacetime sedition bill designed to pro-vide a more firm legal base in peacetime for the pursuit of radicals. A committed, passionate, irrational, antiradical caught in the fury of hysteria, who believes his country can be destroyed by radical agitators, supports such a bill. Palmer proposed it. Palmer supported it. Dozens of Congressmen avidly supported it. Hundreds of publishers—literally hundreds—however, op-posed it and did so vigorously because they thought the bill could be used as a curb on freedom of press. Their opposition was based on a conception of self-interest. There is nothing surprising about this. But it does suggest that pluralist self-interest and pragmatism very much condition the superpatriotic impulse and one's commitment to civil liberties. Prior to the proposed sedition bill, very few publishers showed the slightest interest in freedom of press for radicals. As a matter of fact, many newspapers of national prominence demanded that the government curb radical publishers.

The motivation of publishers is complex but it is not ex-ceptional. Newspaper publishers in this country are Americans and businessmen—often leading Americans and big business-men. We noted that the press overwhelmingly supported capi-tal and was very critical of labor throughout this period. Like

other businessmen, publishers were concerned with the potential growth of a left-wing in the labor movement. As businessmen, why shouldn't they be concerned? Like other Americans,
they are no less prone to the seduction of liberal values, the
only set of political values available in this country. Liberalism
and the American way of life nourished by liberalism is no less
a national faith for them than other Americans. Their literacy
does not exempt them from the national consciousness. In fact,
their definition of their profession and task often leads them
to perceive themselves as special guardians of American truths,
traditions, and the national faith. Historically, their commitment to the American mission and the American dream has
been a powerful wellspring. Their commitment to defend
America against her enemies is no less powerful.

They also define their task as that of transmitting the news.
Much of the news of 1919 and 1920 was made by Palmer and
Judge Gary, Lenin, Calvin Coolidge, and IWW, etc., etc. Palmer raids hundreds of allegedly radical enclaves. This is big
news. He made it big news. It must be reported and promi-
nently reported. Palmer and hundreds of superpatriots, as ini-
tiators and creators of events, even though they may be
contrived or pseudo-events, have a powerful "advantage," as
it were, over the paper that reports the event. They act, the
press reacts. We saw this in the case of Joseph McCarthy. Palmer and McCarthy, by originally defining the situation, have
gone a long way toward making it conspicuous and real. The
situation is "there," as it were, when the press arrives. It is
easier to create than dissect and analyze. It is easier to publish
a Justice Department press release than to do extensive research
yourself. The press, to some degree, is a victim of the "news"
it reports.

The motivation of publishers, like that of many others, was
a peculiar mix of sincerity, self-interest, conscious contrivance,
and victimization.

The press, however, was a prime partner in this pluralistic

enterprise. It "used" other proponents of the conspiratorial myth, as they used the press. The groups that promoted the hysteria could better fulfill their private purpose by cooperating with each other. And they did. Their cooperation was a factor in escalating the menace of the Red menace.

The Department of Justice, for example, not only cooperated with privately employed detectives, labor spies, and corporate offices, but also, in some cases, jointly employed them. The Department also utilized several of its men as agents provocateur. On December 27, 1919, the chief of the Bureau of Investigation and the Department of Justice sent a confidential letter of instruction to a division superintendent in Boston pertaining to the impending Palmer raids.

If possible, you should arrange with your undercover informants to have meetings of the COMMUNIST PARTY and the COMMUNIST LABOR PARTY held on the night set. I have been informed by some of the bureau offices that such arrangements will be made. This, of course, would facilitate the making of the arrests.[10]

The relationship between the department and private detective agencies and corporate officers was intimate. William J. Burns of the Burns International Detective Agency was made director of the Bureau of Investigation. Burns apparently did not even sever his connections upon his appointment and his former agency benefited by its contacts with the department. The department frequently utilized private detectives for special situations. Louis Post, the assistant secretary of Labor, described the relationship.

The detective auxiliary of the Department of Justice drew upon the private detective supply of the country for "special agents" whom it distributed to various points regarded as strategic, and through whom it made cooperative arrangements with local police officials. The detectives were supplied with warrants of arrest from time to time.[11]

It is obvious that some of the evidence advanced by conspiratorial mythmakers, was, in part, actually manufactured out of thin air and that several agencies cooperated, knowingly and willfully at the creation. Corporate officials, labor spies, local police, American Legionnaires, vigilantes, superpatriots, and government agents staged events, printed and distributed radical literature, infiltrated radical parties, promoted radical action, spread rumors, exchanged information, and then cited many of their own creations before Congressional and state legislative investigating committees as "proof" of the conspiracy.

Under Secretary of Labor, Louis Post, who played a major role in developing a counter-community to oppose the Red hysteria, provided a beautiful example of bureaucratic cooperation.

A private detective agency of Pittsburgh had employed an alien with a criminal record to procure "submarine" or "undercover" information about the activities of workingmen employed by one of its clients. His work consisted in part of organizing "radicals" for the purpose of causing them to be deported if the company employing the detective agency were to think best. In the course of this work the "undercover" man cultivated the friendship of Russian "radicals," and to facilitate his operations he joined the Socialist Party and then the Communist Party. Of the latter he became financial secretary locally, and for it he organized "locals" and solicited members. He reported daily to the detective agency that employed him, the detective agency forwarded his reports to its client, and the client furnished information at its discretion to representatives of the Department of Justice.

Upon information so obtained, some of the raids to be described were made. In one of them this provocative agent was arrested along with his dupes. He did not feel disturbed at first, for he had been assured by Department of Justice agents that although he would be deported to Russia with the others, "so as to shield him from suspicion," he would be brought back in due time and be given a job in the Department of Justice.[12]

The flow of undercover information in this instance is interesting and fairly typical of the kind of traffic generally engaged in. The undercover agent reports to the detective agency that employs him. The agency reports to the company. The company "at its discretion" reports to Justice Department agents. The agents report to Washington. The Justice Department, acting as a clearinghouse, then transmits information to a Congressional investigating committee. A small and relatively closed interlocking directorate—mutually supportive—was in operation.

In a revealing bit of testimony before a Congressional committee, Donald C. Van Buren, in charge of military intelligence in the area of the steel strike, described his sources of information of radical activities.

Information comes to us from various sources, all sorts of information, and we try to file, index it, and give it to the proper authorities. Information of that sort came to us from Gary . . . away back in March or April at which time the so-called Reds were planning a nationwide strike in order to free political prisoners. . . .

When we arrived in Gary, we found that the Sheriff had sworn in a great many deputies and that he was running a little intelligence office of his own; the police chief had sworn in a great many policemen, and he was running a little intelligence office of his own; and the Loyal Americans League, composed of citizens who were largely either deputy sheriffs or special policemen—I believe to a man—also had a little intelligence service of its own. So did the American Legion. They were all of them lined up on this Red proposition and had a mass of information.[13]

Military Intelligence apparently acted merely as a passive medium of exchange rather than an active collector of information. It funneled information to the press, the Department of Justice, and to the Congress. It is obvious that if Van Burens' testimony on his sources in Gary is typical, the conspiratorial myth, in part, was based on "evidence" found by highly partisan, unofficial, and untrained intelligence sources, acting as private vigilantes. It is likely, however, that as the information filtered up through Army Intelligence to the Justice Department and then was presented as testimony before Congress—an official public action—or reprinted in *The New York Times*—a highly legitimated source—it became cloaked with legitimacy.

The sources exchange information, protect each other's secrecy, occasionally employ each other, provoke radical acts, and notify their compatriots in advance. One example is reported by Sidney Howard, a muckraking journalist who wrote a series of five articles in *The New Republic* in 1924 on the activities of superpatriotic societies. According to Howard, while labor spies and government agents were not making radicals, some of them, and some antiunion companies, were staging other pseudoevents by reprinting radical documents for ultimate capture by the Justice Department. In at least one case, labor spies were reported to have reprinted copies of the Communist Manifesto for distribution to steel workers so that the Department of Justice could "capture" them and then present them to the Congress as proof of the Red conspiracy. The "planted" word was then converted into the conspiratorial deed.

Howard provides us with another example of the cooperative efforts of the hysteria bureaucracy.

The militant patriots were publicity agents for Mr. Burns. When he hadn't evidence to convict these "so-called liberals" and worse, he turned the patriots loose in his treasure house of rumors and portentous subversive documents. There was meat for them and precious little danger of libel suits, too, with such authority behind them. Dwight Braman sat in the offices of the Allied Patriotic Societies, Inc., and boasted that he was "in almost daily communication with the Department of Justice." Ralph Easley printed the Burns assistance right out in his prospectus of the National Civic Federation's forth-coming Survey of Progress. A survey of progress, by the National Civic Federation, by the way, is not without certain elements of humor. But they had the "cooperation of governmental agencies at Washington." And no one, except possibly Mr. Whitney of the American Defense Society, called more frequently than Mr. Easley on the Bureau of Investigation. These calls provided, one surmises, a convenient link between sworn enemies, Mr. Burns and Easley's pal, Sam Gompers; provided, too, a convenient source of A. F. of L. propaganda against renegade unions.[14]

The creation of manufactured pseudoevents was a major enterprise of the Justice Department. These staged events gain public credence through the legitimacy given them by the press. Therefore, the Department not only attempted to influence newspaper reportage but also attempted to actually create in full, that reportage. A. Mitchell Palmer converted the Justice Department into the major propaganda agency of the Red scare. The Department which was the single most important producer of conspiratorial cues, supplied the press with a steady stream of captured radical documents along with the editorial comment designed to prove that the presence of radical literature was the equivalent of a radical and powerful conspiracy. The press frequently complied and printed material from the Department—another instance of interests cooperating for mutual benefit. In the case of the press, the benefit might have been increased circulation or perhaps reinforcement of the publishers' values.

On January 27, 1920, Attorney General Palmer sent the following letter to newspapers throughout the country.

OFFICE OF THE ATTORNEY GENERAL
Washington, D.C., January 27, 1920

_____ and Associates, Editor _____ Magazine, New York City.

Dear _____:

In order that as one of the leaders of thought of this country you may have before you an authentic source of information as to the significance of the present situation I am taking the liberty of sending to you photostatic copies of original documents published by various branches of the Communist Press in Russia and in the United States. These furnish the purpose, history, and character of the Red Radical Movement, not by hearsay, but under the authoritative sanction of its own progenitors.

Exhibit No. 1 is the Report of Lousi C. Fraina, International

Secretary of the Communist Party of America, describing fully its antecedents, birth and projects, and follows the form of an application of the Communist Party of America to be accepted in the Bureau of the Communist International as a "major party."

Exhibit No. 2 is the manifesto of the Third Communist International adopted at Moscow, March 2-6, 1919, and signed by Comrades C. Rakovsky, N. Lenin, M. Zinerzen, L. Trotsky and Fritz Platten. It is an exhaustive statement of the rationale, principles and program of Russian Bolshevism and its ambition for world-wide dominion. . . .

Exhibit No. 6. "Your Shop" is an evidence of the sabotizing of labor and labor enemies prescribed on the communist program. . . .

Exhibit No. 9. An example of the Russian Bolshevik propaganda among our soldiers in Siberia.

Striking passages in these exhibits are marked for convenience.

The whole is submitted for the furtherance of a more realistic popular appreciation of the menace involved in the unrestrained spread of criminal Communism's unspeakable social treason among the masses.

It is the contention of the Department of Justice that these documents standing alone demonstrate:

(1) That the present aim of the Russian Government and its officers is to foment and incite discontent, aiming toward a revolution in this country. . . .

(2) That the entire movement is a dishonest and criminal one, in other words, an organized campaign to acquire the wealth and power of all countries for the few agitators and their criminal associates . . .

The Red Movement does not mean an attitude of protest against alleged defects in our present political economic organization of society. It does not represent the radicalism of progress. It is not a movement of liberty-loving persons. . . . It advocates the destruction of all ownership in property, the destruction of all religion and belief in God. It is a movement organized against Democracy, and in favor of the power of the few built by force. Bolshevism, syndicalism, the Soviet Government, sabotage, etc., are only names for old theories of violence and criminality.

Having lived at the expense of the Russian people for two years, these speculators in human lives and other peoples' earnings are trying to move to new fields to the East and to the West, hoping to take advantage of the economic distress and confusion of mind in which humanity finds itself after the terrific strain of five years of war.

Its sympathizers in this country are composed chiefly of criminals, mistaken idealists, social bigots, and many unfortunate men and women suffering with various forms of hyperesthesia. . . .

The Department of Justice has a vast amount of other information regarding the radical movement in this country, which is at your disposal. It will give me much pleasure to have one of your representatives call at this office so that you may obtain the information first hand. If you are unable to send a representative, I will be glad to furnish you with any details, either general or in specific cases.

My one desire is to acquaint people like you with the real menace of evil-thinking which is the foundation of the Red movement.

Respectfully,

(Signed)   A. *Mitchell Palmer*[15]

Palmer's letter concludes on the note of the conspiracy as total and apocalyptic and then moves to the domino theory. The prediction of ultimate doom, of course, necessitates total and immediate solutions. As we have seen, it also frightens people and mobilizes many feelings among the masses that prepares them not to actively oppose the repression. For these reasons the prophet of doom is actually a central figure in the pluralist bureaucracy that promotes the hysteria and the repression. To achieve their self-interest, pluralist coalitions had to convince the American people that the overthrow and destruction of America by Bolsheviks was imminent. This prepares the masses to accept the repressive activities of interest groups allegedly designed to curb radicalism but actually designed to enhance self-interest. Lobbyists for the hysteria serve their interest-group employers by defining a situation as real which, in fact, creates a real situation.

Mythmakers prepared for the creation by predicting it in vague and forboding tones. Judge Gary, the chairman of the board of U.S. Steel, for example, spoke of "industrial upheaval

and perhaps social upheaval," and "the control of the government and the establishment of a rule of the minority in American politics."[16]

Senator Miles Poindexter reiterated Judge Gary's dire predictions. "I am convinced," he said on the Senate floor, "that the
increasing number of strikes is based on a desire to overthrow
our government, destroy all government and establish Communism."[17]

"We are facing the direst peril that has ever confronted
our government," writes a superpatriot author in a pamphlet
entitled "Behind the Veil." Another superpatriot writes, "the
signs of the times are full of portents. By the flames of Pittsburgh we can discern approaching a terrible trial for free institutions in this country." A colleague reiterates the theme,
"There has never been in the history of the world a stronger,
more active, better financed, more thoroughly organized coalition, military or otherwise, menacing the peace, prosperity and
democratic ideals of the world. . . . The menace is great; the
crisis is imminent."

Most mythmakers traffic in worlds in collision, ultimate con-
frontations, and life or death. Some, however, continued to
frighten people and mobilize their feelings for the hysteria by
predicting, not ultimate doom but future day-to-day crises.
The day was often May Day or the Fourth of July, and the
Justice Department then, as well as now, served as prophet.
In his book on the FBI, Lowenthal comments on Bureau's
predictions.

In addition to past crimes actually committed, the Bureau concerned
itself also with forebodings for the future. It sent word to Congress
through the attorney general that its undercover informers had
transmitted through secret channels—"information . . . that on a
certain day . . . which we have been advised of, there will be another serious and probably much larger effort of the same character
which the wild fellows of this movement describe as revolution, a
proposition to rise up and destroy the Government at one fell
swoop."

Details were asked of Mr. Garvan when he called on the Senate. What "proposition" were "the wild fellows" making, how were they going to "destroy the government," what was this "serious and probably much larger effort?"

MR. GARVAN: "It all depends on what breaks out in the country. Suppose a July Fourth celebration broke out throughout the country."[18]

The purpose of crying impending doom is to justify numerous demands for numerous interest groups. Judge Gary of U.S. Steel, for example, by stereotyping the strike as Red led and predicting "industrial upheaval" created a public opinion opposed to the strike and elicited the cooperation of the Justice Department in the strikebreaking efforts. The Justice Department utilized the impending doom to justify appeals for budget increases before the Congress. The motivation behind these appeals, according to Lowenthal, was bureaucratic expansion.[19] The greater the danger of a Bolshevik takeover the greater is the likelihood that an interest group can satisfy its self-interest. Labor spies, detectives, Justice Department agents, superpatriotic bureaucrats, etc., prosper in a milieu of doom. Predictions of imminent revolutionary apocalypse by radical speakers and the radical press merely reinforced the sense of danger and excitement, and emergency.

The subtlety of the argument used to weave the myth, and the variety and power of interest group support for the myth is further illustrated by the activities of superpatriotic societies —an integral part of the mythmaking apparatus.

THE SUPERPATRIOTIC
SOCIETY AS BROKER

The mythmaking apparatus was facilitated by the superpatriotic societies which acted primarily as propaganda agencies and brokers for large corporate interests and individual superpatriots. They subsisted and profited from the contributions of corporations and individual business leaders. To maintain such clients, the societies had to produce results. And they did. The largest and most well financed superpatriotic societies concentrated their attack on organized labor, strike demands, the Plumb Plan, the proposal for "one big union," and the proposed nationalization of coal. These societies were the prime agencies in the "conversion" of the open shop into the "American plan," and the closed shop into "Bolshevism in disguise."

Total membership in the societies was small—perhaps 25,000 —if the American Legion is not included. But some were very well financed and their propaganda activities were extensive and well planned. They sought, and succeeded, in reaching primarily opinion leaders. The message that the "best antidote for Bolshevism is Americanism" was sent in thousands of pamphlets to clergymen, school teachers, attorneys, newspaper publishers, businessmen, government officials, and labor leaders and, apparently in the millions, to the general public. The pamphlets appeared under titles such as "The Lying Lure of Bolshevism," "The Enemy Within our Gates," "If Bolshevism Came to America," "Behind the Veil," and "America Asleep."

Their prime themes are expressed in three typical pamphlets, "Reds in America" published by the American Defense Society, "The Spirit of America," published by National Security League, and "The War Against Patriotism," published by the National Civic Federation. The Red conspiracy is gigantic, brilliantly planned, and directed toward almost every group in America.

The most colossal conspiracy against the United States in its history was unearthed at Bridgeman, Michigan, August 22, 1922, when the secret convention of the Communist Party of America was raided by the Michigan Constabulary, aided by county and Federal officials.

Their programs, which are now known, show that their plans for inciting the negroes, the farmers, the government clerks, bank clerks, workmen in industry, members of Congress, to violence against the constituted authorities, have been drawn with almost uncanny appreciation of the psychology of each group.

There is no limit to the activities of the Communist Party of America, to the ramifications of its influence. . . . They have not failed in a single step of their program thus far.[20]

The message that the revolution was imminent and that it would be apocalyptic characterized much superpatriotic literature. The dire prediction is designed to sustain anxiety.

The attempt at armed insurrection may not come for five years, perhaps not for ten, but it will certainly be made in fifteen or twenty years, if the communists are permitted to continue as they have been, with secret conspiracies and "open" organizations to function at the direction of the illegal body; and when that time comes the prostration of business, the paralysis of all industry with its attendant suffering, will be a catastrophe such as this country has never known.[21]

Literally every ill, defined as an ill by superpatriots is traceable to the Red conspiracy, as Mr. Soloman S. Menken of the National Security League made clear.

Their attack has created a disaffection and critical attitude toward our officials which has worked great political injustice and is further reflected in the Socialistic coloring of legislation. A fair example is our tax law. . . . How was the enactment of such a law possible? Because the Reds and Yellows raised a false issue as to what they call predatory wealth, and the politicians were misled into believing that the noise they made was the voice of the American people.

Our course is fatuous in the extreme and we elect to places of trust Frazier, La Follete, and Brookhart, and our young people read the red and yellow journals, and the *Nation* and the *Republic*, with the same perverted sense as those of another time peeked into obscene literature.[22]

Mr. Ralph Easley of the National Civic Federation, in "The War Against Patriotism" advanced a favorite theme of the superpatriots—treason in high places.

. . . it was learned that, under the very dome of the Capitol at Washington, there was an organization made up of a hundred and fifty secretaries to senators and representatives which was completely in the hands of the Reds. It had been in existence for two years, holding its meetings in the caucus room of the House, and yet few persons, even in Washington, had ever heard of it! But Moscow and the Red "liberal" press of all nations had heard of it and knew and exploited the fact that the "United States Congress, Jr." had voted in favor of the recognition of Soviet Russia.[23]

The lonely patriot, trying desperately to awaken good but apathetic Americans to the menace of Bolshevik infiltration was a recurring theme.

We, in the United States, seem to be fighting alone the battle against the Red-ism of the world. If the flood of propaganda against patriotism continues unchecked, its effect will surely be the undermining of our national virility and the extending of an invitation to the bandits of the world to "come and help themselves," for we shall be left defenseless. The question before us today is: "Shall we shrink from the great task which lies before us?" No, a hundred times no—unless we are utterly faithless to our children, to our children's children and to those who "sleep in Flanders' fields?"[24]

The pamphlet was not the only weapon used by the superpatriot. The National Security League created "Flying Squadrons" of volunteer speakers which held about one thousand meetings in dozens of cities. According to Robert Murray, they reached a total audience of 375,000 persons. The League also founded Constitution Day to commemorate, in superpatriotic vernacular, the founding of the Constitution. The support of the governor of almost every state was secured, along with local chambers of commerce, the Sons and Daughters of the American Revolution, and the Boy Scouts. Speakers for Constitution Day included the leading superpatriot, Nicholas Murray Butler, president of Columbia University, and future presidential candidate Judge Alton Parker.

Other societies provided written materials and established

patriotic exercises in the schools. Blacklists of magazines, pamphlets, books, and organizations were prepared which patriotic citizens were urged to boycott. Some superpatriotic societies advocated the purging of un-American statements from textbooks and prepared lists of excerpts to be eliminated. Some school boards, in fact, followed their advice. The American Defense Society prepared pamphlets denouncing the Bolshevik menace which they offered, free of charge, to employers who would be willing to place them in pay envelopes.

The most prestigious and affluent of the societies, however, concentrated on defaming the labor movement. Most of the money contributed to superpatriotic societies was earmarked for this purpose. Four of the major societies—the National Civic Federation, The National Security League, The Better America Federation, and the American Constitutional Association—received most of their funds from industrialists, large corporations, and public utilities.

For example, in 1919, the Congress investigated the finances of the National Security League, which had spent large sums in an effort to defeat Congressmen whose patriotism, in their opinion, was insufficient. Among the larger contributors were J. P. Morgan, John D. Rockefeller, Simon and Daniel Guggenheim, George Perkins of U.S. Steel, Henry Clay Frick of the Carnegie Steel Company, T. Coleman DuPont, H. H. Rogers of Standard Oil, and William K. Vanderbilt. Between 1916 and 1919, Carnegie contributed $50,000 per year. In 1919 the National Security League spent about $100,000.

Support for The Better America Federation, the leading and ultraconservative superpatriotic society of California, came largely from public utilities, many of which attempted to mask their involvement. Hearings before the California Commission of Immigration and Housing, for example, revealed the following:

Thus, in 1920, the San Joaquin Light and Power Company subscribed $300 to the Better America Federation out of "surplus," and charged an additional contribution of $15 to "miscellaneous general expenses!" "Miscellaneous general expenses" are operating expenses. The following year, 1921, the company allowed the Federation $300 out of surplus and $6 as a "miscellaneous general expense." No protest followed these $15 and $6 feelers-out. The company evidently concluded it was safe to make its Better American Federation contribution an operating expense. At any rate, the next year the company boldly so charged its entire $300 contribution to the Better America Federation.

The Southern California Edison Company has its $3,000-a-year Better America Federation contribution more carefully covered up. The $3,000, given in $250-a-month installments, was in 1921, and again in 1922, charged to "miscellaneous general office supplies and expense," all of which are finally included in operating expenses. The contribution is made to the Los Angeles "Americanization Fund." This so-called Los Angeles "Americanization Fund" is supported by pledges aggregating $160,000 a year for five years, $800,000 in all for the support of the Better America Federation.[25]

The American Constitutional Association, the leading super-patriotic society of West Virginia, whose manifest function was the defense of constitutional principles and whose latent function was the defense of coal operators in their fight against union demands, was supported primarily by coal companies. In a revealing trial, a professional solicitor of funds for the Association sued his employer for inadequate compensation. During the testimony, it was revealed that Judge Elbert Gary of U.S. Steel, a major coal operator, contributed $5,000 to the association. The self-interest and pluralist base of superpatriotism is nicely revealed by the fact that contributors to the defense of our constitutional principles included: the Pocahontas Coal Company, William McKnell Coal Company, Carnegie Gas Company, West Virginia Utilities Company, Harry Bowen of the Bowen Coal Company, William Ord, president of the McDowell Coal Company, Bottom Creek Coal Company, Crystal Block Vaol Company (a subsidiary of U.S. Coal Company), Manufacturers' Light and Heat Company, Colonel Leckie of Leckie Coal Company, Atwater and Company, dozens of coal buyers, and the Dollar Savings Bank of Wheeling.

The National Civic Federation, originally a fairly progressive organization of America's most prominent businessmen and labor leaders, had become, by 1918, militantly superpatriotic and hysterically antiradical. A list of its major financial supporters includes Carnegie, Morgan, Belmont, Rockefeller, Judge Gary, Otto Kahn, Perkins, and Vanderbilt.

The boards of directors of several societies overlapped. The same men contributed to several societies. Several companies contributed to more than one society. Some employees of one superpatriotic society worked, for compensation, for other societies. Societies exchanged information. Superpatriotic pamphleteers quoted each other. Cooperation between superpatriotic societies and employers associations was often close. Some leaders of some employers associations were members of the boards of some superpatriotic societies. We are speaking of interlocking directorates and pluralist combinations fed by communality of purpose and the pursuit of self-interest.

In its creation and pursuit of the Bolshevik menace, the government used the superpatriotic societies and the superpatriotic societies used the government. The Bureau of Investigation of the Department of Justice permitted some leaders of superpatriotic societies to see confidential files containing information on radicals. Superpatriotic societies then used some of the confidential material in propaganda pamphlets. Superpatriots supplied secret service agents and lawyers from the Department of Justice with information on alleged radicals which the government then used to prosecute radicals. Much of the "evidence" proved to be spurious. Superpatriotic societies also supplied to public officials material which was used in speeches and reports. According to Hapgood, a leading authority on superpatriotic societies, Ralph Easley, director of the National Civic Federation raised funds to finance efforts of William Burns of the Bureau of Investigation to investigate and prosecute Michigan communists' efforts which could not in their entirety be financed by public funds.[26] Although the material seized by the government in a raid of Michigan communists was government property seized by search warrants, Burns permitted R. M. Whitney of the American Defense Society to use some of the material in newspaper articles and to use it prior to the trial of the Michigan communists. While providing superpatriotic societies with information from confidential files, Burns replied in the negative to a request from the National Council for the Prevention of War for material used by Burns in an attack upon the Council: "I must advise you that it has long been the practice of the Bureau to hold its files confidential and available for confidential use only; and I regret that under this rule it would be impossible for me to answer your inquiry."[27]

During the Red scare and its aftermath, Army and Navy officers and officials in the War Department continuously attacked pacifist and disarmament groups. When the Red scare terminated, several superpatriotic societies turned their hand to pacifism. The relationship of these officers and officials to certain patriotic societies, most particularly the American Defense Society, was close and mutually profitable.

Major General Eli Helmick, Inspector General of the United States Army, speaking on the "Menaces Facing Our Country Today," attacked "advance revolutionary pacifists" and argued that "the arm of the Soviet had reached into Vassar and Bryn Mawr Colleges." One military man spoke of "paid agitators, sentimental sob sisters and Reds who are seeking to undermine our form of government." The Army and Navy Register, in an article published three years after the Red scare terminated, reiterated Red scare themes when it reported that $3,000,000 in gold had been sent to the United States by the "Communist International" for a campaign to eliminate the army and navy "so that when the Red uprising comes the country will be at its mercy."[28]

Several of these attacks were based on material, paraphrased or reprinted verbatim, from superpatriotic pamphlets published during the Red scare. In 1926, five years after the Red scare, the *Army and Navy Journal* published antipacifist and antiradical articles by Fred F. Marvin, the leading publicist of the American Defense Society. Other military men used R. M. Whitney's "Reds in America," one of the most virulent Red scare pamphlets, as a major source. Other major sources were the congressional and state investigations of alleged radicalism conducted in 1919 and 1920.

The mutually supportive relationship between the military and superpatriotic societies, and the business community and these societies, is not surprising in view of the communality of their world view and self-interest. If a gigantic Bolshevik domestic conspiracy threatens America from within, and if America is threatened from without by the international communist menace, it is necessary to maintain a strong military establishment which pleases the military, many prominent businessmen, and antiradicals. The emphasis on radical threats to America heightens the commitment to the American way of life which is understood, in part, to be a business civilization, laissez faire, and a nonradical labor movement. A by-product, frequently intended, of political hysteria is heightened conservatism, a defense of the status quo, and a strong military posture. Superpatriots, the military, and the business community have, therefore, a common interest which accounts for why they cooperate and why, in their Red-baiting propaganda, they quote each other as authoritative sources.

The superpatriotic societies saw advantage in the growing fear of radicalism. They feed that fear in the guise of patriotism. While the government was not concentrating on the Red menace, superpatriotic societies took up the slack, continuously built up the excitation, and thus contributed to the unanimity of conspiratorial cues which made it very difficult for the average American to withstand the conspiratorial message. We noted that the fact that so many of America's most respected and most successful men publicly supported these societies legitimated the message and therefore made it all the more irresistible.

The mutually supportive relationship of superpatriotic societies, the military, employers associations, the press, the Justice Department, and dozens of other groups is an example of interest group pluralism—the coalition of interest groups in the pursuit of mutually advantageous self-interest. The fact that these groups rallied around the issue of antiradicalism makes their activities no less a pluralist phenomenon than had they rallied around the issue of oil depletion allowances, rent control, or pollution. As a matter of fact, the grand interest group coalition of the post World War II era—the military-industrial complex—is formed around precisely the issue of the Red scare, to wit, an international communist conspiracy which threatens to destroy the American way of life. More economic advantage probably accrues to more powerful interest groups through the exploitation of the antiradical issue than any other. Contemporary American pluralism is balanced much more on a fulcrum of antiradicalism than one might suspect.

The hysteria expands because increasingly larger numbers of interest group pay-offs become available. The repression mounts because more groups seek the elimination or restriction of their opponents. The hysteria, however, also escalates because it is necessary to continuously frighten the American people. Their support is based, in large part on anxiety—anticipation of future conspiratorial danger. So, periodic "proofs" of this danger must be offered and the number of suspected radicals must grow. The web of suspicion must expand. The hysteria and the repression, therefore, are governed by an internal dialectic of escalation.

This totalism and escalation is, for the proponents of hysteria, not a matter of choice but of necessity. The proponent of political hysteria must maintain high levels of anxiety and justify extreme means to eliminate the threat. The threat, therefore, must be portrayed as enormously powerful and totally evil. This apocalyptic version of the conspiratorial theory of history is a functional necessity.

After his report on Bolshevik propaganda was made, Senator Overman stated that, "We must bring home to the people the truth that to compromise with Bolshevism is to barter away our inheritance." The conspiratorial threat to America is so gigantic that no compromise is possible with the radical menace. The threat must be totally eliminated. The traditional *modus vivendi* of American politics—incremental solutions and bargaining—cannot be utilized in resolving the apocalyptic radical conspiracy. Complete dehumanization of the victim and his total obliteration are demands that characterize periods of political hysteria. The total evil of those who threaten America maintains high levels of anxiety among the people.

The fact is, however that the repression is administered incrementally, and in large part, via the avenue of law, indictments, convictions, judges, juries, deportation, and legislative investigations. The repression is largely legal and those few who are in fact convicted and indicted serve the symbolic function of intimidating liberals who adopt a posture of quietude. The rhetoric of hysteria is extremist and apocalyptic. The demand for repression is sweeping. But the repression is, with many exceptions, pluralist sponsored and legally administered. Democratic repression is demanded by highly legitimated business leaders, and publishers, and office holders—some of our most prominent figures—and it is administered not by thugs, or vigilantes, or mobs, but by attorneys general, administrative officials, judges, congressmen, senators, state legislators, and public opinion. The concentration camp is unnecessary and archaic. The repression unfolds in, around, and through the law.

But totalism and escalation are necessary components of the

rhetoric of hysteria. The radical is not merely evil, he is monstrously evil. The radical plans not a takeover merely of the American government, but of the totality of American life and all American institutions. The radical plans not only to take over everything but to transform everything in a completely anti-American way. The Red conspiracy is not merely a conspiracy, but the greatest and most malevolent conspiracy in the history of man. The radical plans not merely to displace the officers of the government and dismantle the home and the church, but to murder, rape, burn, and pillage. The crusade to eliminate Bolshevism must expand. The role of suspected radicals and agitators must be widened. The expansion, however like the hysteria itself, is governed by a dialectic.

THE WEB OF SUSPICION

We noted that as the hysteria expanded ever larger numbers of individuals and institutions were tagged as Red or Red-infested or sympathetic to Bolshevism. Suspected radicals were found first in the labor movement, then in the universities, the clergy, the public schools, the ghettoes, Hollywood, the press, among social workers, people with dramatic and unusual lives (Helen Keller), civil libertarians, liberal politicians, congressional staffs, Democrats, Republicans, Progressives, and finally in the highest levels of government. The web of suspicion ultimately came to include the opponents of hundreds of interest groups that assumed they could profit by tagging their opponents as Reds. For "Wets," "Drys" are suspected Bolsheviks. For "Drys," "Wets" are undermining the Republic as part of a gigantic international conspiracy.

The pattern by which the web of suspected radicals widens is not accidental but purposive and utilitarian. Hundreds of interest groups came to see the utility of tagging their particular opponents as Red. The Boy Scouts were not tagged as

Red, in part, because they opposed no significant interest group. Another criteria used in the selection of Bolsheviks has to do with the relationship—potential or actual—of a group or individual to the existing distribution of property and/or political power. Labor was the prime target of almost every elite that promoted the antiradical hysteria, particularly those groups within the labor movement that advocated alterations in the existing pattern of ownership or power—advocates of the nationalization of coal or railroads and proponents of the closed shop and "one big union." Individuals who were not committed to the labor movement but were critical of fundamental economic and political arrangements were also tagged as Bolsheviks. Conservative politicians and party bosses often referred to advocates of the initiative, referendum, recall, as Reds—not to mention those who proposed suffrage for women. Landlords often typed social workers as Reds.

Professors, school teachers, and clergymen were frequently typed as Reds or dupes of the Bolsheviks. The criteria here is the ability to affect the ideas of young people. We have seen that Bolshevism was often referred to as a disease which is highly infectious and which can be resisted only by mature men of strong character and good mental health. The young, and those not yet fully Americanized, or members of backward races are particularly susceptible to this infection. That is why, according to superpatriots, agitation among immigrants and Negroes is particularly dastardly and suspect. It is like the selling of dope to children.

Another criteria for determining who shall be attacked was the willingness of a person or institution to defend the rights of radical minorities. The American Civil Liberties Union was a major object of attack as were liberal journals like *The New Republic* and *The Nation*.

As the hysteria mounts, the Bolshevik label becomes a catch-all, and distinctions—subtle and gross—begin to vanish between liberals, social reformers and critics committed to the system, Progressives, civil libertarians, open shop advocates, IWW's, revolutionary socialists, and communists committed to revolutionary tactics. All are labeled Red. "For our purposes," writes Ralph Easley, the superpatriotic director of the National Civic Federation, "socialism, IWW'ism, syndicalism, and Bolshevism, are one and the same menace. While these bodies vary in their methods and machinery they all mean the same thing. . . . Karl Marx's *Capitalism* is the bible of them all."

Distinctions vanish because large numbers of disparate groups wish to exploit the hysteria by stereotyping large numbers of disparate groups. Obviously, rigorous and rational criteria for determining who is Red would hinder the utility of the hysteria. The criteria become functional. A Bolshevik is any person or group whose opposition one wishes to lessen or eliminate.

As the web of suspicion widens vague criteria of who is Red are developed. Persons are stereotyped, not precisely as Red, but as "leaning towards" Bolshevism. The possession of radical literature in one's home, meeting place, or university classroom then becomes a criteria for "proof" of radicalism. At this juncture, criticism of significant American economic or political institutions—even modest and mild criticism—become criteria for defining radicals. The assumption then is made that if one is not a conservative, one is a radical. Radical action becomes no longer even an element of the definition. In fact, the absence of conservatism becomes the definition of radicalism, and this is precisely what conservative business interests who support and attempt to exploit the hysteria wish to accomplish.

As the web of suspicion widens, the language used to attack specific individuals and groups becomes more bombastic, extremist, and apocalyptic. The demand for extremist remedial action to counter the threat is made by larger numbers of interest groups and made more vociferously. The targets become increasingly arbitrary and come to include very prominent institutions and individuals (Columbia University and Professor Charles Beard) and completely obscure individuals, like teachers in grammar schools. Like the system of terror utilized in some African tribes[29] and in modern totalitarian states—a system which terrorizes through the fear engendered by the arbitrary and capricious selection of victims—democratic repression in America uses random attacks and vilifications and essentially arbitrary criteria of selection. The arbitrariness keeps everyone on the defensive because no one quite knows who will be struck next. The ease and rapidity with which liberals were intimidated and silenced during 1919 and in the 1950's, until the repression was well developed, is among the more impressive aspects of political hysteria.

Despite the demand for the total elimination of radicals, the number of persons who are actually discharged, deported, or indicted and convicted is very small. During the entire Red scare probably not more than two thousand persons lost their positions, were sentenced to terms in jail, or deported. About another two thousand—mostly victims of Palmer raids—had their civil liberties grossly violated and most of these for only a few days. And this brings us to the fundamental quality of democratic repression—its lawful and legal nature. Despite the claims of our most eminent authority on free speech, Zachariah Chaffee, to the effect that "the attorney general [Palmer] carried through the greatest executive restriction of personal liberty in the history of this country . . . ,"[30] the fact remains that the political hysteria and the repression were initiated, sustained, and escalated with little recourse to violations of law. The repression unfolds primarily by lawful process, and when it does not use the law directly, it moves around the law, as it were, above it and below it. In the first place, relatively few people—a few thousand—were actually indicted, convicted, sentenced or deported. Relatively few had their civil rights grossly violated—perhaps another few thousand —probably fewer than have their rights violated in this country on any given day through electronic surveillance alone. And the violations of the Red scare occurred during a period of about eighteen months.

As we noted, judges, juries, the law, and administrative decision are the *modus operandi* of political hysteria, not vigilantes or concentration camps. They are not necessary and, from the vantage point of sophisticated mythmakers who utilize the democratic capacity for repression, they are dysfunctional and superflous. They may evoke organized opposition by civil libertarians. Unsophisticated proponents of repression in America utilize the bludgeon. Bright exponents of repression use the law—particularly the law of conspiracy—and then they use the law only occasionally to indict, convict, incarcerate, and deport the alleged enemies of the United States as examples of what can occur to those who violate American mores. Intimidation is the purpose.

The few thousand who suffer detention, deportation, or the loss of employment serve the symbolic function of reminding millions that it can happen to them. Fear of being thought of as radical and hatred of radicalism were introjected long before the hysteria unfolded. The hysteria builds on these fears; the hysteria strengthens them; but the hysteria does not inaugurate them.

Proposals by prominent public officials and private persons to restrict civil liberties are made. A peacetime sedition law is proposed. Legal niceties do come under attack. Some laws are actually passed which do restrict civil liberties, but very few radicals are actually convicted. Laws which have been in effect for years are more than adequate.

The Red scare vindicates Gabriel Kolko's wise judgment about civil liberties in the United States during periods of social tension.

For though freedom is a posture decision-makers tolerate among the politically impotent, those in power act to make certain that all others remain ineffectual. When their own policies are subject to severe trials, or appear to be failing, they cannot afford the luxury of organized opposition and functional freedoms which can shatter their hegemony over the normal, usually passive social apathy. The history of civil liberties in the United States is testimony to the fact that when freedom moves from rhetoric to social challenge it is suppressed insofar as is necessary. Functional freedom is the ability to relate to power or forces with the potential for achieving authority, that is, the decision-making establishment of those who seek to transform or replace it. So long as intellectuals or the people exercise this right "responsibly," which is to say to endorse and serve the consensus their rulers define, abstract freedoms flourish in public pronouncements and slogans because they lead nowhere. Hence the dissenter has the freedom to become a victim in the social process and history, and a battery of sedition, espionage, criminal anarchy, or labor laws exist in readiness for the appropriate moment of social tension and the breakdown in the social and ideological consensus which exists during periods of peace and stability. The celebrants of American freedom rarely confront the concepts of order that underlie the large body of law for suppression that always exists in reserve.[31]

The democratic repression that is a fundamental aspect of America is based in part on the popular illusion that formal or abstract freedom is functional freedom. Abstract freedom flourishes in America and it is even promoted by the state and the leaders of power groups because such freedom does not significantly affect the distribution of power. Abstract or formal freedom—which is defined as the heart of liberalism—is also encouraged because it neither questions nor attacks the fundamental values of Lockian liberal politics and capitalism. As a matter of fact the practice of nonfunctional freedoms is encouraged precisely because the people who practice them take them to be functional—that is, they really believe freedom exists in a form which permits them to affect significant decisions and distributions of power. Their illusion of possessing real freedom commits them to belief that America is precisely what it is supposed to be—the leader of the free world. It commits them to the belief that America has representative government, popular sovereignty, and operational freedom. The illusion thus reinforces the American identification with the American way of life and this further forecloses transcendent perspectives. As the identification with the American way becomes passionate and compulsive, few think of challenging it because it becomes, in the popular mind, even more the embodiment of self-evident truth. After all, people do practice the very freedoms that these ultimate truths bestow upon them; thus, the need of the state and business elites to utilize the battery of sedition, espionage, criminal anarchy, or labor laws lessens because people lose the will to engage in transcendent speculation. As America achieves more militant liberal unanimity, the American achievement becomes, as Marcuse points out, the achievement of all large modern technological states —to wit, the containment of qualitative social change, the dominance of the status quo, and the smothering of transcendent impulse. Repression of the traditional sort—secret police, detention camps, political trials, political purges, raids on party headquarters, and the like, will become increasingly archaic and looked upon as a primitive and crude technique of tension management and system maintenance. The achievement of America and other modern nations is a far subtler form of tension management. But more of this in the last chapter.

Large numbers of interest groups utilizing the techniques of pluralist politics, coalesced in the pursuit of self-interest and promoted a hysteria and democratic repression—legally and non-violently. This is true pluralism producing the politics of mass society—a politics infused with highly moralized issues and ideological concerns, a politics based on appeals to the irrational, a politics of repression and intolerance. This is pluralism producing messianic politics—precisely what it is not supposed to produce—according to its wisest theorists. Certainly, when literally the entire fabric of American pluralism which is, in theory, supposed to nourish democracy, tolerance, and a pragmatic politics, in fact, promotes repression, intolerance, and ideological politics, something is wrong with the theory. When the allegedly countervailing forces of pluralism and the institutional restraints of American politics—federalism and checks and balances and separation of powers and due process of law—not only fail to prevent irrational, mass politics but are the prime means used to promote it, critical reevaluation of pluralist assumptions is appropriate.

A host of America's most prominent social scientists—Richard Hofstradter, Daniel Bell, Seymour Lipset, Robert Dahl, Talcott Parsons, to mention the most prominent—began to argue in the 1950's—partly in response to McCarthyism—that social stability and democratic practice were promoted by large numbers of interest groups, balancing and moderating each other's aggressivity, through the pursuit of self-interest, according to democratic rules of the game. Stability and democracy were allegedly enhanced because these groups avoided the ideological and moral issue in favor of immediate and particular and concrete issues. They were concerned with bread and butter issues rather than justice and truth, good and evil. These groups allegedly imposed rationality on their members; that is, steered them in a course of self-interest and taught them that it was necessary to bargain and tolerate the presence of opposing groups and opposing points of view. The leaders of these groups, allegedly, are better informed than the masses, more moderate, more committed to democratic values and more willing to compromise. Group leaders, in other words, because of these attributes, comprise elites that are committed to the preservation of democratic forms. These group leaders, therefore, prevent irrational, passionate, moralistic, ideological mass politics which might become crusades and polarize society. By nourishing a pragmatic, moderate, tolerant, antiviolent incremental, dollars-and-cents approach, they help to democratize their members and keep American politics down to earth.

Again, they do this because it enhances group self-interest, their own self-interest, and because they are committed to the democratic way.

According to theorists of pluralism, mass politics, populism, agrarian radicalism, McCarthyism—not democratic pluralism —in a capitalist society, produce extremism, intolerance, instability, and large-scale repression. Mass politics, according to pluralists, caters to the irrational, to psychological grievances, to status concerns, to nativist and jingoist impulse, and to conspiratorial prospective. The promoters of mass politics raise the ultimate questions of justice and attempt to play upon generalized resentments stemming from the deeper layers of personality. The politics of mass society does not focus on concrete and group demands, but on generalized moral objectives. The political traffic is in moral absolutes and grotesque conspiracy. The purpose of such politics is the defense of ultimate truth. Antipluralist politics allegedly denies legitimacy to diverse points of view and has low tolerance for ambiguity. The constituency of mass politics is the people qua mass and the nation—not interest groups.[32]

The fact is, however, that pluralist leaders can, and frequently do, promote mass politics and that mass politics can be used to advance the cause of individual interest groups and group leaders. The distinctions which pluralists make between pluralist and mass politics are much too neat. And these distinctions are central to the support which Hofstadter, Bell, Dahl, Parsons, Lipset and American politicians grant to pluralism and which form the basis for their condemnation of mass politics. They were impressed and disconcerted by the rise of McCarthyism which they perceived as a deviation from pluralism and an example of what mass politics can produce. They perceived McCarthyism as rooted in the perspectives of populism.

But interest groups can produce mass politics through the techniques of pluralism. And mass politics, based on pluralism, can feed the self-interest of hundreds of groups. The Red scare

is, I believe, the classic example. Numerous group leaders promoted the Red scare for reasons of self-interest. They did this
by coalescing and cooperating. And they used, with some exception, traditional pluralist techniques: they lobbied; they
formed pressure groups; they financed pressure groups and public relations agencies (superpatriotic societies); they testified
before legislative committees, they masked self-interest behind
the guise of public interest; they demanded legislative investigations and the passage of self-serving law; they did not advocate, with rare exception, direct action or violence; they did
advocate the use of lawful procedure; and they had a clear conception of their concrete self-interest. They violated almost
every standard of public behavior expected of the democratic
elitest. They consciously lied to the public. They spread rumors.
They hired labor spies. They created fictitious conspiracy. They
planted stories in newspapers. They occasionally provoked violence. They used inflammatory rhetoric. They trafficked in
apocalyptic confrontation, moral absolutes, and ultimate truths.
They structured political issues in terms of life and death. They
were not in the least concerned with the rights of minorities.
They did not believe that "the opposition" was legitimate. They
argued that opponents can be neither reasoned nor bargained
with. They eliminated compromise and incrementalism as approaches to the problem. They appealed to repressed wishes
and fears of the masses. They stimulated nativism and jingoism,
and nationalism and ideology, and they portrayed politics as
the pursuit and defense of truth.

In other words, the leaders of interest groups—many of whom
belonged to several groups—men of the highest social standing,
men deeply socialized in American belief, men allegedly committed to pluralism and democracy, promoted an extremist
hysteria. Mass politics in America can be an excellent mask for
privilege and pluralist self-interest. As the pay-offs available in
hysterical mass politics became clear to larger numbers of interest group leaders, they joined in the creation—just as the

theory predicts. Democratic elitists did what the purveyors of mass politics allegedly do and democratic elitists do not do. Mass politics is seductive precisely because it basically is pluralist, and legalist, and nonviolent. The political hysteria that was the Red scare could not have developed without the support of dominant elites. It was largely their creation.

The Red scare and McCarthyism were not aberrations; they were rooted in the mainstream of American political rhetoric. The elites which promoted the Red scare revived the ancient rhetoric of American Whiggery, the rhetoric of big property, the rhetoric of democratic capitalism: we are all democrats; we are all capitalists; every working man is a potential capitalist; America has no classes, no exploitation, no structural inequities, only infinite plasticity and mobility; what inequality exists, results from individual effort, not from power differentials. The superpatriotic pamphlet is a melange of Social Darwinism and Algerism—an idealized capitalism. Political hysteria is a version of the conservative ideology, and democratic repression is designed to preserve capitalist fact.

Conservatives throughout our history have attacked their radical or liberal opponents as despoilers of American morality and self-evident truth. They have frequently predicted that the success of their opponents would produce total destruction— the end of the American way. They frequently portray their opponents as part of a colossal and malevolent conspiracy, and the confrontation as one of good and evil. In attacking those who wish to innovate, conservatives have utilized moralistic perspectives, and they have attempted to excite latent and irrational fears and impulses. This is the way Federalists circa 1820 attacked those who would abandon the property qualification for voting. This is the way that Whigs attacked Jackson. This is the way Social Darwinists attacked liberals. This is the way conservatives attack Populists and Progressives. This is the way Republicans first attacked the New Deal. When it suited their purposes, Conservatives and Pluralists, and Whigs, and Democratic elitists—whatever one might call men committed to existing structures of power and property—utilized precisely the techniques and rhetoric which are commonly held to be unique to mass and antipluralist politics.

Pluralist heroes can be extremist progenitors when it suits their self-interest. Remember the apocalypse and the creeping Bolshevism that Republicans predicted upon F. D. R.'s election —good Republican rhetoric. The appeal to the masses, to their greatest fears and deepest prejudices is very much a part of good solid American politics. It is very much a part of good solid American conservatism. The paranoid style is not only substantially less aberrant than Hofstadter believes, but must be considered closer to the center of American history than has even been admitted. The paranoid sense of the enemy, the conspiracy, and the apocalyptic confrontation which have been central to our history are hardly new.

We have hinted at the idea that below the calm and seemingly rational surface of the American mind lies a pocket of political dynamite—a passionate and visceral identification with the American way of life, with the liberal traditions of Locke and Smith converted into national symbol and cliche, transformed into a powerful Americanist nationalism and dogma, ritualized and "Fourth of Julyized." There is force and thrust and ferocity and religiosity below the passionless surface of American incrementalism; and it can come to the surface, during stress, in the person of Palmer and McCarthy, Wallace, and Agnew, the Klan, the Legion, and John Birch. The liberal tradition is the only tradition we have and have ever had—no left, no right, merely an omnivorous center which has the potential ferocity of a national crusade.

We turn now to the roots of the American political culture that nourish this ferocity and these crusades.

6

THE DEMOCRATIC
CAPACITY FOR
REPRESSION

THE great scare was not an exotic aberration outside the nation's history. It was not primarily the work of psychotics and paranoids. The political hysteria of 1919, like McCarthyism, was an exaggeration of the American commonplace—a very American mixture of American conservatism, pluralism, legalism, antiradicalism, racism, and nativism. The hysteria utilized very American techniques of interest group politics. The hysteria was promoted by elites, most of whom exploited it for reasons of self-interest. Again, the hysteria succeeded without violating the civil rights of more than perhaps four thousand people. With exception, it was a "lawful" and nonviolent operation. The pluralism and legalism of democratic repression can make it very seductive to American elites and to the American people.

The hysteria, in other words, was the product of forces deeply rooted in American culture. It was perceived by most Americans as a perfectly sensible and American way to defend the American way of life against serious danger. Repressive political hysteria is, among other things, the product of passionate nationalism—an intense and emotional identification with the American way of life. This identification with America is profound, very old and very American. The Red scare was a defense of America—an attempt to revitalize American values.

It was also, from the vantage point of elites, a technique for managing tension and maintaining power. This makes political hysteria appealing to men of power who feel threatened.

The hysteria was national—not sectional. The hysteria was pervasive—not superficial. The hysteria was not a manifestation of a particular class nor ethnic group. Nor can it be discounted solely as the work of a few Machiavellian publicists, and government, and business elites, manipulating an unwilling public. The American public was susceptible to the appeals of the conspiratorial myth and accepted the alleged antiradical repression. The Red scare was a product of the American people manipulating themselves as well as the American people responding to manipulation.

This is its most significant and disturbing feature. The seeds of the conspiratorial myth must have been sown in the minds of America's true believers long before 1919. The propensity to react and act toward radical dissent in such a visceral and passionate manner must have been the result of prolonged training. The mythmaker needed an accepting and compliant public. This is precisely what he had. American perspectives prepare America for particular conspiratorial myths and for particular forms of political hysteria. An antiradical and democratic repression (pluralist, legal and nonviolent) is the manifest expression in America of deeply rooted latent forces. This is why it recurs.

Louis Hartz, in a most perceptive book on American political thought, entitled *The Liberal Tradition in America*, suggested that the Red scare represented "Americanism" in its purest form —that the Red scare was based on forces always present in American culture but customarily latent.[1]

With respect to why America pursues radicals and pursued them so vehemently during the Red scare, although America has so few radicals, Hartz writes:

We must not assume that the substitution of Republican "Americanism" for the Democratic "Americanism" wholly explains the movement: it is what they had in common that really produced it. True, the embroidering of the Bolshevik menace was a natural technique for a Whiggery which had since the Civil War, tried to discredit its opponents by labeling them as "socialist" and "un-American." But the technique was possibly only because the nation as a whole was inherently sensitive to the symbol of socialism and Wilson was as much a party to this sensitivity as Harding was. He denounced Bolshevism as "poison." . . . the heart of the matter lay in the American general will . . . in a land where Communism is truly "alien" what is more sensible than to get rid of it simply by throwing out the men who brought it over . . .

The Red Scare mentality displays the American absolutism in its purest form.[2]

If Hartz is correct and the Red scare is a manifestation of the American general will—of American absolutism—then the problem of political hysteria in America is best approached by delineating the essence of that will and the nature of that absolutism. One must discover America to understand the hysteria: One must discover why only America, of all the Western nations, reacts so violently and irrationally to socialism. One must discover what, in liberal America, constitutes this American absolutism. If the origin and nature of this absolutism can be delineated, and if the Red scare mentality exemplifies it in its purest form, then to understand the hysteria is to perceive something that apparently is fundamental to America and to perceive it *in extremis*. America produces the hysteria and the hysteria illuminates America.

Utilizing concepts like the American general will, or the absolute essence of America, or American absolutism is a treacherous undertaking because America is a very complex place—in many ways quite unsettled, in many ways very fixed and rigid. The alleged national identity or national character of Americans is ridden with contradictions. Scholarly lists of American traits invariably contain opposites. Americans are described as idealistic and materialistic, venturous and con-servative, conformist and individualist, tolerant and intolerant, physically mobile and intellectually rooted, charitable and selfish, committed to equality and insensitive to discrimination, all at the same time.

If an American general will or essence or absolutism exists, it must be the product of the interplay and resolution of numerous polarities. Erik Erikson has made the useful observation that ". . . a nation's identity is derived from the ways in which history has, as it were, counterpointed certain opposite potentialities; the ways in which it lifts this counterpoint to a unique style of civilization, or lets it disintegrate into mere contradiction."[3]

America is, in many fundamental ways, a unique civilization. There is an American national style despite the presence of contraries. Americans, millions of Americans, perceive themselves, their country, and its relation to the world in a manner quite different from any other nation.

Yet all Americans do not perceive America and the world in the same way. All Americans do not react to the same situation in the same way. But enough Americans do perceive and do act in concert, within limits, and in a predictable manner, so one may speak broadly of an American approach or an American response, or for that matter, of an un-American way.

The problem is to delineate some essential features of the national style and some significant polarities of American life which are related to the dominant proclivities in times of stress. The Red scare and McCarthyism are, among other things, very crude attempts to manage and mitigate important polarities— most particularly the liberal thrust toward variety and dissent and the illiberal thrust toward homogeneity, restraint, conformity, and unanimity of opinion. Lockian liberalism, the root of American political thought, guarantees those inalienable natural rights of speech, press, and worship, which, if taken seriously, provide the means for substantial variety of life style and dissent—religious as well as social and political. America has a commitment, at least in theory, to variety and to dissent. Other forces in American history, however, greatly reduce the potentiality for variety and dissent, and more significantly, foster a near unanimity of opinion and life style.

The tension between conformity and nonconformity is not an epiphenomenon. It is a major American problem. The efflorescence of individual differences in extremes can destroy the cohesion necessary for a viable society, particularly a society where dissent is legitimated and sometimes even protected by the state.

These tensions can not be eliminated without a serious commitment to repression and they will remain as long as inequitable power arrangements drive some to seek relief from the power of others. These tensions and polarities, however, may be managed or mitigated—and usually are. The repressive political crusade is one of several techniques periodically utilized to manage tension. It is designed, in part, to lessen variety and heighten conformity, to revitalize the highly emotional commitment to the American way of life, to conservatize America, and to stabilize American elites to recommit Americans to America.

The polarities, of course, are managed in many other ways. Until very recent years the polarity was mitigated primarily by a highly efficient socialization process which turned out "good" citizens—good Democrats or good Republicans—committed to America. Deviance—political and social—in other words, was managed by preventing its development during the early years of life, through highly efficient socialization into America. The threat to the American way which might be posed by critiques of Lockian political liberalism and capitalism rarely materialized because indoctrination in Locke and Smith—at least as cliché and symbol—is so powerful and so total. The thrust toward variety is also blunted by a commitment to the rights of free speech and press which are more verbal and symbolic than deeply felt. American liberalism, understood as true commitment to variety, is largely lip service liberalism. The tensions of variety are also mitigated by a commitment to equality which is largely verbal and symbolic—a commitment which masks and rationalizes considerable inequality. Tensions are also managed by a more stringent and emotional commitment to the rule and right of majorities—also highly symbolic and largely artificial—than to the rights of dissenting minorities.

These polarities are manifested in historical forces and social and political movements. They find expression in political parties, protest movements, legislation, decisions of courts of law and the allocation of scarce resources. The polarities are also manifested intrapsychically. The identity of Americans, their sense of who they are and where they are, and what they can and cannot do, and how they should relate to society and to America and to each other are also affected by conflicting cues—cues condemning and condoning variety and dissent, equality and inequality.

Political hysteria, and some of the other techniques utilized to manage conflict, are designed to resolve economic and political tensions and intrapsychic conflicts. The management of tensions is necessary on both levels—personal and social.

Individuals can revitalize their values, reaffirm their sense of self, and experience self-righteous pleasure by participating in the extirpation of un-American heresies, and American elites can resolve power struggles, and reaffirm the status quo.

To understand the roots of the hysterical impulse we must understand these polarities. We must understand the rooted and rootless quality of the American identity. We must understand that peculiar and awesome love affair which Americans have with America—that love affair which causes Americans to respond so fervently when America appears to be threatened, whether the threat is real or not.

AMERICAN POLARITIES

Alexis de Tocqueville, whose classic, *Democracy in America,* was written during the age of Jackson, raised the question of whether a stable society could be maintained where aristocracy was absent and substantial social equality present. To a sophisticated European, prescription and tradition served as a basis for identity. Aristocracy served as the fount of authority and the cement which bound the social system together. What and who in America would fulfill these functions? Tocqueville argued that equality was a solvent of social bonds and, as such, tended to produce, not a society, not a *communitas,* but an aggregate of rootless, undifferentiated, and anarchic individuals—a mass without form or consciousness of self.

Tocqueville understood that in America, with ancient class hierarchies and traditional functional relationships absent, it would be difficult to develop a sense of rootedness and place—a well defined identity. He understood that many of the virtues of equality were countered by the fact that although one among undifferentiated equals may be fiercely independent and individuated and self reliant, one may also feel terribly lonely and isolated—cut off from a rich and differentiated group life. Man, in a situation of equality, would need to create symbolic and institutionalized substitutes for aristocratic authority and for the group affiliations that medieval Europe provided. Tocqueville's prediction that Americans would form and join endless groups in an effort to find fraternity has, of course, proven correct. The American substitute for aristocratic authority, he predicted, would become the power and authority of the majority—a power, he taught, of potentially tyrannical dimension.

Some fundamental polarities of the American national style

emerge from this peculiar historical circumstance—the impulse toward independence and reliance on self and the impulse toward dependence and reliance upon public opinion and majority will. America produces individualists and conformists—those who refuse to join the lonely crowd and those who succumb to it. America, in a sense, creates the crowd, for it can transcend the loneliness of equality. The crowd allegedly will provide some fraternity and security. But the crowd is lonely. The crowd invariably disappoints those who seek fraternity because in an egalitarian and individualistic society, it is primarily an aggregate and not a *communitas*. The mass is cold, but because it becomes the individual man writ large, it has power and authority. So the American may choose between the pleasures of independence countered by loneliness, or the promised fraternity of the mass which is negated by surrender to it. We are speaking of characteristic psychological responses to comprehensive social equality—one of the fundamental facts which shaped American history. The democratic situation characterized by social equality contains the potentiality for submergence in the mass. The power of the mass nourishes a one-dimensionality which can negate variety and which can become a resource for promoters of political hysteria. Is it not possible that in his search for roots and fraternity the American may find in the nation, the very fraternity which is so conspicuously absent in his daily experience? When local bonds are weak, is it not possible that man will identify with larger wholes? Is not superpatriotism possibly an effort to become part of a larger family? Can the superpatriot be the man who is especially lonely —the man without "family?" The symbolic use of America as a wider family, we will see, is facilitated by the fact that America, because of historical accident, has been an identifiable and definable entity—a liberal entity and little else. We often talk of the American way of life. If there is such a thing, it can be used all the more readily as nourishment for the impoverished and lonely. This loneliness, this lack of continuity, this difficulty in rooting an identity in America was beautifully described by Tocqueville.

Among democratic nations new families are constantly springing up, others are constantly falling away, and all that remain change their condition; the woof of time is every instant broken and the track of generations effaced. Those who went before are soon forgotten; of those who will come after, no one has any idea: the interest of man is confined to those in close propinquity to himself. As each class gradually approaches others and mingles with them, its members become undifferentiated and lose their class identity for each other. Aristocracy had made a chain of all the members of the community, from the peasant to the king; democracy breaks that chain and severs every link of it. . . .

Thus not only does democracy make every man forget his ancestors, but it hides his descendants and separates his contemporaries from him; it throws him back forever upon himself alone and threatens in the end to confine him entirely within the solitude of his own heart.[4]

It is difficult to tolerate this aloneness. The failure to produce fraternity and develop a *communitas* remains, today, one of America's most conspicuous failures.

America remains an aggregation, not a nationhood with a healthy counterpoint between independence and *communitas*. Equality can be both an asset and liability. It can produce independence but it can produce mass cult—the subtle and unrecognized intrusion of the mass. Seen as the power of the people and the culmination of their democratic consent, it can become the most powerful of voluntary repressions. Tocqueville sensed this possibility.

. . . At periods of equality men have no faith in one another, by reason of their common resemblance; but this very resemblance gives them almost unbounded confidence in the judgment of the public; for it would seem probable that, as they are endowed with equal means of judging, the greater truth should go with the greater number.

When the inhabitant of a democratic country compares himself individually with all those about him, he feels with pride that he is the equal of any one of them; but when he comes to survey the totality of his fellows and to place himself in contrast with so huge a body, he is instantly overwhelmed by the sense of his own insignificance and weakness. The same equality that renders him independent of each of his fellow citizens, taken severally, exposes him alone and unprotected to the influence of the greater number. The public, therefore, among a democratic people, has a singular power, which aristocratic nations cannot conceive; for it does not persuade others to its beliefs, but it imposes them and makes them permeate the thinking of everyone by a sort of enormous pressure of the mind of all upon the individual intelligence.[5]

The master to whom all submit is man en masse, the majority, the cult, the dominant opinion. It is the tyranny implicit in a society of equals, and it can be an awesome tyranny because it operates silently and "voluntarily." It relies not on external coercion or violence—not on armies—but on internal predisposition, habit, and socialization. The illusion that dominant opinion is voluntarily entered into makes that opinion all the more powerful. Perceiving its one-dimensionality as voluntary, Americans will certainly define it as pluralism and defend it, with passion, when it appears to be threatened.

To have one's opinions prefabricated can be a source of great comfort and relief. It relieves one of the responsibility of choice. It provides one with a preselected identity. It is a fount out of which a stable and rooted identity may be built, and it has the continuous and powerful thrust and authority of society behind it. The authority that replaces the aristocracy is the people. Since we speak of a society allegedly composed of equals there is little reason to distrust or reject the opinion of the people, because the people is merely the sum of the judgments of equal men. Its weight grows with its numbers. Men need not fear their equals. Confidence in the wisdom of the people is high because the people are the totality of combined wisdom. The political leader, in this milieu, presents himself as the projection of popular will—a passive mediator of the common voice.

If each man passively receives and introjects the master's voice, each man comes to resemble all others, and the potentiality for variety collapses into a stultifying one-dimensionality.

Anticipating aspects of Marcuse's thought by more than a century, Tocqueville described this one-dimensionality.

In America, even more than Europe, there is only one society. It may be either rich or poor, humble or brilliant, trading or agricultural; but it is comprised everywhere of the same elements. The plane of a uniform civilization has passed over it. The man you left in New York you find again in almost impenetrable solitudes; same clothes, same attitude, same language, same habits, same pleasures.[6]

The power of the majority in America stems not only from the need, in a society of equals, to create roots of authority, but also from the fact that in America the entire political ethos is built around the concept of the right of the majority to vote. Lockian liberalism sets the process in motion. The power of the majority—not necessarily in fact but rather in the eye of each man—is supported by natural right. It is legitimated by hoary tradition. It is legitimated by the founding fathers building on Locke. And all of these imperatives are reinforced by a fundamental fact of American society—the need to transcend the authoritylessness implicit in a society of equals. All of this enhances the power of majoritarian consensus. The loneliness of each man leaves him weak before the weight of the mass.

The power of consensus which becomes a root of the American absolutism is impressive. Developed through socialization and transmitted from generation to generation in a passive and voluntary way, it gains strength and legitimacy because it is enforced through the introjection of values rather than violence. Because it is accepted voluntarily, it appears not to have the coercive power which, in fact, it has. And this illusion of self selection and self control increases its power. When the will of the people, raised to the level of community authority, is threatened, in fact or fantasy, it is necessary to defend that will. It is necessary to revitalize ancient and sanctified values and maintain each man's sovereignty writ large in the popular will. This is a root of political hysteria.

The rootedness and certainty of the American political identity which gains its power and right from the people's will and authority can be used to justify the elimination of dissent. The certainty of right and the weight of the authority transforms the elimination of dissent into a moral and self-righteous act. And the morality of the act gives it a power, a passion, and a force not common to American politics. This is the passion behind the Red scare. This is a source of its irrationalities. This is why Americans are prone to greatly exaggerate the dimension of threats and set in operation repressive measures which go far beyond reason and need. The irrationalities, the emotional outbursts, the profound misperceptions, and the hysterical contagion which characterized the Red scare, and McCarthyism, and the Cold War, stem from the highly affective identification with the Americanistic national credo which appears to be so benign yet is so precisely because it is perceived simply as the sum of the wills of each man and his neighbors.

The hysterical pursuit of radical dissenters not only involves a defense of the majoritarian homeland but an attack on radicalism. The visceral antiradicalism of America obviously has something to do with the fact that America is, in a very special way, a very conservative country. The conservatism of the American national character, upon which dozens of Americanists have commented, is also related to the way that Americans responded to social equality. Tocqueville suggested that the American was a venturous conservative—entreprenurial, innovative, venturesome, and risk taking in the pursuit of wealth, but extremely bourgeois, conservative, property oriented, and possessive, once he has achieved success. A commentator on Tocqueville has described the process by which the values of the venturous conservative are shaped from a condition of equality.

A comprehensive social equality is the common point of departure. Along one line: a world of almost-equals creates an anxious urgent, flexible seeker of the next, most precious, most elusive increment of wealth and status: a seeker out of fear for his possessions and hope for his opportunities, becomes a firm conservative on property matters; and, one who, from the depth of his material preoccupations, has little concern for radical revaluation of his moral universe. Along the second line: the masterless man, free to invent a fresh world, finds all the important value answers . . . given in familiar, comfortable form by his own self image magnified to authoritative dimensions—by the majority. In this direction little adventure survives; only a sort of surface confusion masking a congealed mass of values.[7]

The venturous conservative is venturous, risk-taking, entreprenurial, innovative, and amenable to economic change. He is extremely radical in his approach to economic development. One might expect this type also to be receptive to innovating ideas in general, even to radical ideas relating to social and economic change, but this is precisely what he is not. He may be venturous but he is a conservative who is deeply wedded to private property and the ethic of possessive individualism.

His orientation toward risk taking and innovation is limited to the area of economic entreprenurialism. His economic ideology is staunchly conservative and it has been that way since the founding of the Republic. He is profoundly materialistic and his life style is bourgeois to the core. America's commitment to the Protestant Ethic, to a definition of the good life as a life of expanding affluence and materialism, and to the virtues of property ownership converge, and reinforce and legitimize the conservative and bourgeois life style. The American identity becomes rooted as bourgeois values define its bounds and the affective quality of the identification with capitalism is reinforced from generation to generation. Americans know that the business of America is business. And the businessman, at least on the surface, is secure in the role and identity America defines for him. His certainty in the virtues of his role and of free enterprise make him particularly sensitive to and threatened by radical and egalitarian schemes. His identity is so intertwined with bourgeois values that radical ideas not only threaten his livelihood but also his sense of self. This, perhaps more than potential economic loss, is what mobilizes him for mythic radical conspiracies and antiradical crusades.

The radical threat is a threat to existential identity. The threat evokes a visceral and affective defensive response because the identity is so rooted. The affectivity and irrationality of the response is determined by the affectivity of the identification. The antiradical hysteria derives much of its force from this affectivity. The power of the American way of life produces the power of the defenses designed to protect it.

Tocqueville has suggested why the definition of the good life in America is almost exclusively in terms of economic success and why the pursuit of wealth is the national passion; which, of course, would make the pursuit of levelers a national passion.

In America one cannot gain status and achieve permanent place through admission to aristocratic orders or through ascription. The open and avid pursuit of rank, privilege, honor, and intellectual distinction even has a somewhat aristocratic taint, and therefore, is often frowned upon in America. Money and goods become the prime criteria of place. They are pursued with unusual ardor because other traditional roots of identity are absent or weak. The abundance of free land, the presence of much actual opportunity, and a condition of relative social equality also enchance the pursuit of affluence. Wealth becomes the basis of a new pseudoaristocracy. Wealth becomes the measure of man; not of course, without much apprehension and much anxiety.

When, on the contrary, the distinctions of ranks are obliterated and privileges are destroyed, when hereditary property is subdivided and education and freedom are widely diffused, the desire of acquiring the comforts of the world haunts the imagination of the poor, and the dread of losing them that of the rich. Many scanty fortunes spring up; those who possess them have a sufficient share of physical gratifications to conceive a taste for these pleasures, though not enough to satisfy it. They never procure them without exertion, and they never indulge in them without apprehension. They are therefore always straining to pursue or to retain gratifications so delightful, so imperfect, so fugitive.

. . . the love of well-being has now become the predominant taste of the nation; the great current of human passions runs in that channel and sweeps everything along in its course.[8]

"It would be difficult," Tocqueville writes, "to describe the avidity with which the American rushes forward to this immense booty that fortune offers. . . . Before him lies a boundless continent, and he urges onward as if time pressed and he was afraid of finding no room for his exertions."[9]

The avid pursuit of wealth and the degree to which Americans define each others' place and their own identity in terms of wealth, creates a passion for possession and a deep commitment to private property. The passion and the commitment are so closely interwoven with the average American's sense of self, that radical threats to acquisitiveness and possessive individualism are threats not merely to one's property but to the nation's definition of its entire purpose for being, and to the individual citizen's definition of the meaning and worth of his life. To threaten the structure of property relations is to threaten the quintessential America. This is, in part, why America transforms mere radical rhetoric into apocalyptic dispossession. This is a source of America's extraordinary and irrational pursuit of the radical heresy and of America's tendency to vastly exaggerate the dimensions of American radicalism. The national purpose is threatened. The individuals' existence and identity are threatened. The American root and branch is the issue and it is threatened. Antiradical hysteria is a reaction formation and counterpoise to the avid pursuit of being through possessions.

The problem, however, has deep roots in reality as well as fantasy. The issue is not merely one of mythic and artifacted radical conspiracies and imagined threats to property and identity. Money and property, and the status and security it brings, can be—and in America frequently are—lost. The vicissitudes of capitalism make economic security a much less certain source of identity than a lordship or a position in an ancient feudal bureaucracy. "The desire of acquiring the comforts of the world haunts the imagination of the poor, and the dread of losing them, that of the rich."

An American identity rooted in money, potentially unstable, carries with it, below the surface, an immense anxiety. This anxiety, according to Tocqueville, has to do with the fact that

The bold pursuit of success perpetually retires before them, yet without holding itself from their sight, and in retiring draws them on. At every moment they think they are about to grasp it, it escapes at every moment from their hold, they are near enough to see its charms, but too far off to enjoy them; and before they have fully tasted its delights they die . . . In democratic times enjoyments are more intense than in the ages of aristocracy, and the number of those who partake in them is vastly larger; but, on the other hand, it must be admitted that man's hopes and desires are often blasted, the soul is more stricken and perturbed, and care itself is more keen.[10]

America's proneness to political hysteria and the intense pursuit of alleged but usually nonexistent radicals is related to this "stricken and perturbed" soul. The instability of status achieved through the acquisition of wealth makes many successful Americans edgy and anxious, fearful of loss and defensive, and very quick to respond to threats to economic security. This heightens our antiradical posture. The actual loss of wealth, or, even the relative status deprivation experienced by those who are bypassed, is particularly crushing. When the principles of capitalism become transformed into universal and self-evident truths, and when possessions are the meaning of one's being, the antiradical impulse is powerful and easily mobilized. It becomes the first response to any threat of sudden change.

The instability of bourgeois identity is anxiety inducing and the anxiety when mobilized is conducive to overarching and irrational bursts of repressive political action.

The presence of relative social equality in America and the commitment to equality of opportunity, like many other fundamentals of the American situation, contribute to the polarities of the national style. Equality of opportunity and condition opens the possibility that millions will succeed economically and, therefore, stabilize their identity and achieve some security. Yet the fluidity and instabilities of American capitalism periodically threaten this identity.

Describing Americans as "the freest and most enlightened men placed in the happiest circumstances that the world offers," Tocqueville then noted a paradox. "It seemed to me as if a cloud habitually hung upon their brow, and I thought them serious and almost sad, even in their pleasures."[11] The sadness and rootlessness that accompanies this anxious materialism has perhaps never been more poignantly described than by Tocqueville.

In the United States, a man builds a house in which to spend his old age, and he sells it before the roof is on; he plants a garden and lets it just as the trees are coming into bearing; he brings a field into tillage and leaves other men to gather the crops; he embraces a profession and gives it up; he settles in a place, which he soon afterwards leaves to carry his changeable longings elsewhere. If his private affairs leave him any leisure, he instantly plunges into the vortex of politics; and if at the end of a year of unremitting labor he finds he has a few days vacation, his eager curiosity whirls him over the vast extent of the United States, and he will travel fifteen hundred miles in a few days to shake off his happiness. Death at length overtakes him, but it is before he is weary of his bootless chase of that complete felicity which forever escapes him.[12]

Tocqueville understood that this anxiety and restlessness characterized an American identity which was, in many ways, existentially rootless and fragile. This insecurity springs, in part, from the egalitarian character of American life. In a culture which places great emphasis on equality, and which does not have traditional hierarchical differentiations, it becomes difficult to distinguish yourself very much from others, it becomes difficult to locate yourself in space and time, it becomes difficult to know, with a high degree of certainty, who you are. Indeed, you are not supposed to be too different, in America. The forces that prevent people, in an egalitarian culture, from becoming separate, unique, individuated, and therefore psychically free are formidable.

A uniformity of culture and personality tends to develop an identifiable one-dimensionality. On the one hand one feels entitled to differentiate oneself from one's peers and the rest of society; on the other hand, the very equality which allows this consideration mitigates against its implementation: you are not supposed to think of yourself as different! This tension expresses the essence of Tocqueville's insight.

The forces producing a uniformity of values and life style are powerful. But this is customarily hidden from public view by numerous popular illusions. The authority which Aristocratic opinion has in feudal society was transformed in nonfeudal America to public opinion. Its authority became compelling because the illusion was sustained that the opinion of the public was merely the idealized small men next to the large. The compulsive uniformity of America does not appear to Americans to be a forced or restrictive uniformity, but merely a voluntary aggregate of self wills. This sustains the illusion of self-determination. It feeds the illusion of representative government. It masks the compulsions imposed by the uniformity. And it draws attention away from the possibility that some combination of power groups rule.

Nevertheless, to be an American means to be separate, to be different, to be an individual. The polarities of the American identity are sharp—dependence on the will of the majority and independence, an apparent individuality which is actually a conformity, a conformity which appears to be a sum of individualities, a sense that differences of life style and values are deviant and should be avoided and a sense that such differences are legitimate and should be sought.

The tensions and polarities of such a national style are intimately related to the proclivity for repressive political hysteria. The American who is different, who poses alternatives to the dominant political and economic ethos and dominant life style, violates the compulsive and legitimated consensus. He must be curbed. Nevertheless, the American who is different, is, in another sense, doing what the culture defines as good. In fact, he may be doing what Americans secretly wish to do. This may arouse the conformist's anger because it taps his secret wish. He can repress his wish by repressing the man who defies the very consensus he might like to defy.

The polarities and instabilities of the national style and the consequent need to introduce stability and manage tensions are exacerbated by the enormously rapid technological and social change that occurs in this country. The active, changing, driving, transitional, rootless quality of the American environment did not escape Tocqueville's attention. As noted, "in the United States a man builds a house in which to spend his old age; and sells it before the roof is on. . . ." A stable and traditional environment did not exist and could not have become a source of identity development. Indeed, precisely the reverse occurred, the rapidly changing character of the environment became a source of identity confusion, instability, and rootlessness. This enhances the need for roots. This makes threats to national identity, real and imagined, appear more unsettling and frightening than they may in fact be.

But the velocity of change is also related to the need to repress the deviance which the superpatriot may secretly wish for. Erik Erikson has addressed himself to this point.

Most of her (America's) inhabitants are faced, in their own lives or within the orbit of their closest relatives, with alternatives presented by such polarities as: open roads of immigration and jealous islands of tradition; outgoing internationalism and defiant isolationism;

boisterous competition and self-effacing cooperation; and many others . . .

Thus the functioning American, as the heir of a history of extreme contrasts and abrupt changes, bases his final ego identity on some tentative combination of dynamic polarities such as migratory and sedentary, individualistic and standardized, competitive and cooperative, pious and freethinking, responsible and cynical, etc. . . .

While we see extreme elaborations of one or the other of these poles in regional, occupational, and characterological types, analysis reveals that this extremeness (of rigidity or of vacillation) contains an inner defense against the always implied, deeply feared, or secretly hoped for opposite extreme.[13]

The extreme contrast and the abrupt change can be difficult to absorb and resolve. The result is an identity, tinged with tentativeness, an identity which, even when superficially settled, remains potentially threatened by dramatic social change. The rootedness of American identity always confronts the rootlessness of American life. That rootlessness creates the powerful urge for rootedness—an urge exacerbated in times of stress. And it is here that the connection can be made between the tensions and contraries of national identity or style and the American proclivity for extremism. The search is for roots—stable, changeless roots. The nation, the American way of life, ancient American principles, Locke, Smith, Alger, ancient, venerated, and changeless American institutions and values become the stable rock upon which America can rest.

The prime source of the American identity—political and otherwise—is eighteenth century values and political institutions carried, little changed, into the twentieth century. The American identity is built on a bedrock of changeless principle. The American principle—selected bits and pieces of John Locke and Adam Smith—rigidified through two centuries of unchallenged dominance and steeled in the crucible of Horatio Alger, has become the American absolute. That absolute, manifested as the will of the majority, becomes particularly compelling. The American identity and perspective is liberalism—Locke in politics and Smith in economics—visceral, dogmatic, affective, compulsive, unanimous, unchallenged liberalism.

And this identity, which structures the American world view, is old. In terms of the time span of American history it is, in fact, ancient. Ancient habits are resistant to change. The American style is truly classic. Formed during the infancy of the Republic, it has become deeply rooted—an ancient habit, reinforced through socialization and strengthened because it was unchallenged. The significance of this ancient imprinting for political studies is twofold: such identities are little amenable to alteration; and such identities produce powerful defense mechanisms—mechanisms designed to defend against threat and change, real or fantasy. The power of the identification with such habituated ways is great and so is the power of the mechanisms designed to protect that identification. Resistance to fundamental change should be a bulwark of American political culture. And it is. During times of stress, the resistance should be vigorous.

The changelessness of our fundamental values and political institutions, the carry over of Locke and Smith from the eighteenth to the twentieth century, is frequently overlooked because of the tremendous amount of economic and technological change and the great physical movement of the American people. Tocqueville hinted at this when he noted the contrast between the velocity of change in economic relations, physical location and daily life, and the stability and traditionalism of political and religious ideas. This struck him as a paradox of major proportions. It is a paradox and it has important ramifications for the American national style and the American proneness to political hysteria. Americans, Tocqueville noted, "love change but dread revolutions."[14]

Two things are surprising in the United States: the mutability of the greater part of human actions, and the singular stability of certain principles. Men are in constant motion; the mind of man appears almost unmoved. . . . In the United States general principles in religion, philosophy, morality, and even politics do not vary, or at least are only modified by a hidden and often an imperceptible process; even the grossest prejudices are obliterated with incredible slowness amid the continual friction of men and things.[15]

Obviously a country that loves change but hates revolution, is not going to warmly receive radicals and radical ideas, particularly when it can find a source of psychic stability in a deep commitment to unchanging principles.

Ideology is of prime importance to Americans. The liberal ideology, both in politics and economics, has been so stable in such a very unstable environment that it has become a major source of identity. It plays a role in our history which is much greater than is generally appreciated.

American politics, in a peculiar sense, is highly ideological. Our Lockean and Smithian ideology, because it has never been challenged by a mass movement of the right or left, has become all that we have, and, like most ancient and unchallenged beliefs it has become so dogmatic and rigidified that we are scarcely aware of it. Americans find their definition in it. Naturally they rise to its defense when it is thought to be under attack.

THE LIBERAL DOGMA

Tocqueville's analysis of America is based upon developing the implications for the social system of a society without aristocracy and with substantial social equality. Louis Hartz has built on Tocqueville and developed a theory of American political culture that also illumines the American capacity for repression. Hartz's analysis is based upon developing the implications of the fact that Americans unanimously and passionately and compulsively identify with liberalism because liberalism has been the totality of the American experience and, as such, has become the American absolutism and the American compulsion.

On the first page of *The Liberal Tradition in America* Hartz states that his analysis

> . . . is based upon what might be called the story book truth about American history: that America was settled by men who fled from the feudal and clerical oppressions of the Old World. If there is anything in this view, as old as the national folklore itself, then the outstanding thing about the American community . . . ought to be the nonexistence of those oppressions, or since the revolt against them was in the broadest sense liberal, that the American community is a liberal community.[16]

Born relatively free, America was forced neither to resort to transcendent political speculation nor revolution to become free. Revolutionary traditions with transcendent schemes of political philosophy were and are conspicuously absent in America. In fact, America lacks a tradition of original and creative political philosophy. America inherited Locke, americanized Locke, and remained with Locke. Lacking a revolutionary tradition, America also lacked a tradition of reaction. Indeed there was no feudality or aristocracy that America could return to since neither existed. The absence of a genuine aristocracy and a reactionary medieval Catholic church advocating traditional European conservative ideology of the brand of Burke or of De Maistre is a fundamental fact of American history.

The absence of a conservative tradition hastened the truimph of liberalism and contributed to the totality of its victory. The absence of conservatism denied to Americans an alternative model to liberalism. The absence of conservatism made it an unknown, and, therefore, a frightening and alien European doctrine. Liberalism triumphed early in the history of the Republic and its triumph was total. The speed and the sweep of that triumph fixed the liberal mold so that the unfolding of American history is the unfolding of liberalism.

Because relative social freedom for white men was widespread at the time of the founding of the Republic and because the

English inheritance was, by continental standards unrepressive, the American Revolution remained a political revolution, not a social upheaval. The American Revolution was justified by resort to ancient canons of English constitutional law—the historic rights of Englishmen—modified by the widely accepted views of some Enlightenment philosophers. The revolution was conservative. It was designed to preserve the goodness of the English past, not to remake the world.

Aristocracy was absent. European conservatism never took root. A reaction was impossible. America, as it were, was "born" with these characteristics. A good deal of social equality, however, was preserved and expanded because land was abundant and access to it was not inhibited by feudal property arrangements and restrictions on movement. And the triumph of the Protestant ethic helped to sustain and create a relatively flexible social structure. Americans, Tocqueville noted ". . . are born equal, instead of becoming so."

The liberal inheritance of America, the abundance of free land, and the presence of substantial equality militated against the development of a class-conscious and radical proletariat espousing revolutionary doctrine. A mass based radicalism and a competitive Socialist Party are conspicuous in America by their absence. America is the only powerful and advanced industrial nation without a serious socialist movement. The absence of socialism, surely a prime fact of American life, is related to the absence of feudalism. Hartz writes:

It is not accidental that America which has uniquely lacked a feudal tradition has uniquely lacked a socialist tradition. The hidden origin of socialist thought everywhere in the West is to be found in the feudal ethos. The *ancien regime* inspires Rousseau; both inspire Marx.[17]

The absence of a bleak feudal conservatism has denied radicalism one of its prime targets and roots, for Marx attacked the remnants of feudalism as well as capitalism. The absence of a radical tradition hastened the triumph of liberalism and contributed to the totality of its victory. The left never seriously challenged the liberal hegemony. The absence of radicalism denied to Americans an alternative model to liberalism. The absence of radicalism made it an unknown and, therefore, frightening, and alien European doctrine.

Radicalism and conservatism were unknown, and the unknown is frightening. Their absence meant that the liberalism imported to America from England went unchallenged, and being unchallenged it triumphed quickly and became all that there was. As liberalism triumphed, alternatives to liberalism waned, and liberalism became the American doctrine, the American ethos, the American way of life. Liberalism as a unanimous ideology became a powerful and passionate nationalism. When this occurred, radicalism became increasingly un-American and opposition to radicalism became an essence of patriotism and an important way to define one Americanism.

With conservatism and socialism absent, with aristocrats and proletarians absent, America developed a political ethos unique to the West—a unanimous Lockean liberalism, a liberal way of life, a massive middle class society—bourgeoisie to the core —which has never been seriously threatened by extremist political movements of any magnitude. Facing no serious opposition, this liberalism could only become unanimous. It could only become the totality of our political consciousness— a unanimity—strengthened over time and reinforced by generations who knew of no other tradition. This Lockean liberalism could *only* become an enormously powerful nationalism—an American way of life and unconquerable giant—which, like most totalisms, became over time, dogmatic, compulsive, rigid, visceral aggressive, unconquerable domestically, and militant abroad.

"Surely then, it is a remarkable force," Hartz writes, "this fixed, dogmatic liberalism of a liberal way of life. It is the secret root from which have sprung many of the most puzzling of American cultural phenomena."[18]

The greatest puzzle, of course, may be expressed in Talmudic form: how can a country that is so good—so sensitive to the rights of minorities and so caring of individualism, so committed to the expansion of freedom—be so conformitarian, so frightened of dissent, so opposed to substantial social and economic change, so racist, and so prone to irrational fits of regressive patriotism? How can the same country produce Thomas Jefferson and Joseph McCarthy, Walt Whitman and A. Mitchell Palmer, the Ku Klux Klan and the American Civil Liberties Union?

The liberal tradition in America, Hartz writes,

. . . is riddled with paradox. Here is a Lockean doctrine which in the West as a whole is the symbol of rationalism, yet in America the devotion to it has been so irrational that it has not even been recognized for what it is: liberalism. There has never been a "liberal movement" or a real "liberal party" in America: we have only had the American Way of Life, a nationalistic articulation of Locke which usually does not know that Locke himself is involved. . . .[19]

The paradox emerges from the nature of the identification which Americans make with the liberal tradition and with the substance and polarities of the tradition itself. Because alternatives to liberalism were absent and never seriously developed, Lockean liberalism became the sum and substance of America. Because challenges were absent, liberalism became the natural terrain—the obvious normal, unquestioned basis of America's being. Liberalism, again, became America's "given." Because challenges were absent, Americans were not forced to evaluate the merits of liberalism. And Lockean liberalism, as the only American tradition, became the powerful nationalism it is. Liberalism became ". . . a universal, sinking beneath the surface of thought to the level of an assumption, then, it is reborn, transformed into a new nationalism . . ."[20]

As a totalistic nationalism, American liberalism has enormous power. As a hidden assumption, it works in wondrous, unconscious, and deterministic ways. The American labors under the illusion that he has voluntarily selected his ethos when, in fact, it has been imposed upon him by society, since it is the only set of values available. His illusion of self-selection heightens his belief and his commitment. One hears endless talk of the free expression of ideas, when, in fact, America presents to its citizens only one fundamental perspective on politics and life. This is the unidimensionality Tocqueville noted. The liberal ideology thus becomes a moral absolute. As Hartz puts it, ". . . a national essence, a veritable way of life."[21]

Nothing in politics is more powerful than an ideology which has become the sole national credo, which is taken for granted as self-evident truth, and which appears to be an absolute.

The identification of Americans with the national essence is highly affective and compulsive. Liberalism is not merely a political perspective in America competing with other perspectives. It is self-evident truth taken as universal truth, and, as such, the existential identity of Americans is firmly rooted in it. It is so pervasive that it is called the American way of life. Hartz has shown that that national ethos, for which Locke was the source, provided many services for the citizen. It "gave the citizen a glowing sense of nationhood, a national anthem to sing and communicate to his children. . . ." ". . . A shield against the Saracen, the only imaginable moral way of dealing with the man outside the West."[22]

This highly affective identification of the American people with the Americanist nationalism is precisely what elites who promote hysteria attempt to activate. The Red scare was felt by millions as a symbolic, but nevertheless critical, identity crisis. Although those who originally promoted the Red scare argued that the Red conspiracy would rob Americans of their property, money, and place, the threat was basically not experienced as a threat to material well-being; but rather, to Americanism, to the American life style, to the American way. The threat was to the American existential being in almost all its aspects. The crisis was one of identity. There is an apparent paradox here.

If the American identity is so well rooted in the American way—so secure—it should not be so readily threatened. People who truly know who they are, and are at ease with themselves, and whose security and well-being permits them to test reality fairly accurately, do not react with such irrational fervor to threats to their being, especially when those threats are more fantasy than real. This paradox may be resoluble if one can suggest that the American identity is firmly rooted but also, in a peculiar way, infinitely compulsive. We have already suggested that the rootedness is constantly threatened by the vicissitudes of the marketplace.

In one sense, the American identity is well-rooted and has been well-rooted since the eighteenth century when Americans defined their experience and being as bourgeois and liberal. Americans know what an American is supposed to be. They know the "self-evident truths" that define the American ethos. Something called Americanism does exist, and something called un-Americanism also exists. Americanism is a commitment to representative government, a conviction that representative government is the best of all possible political worlds, and a conviction that America embodies it. Americanism is a commitment to capitalism and Horatio Alger, a conviction that the market economy is the best of all ways to organize the economy for the betterment of all. Americanism is the belief that one can "make it" if one pursues the work ethic.

The details and adjustments of American life and the struggle for place and power unfold within the context of Lockean and capitalist perspectives. Locke, Smith, and Alger, bourgeois values, and antiradicalism frame the American experience. The identity nourished by this experience is bounded, and thus known—it is old and thus deeply ingrained, and it has never been seriously tempted by alternatives or challenged, which makes it all the more firm and dogmatic.

This Americanism, this way we define our being, is a powerful force and a source of much security. It tells us who we are and are not, who are our allies and enemies, what is proper and what is not. But it even tells us what is truth and antitruth, heresy and heretic. And this truth is not only truth, but self-evident truth, a truly beautiful thing because it can serve as a commandment and guide throughout life, a guide to the perplexed, to the untutored and the savant because this truth is bold, clear, and self-evident.

There is much security to be found here. The self-evidence of America's norms makes the American more certain of his place and more certain that the attack on un-American heresy is justified. The Declaration of Independence, after all, does state that "we hold these truths to be self-evident. . . ." For the American, truth exists and, whatever it is, it is self-evident, obvious even to the untrained eye and the untutored mind. Now the truth is a powerful thing because it makes the possessor of the truth authoritative and transforms the defender of the truth into a defender of the faith. It is the stuff out of which crusades, inquisitions, and purges can be made.

When that truth is self-evident and an integral part of the national psyche, its power is almost without limit. He who counters self-evident truth appears in only one of three guises: a mental incompetent who is simply not bright enough to perceive the truth; an alien who has not yet been Americanized and who, therefore, isn't familiar with the truth, or a heretic who willfully and with evil intent seeks to smash the truth. The mental incompetent may be educated, given therapy, or hospitalized. The alien may be Americanized and, if that doesn't work, he may be deported. The willful heretic, however, must be investigated, incarcerated, or eliminated.

The rootedness of the American identity is nourished in certitude of the right and the just. The man who is so secure in his being and conviction will hunt heresy fiercely and sincerely. And this is the point. The pursuit of Reds, at least from the vantage point of the average American, is sincerely motivated. The Red is pursued because people do believe—with the highest conviction—that he is a vicious purveyor of anti-truth. Elites may be more sophisticated and contriving. They may know the Red menace is no menace at all. But for the American people the power and passion of the Red scare and McCarthyism and the entire paranoid style in American politics —international Russo-Chinese conspiracy et al.—is a power and passion based on sincere conviction and on true belief. To most of America it is a very real thing. That is why elites get the response and support they seek.

The liberal unanimity which defines the American being has been transformed into a passionate nationalism and, as such, it has the quality of an irrational compulsion. The liberal unanimity does provide America with roots and definition and identity, but the identity is highly affective. When that passionate definition is threatened—in fact or fancy—the defense is visceral, passionate, and automatic. The totality of the pure American experience is involved. It is as if the slightest deviance threatens the purity and integrity of the whole—as if a minor infection could spawn an epidemic. Unanimity breeds unanimity—compulsively. Unanimity cannot tolerate diversity —compulsively. Can Americans act otherwise when they are told by no one less than their attorney general or their president that the national homeland and the true faith are threatened?

The unique contours of American history—no aristocratic conservatism, no proletarian radicalism—have produced a unique political constellation—a unanimous, compulsive, and dogmatic liberalism. The identification with liberalism in America approaches unanimity. It is highly affective and binding. And it is compulsive in the sense that Americans are habituated to the one American way through a process of exquisite socialization which has been reinforcing liberal attitudes for generations. It is irrational, in the Freudian sense—compulsive, omniverous, and largely inarticulated. The American psyche frames its perception of America and the world in rigid liberal categories and, of psychic necessity, can perceive it in no other categories.

America's liberalism has been so total and pervasive, and challenges to it have been so petty and ephemeral, that liberalism in America has become an unconscious and unarticulated premise—a first principle which is rarely tested and examined. In this sense Americans do not know liberalism in a fully dimensional way. And this is one prime source of the power which liberalism exerts in the American mind. As an unrecognized and untested and universally accepted first principle—an unconscious force, as it were, operating below the surface of conscious thought—it is all the more powerful. It is so taken for granted, and so rooted in our being that it frames our posture, without our being conscious of its power. The American being is determined in the sense that no other is available. Can one opt for socialism in the sixth grade in Mobile, Columbus, Madison, Topeka, or even in New York City? Where are socialist teachers to be found?

We are speaking of determinism and free will. With aristocracy and bleak feudal conservatism absent and with no proletarian well spring for radical class consciousness to develop, en masse, could America have been anything but the unfolding of liberalism? American origins shaped American history. We are speaking of social Freudianism where the infancy of a nation is in the critical period for the formation of its character. The original thrust of liberalism confronted with no opposite force simply continues in motion.

Tocqueville understood this and brilliantly described the process.

I have already observed that the origin of the Americans, or what I have called their point of departure, may be looked upon as the first and most efficacious cause to which the present prosperity of the United States may be attributed. The Americans had the chances of birth in their favor; and their forefathers imported that equality of condition and of intellect into the country whence the democratic republic has very naturally taken its rise . . . the early settlers bequeathed to their descendants the customs, manners, and opinions that contribute most to the success of a republic.

When I reflect upon the consequences of this primary fact, I think I see the destiny of America embodied in the first Puritan who landed on these shores . . . It has been effected with ease and simplicity; say rather that this country is reaping the fruits of the democratic revolution which we are undergoing, without having had the revolution itself. . . .

The emigrants who colonized the shores of America in the beginning of the seventeenth century somehow separated the democratic principle from all the principles that it had to contend with in the old communities of Europe, and transplanted it alone to the New World. It has there been able to spread in perfect freedom and peaceably to determine the character of the laws by influencing the manners of the country.[23]

Political identity in America, in other words, was fixed at the point of origin. Challenges were absent and this caused America to lapse into what Hartz calls "three hundred years of liberal immobility." A vital part of America has not grown. In a sense, America has not had the opportunity for choice. The freedom of will which might have permitted America to opt for non-liberal choices was negated by the power of her liberal infancy.

The American remains self-conscious politically, unindividuated, and, therefore, immature. His ability to control himself is limited. It is as if his growth terminated with the end of his infancy. He remains a child—a child of habit—and a dangerous child because he has power. He perceives and responds in the twentieth century with little more sophistication than he did in the eighteenth. It is as if his ideological parents continue to dominate his life. He rarely makes a move without consulting them. Like the neurotic, he finds it difficult not to repeat the self-destructive but identity-preserving errors of his youth.

The identity which is so rooted and so secure is also immature, and here we have another key to the Red scare and McCarthyism. Political hysteria is an infantile fit. This immaturity is a fundamental fact of American politics and a tragedy. The experience with the Red scare did not prevent us from producing McCarthyism, and Korea did not cause us to avoid

Vietnam and Cambodia and Laos. They are, in part, products of the national compulsion and myopia. There is a sense in which the American Legionnaires, who hung a Wobblie from a bridge in Centralia in 1919 and then castrated him, could have done little else. Their identification with America, and the irrational rage which radicalism evokes in them, are not of their own making. They are not the product of conscious will. They are, psychologically speaking, visceral and compulsive responses.

Hartz has commented subtly on the compulsive and automatic character of the Red scare response.

. . . the psychic heritage of a nation "born free" is, as we have abundantly seen, a colossal liberal absolutism, the death by atrophy of the philosophic impulse. And in a war of ideas this frame of mind has two automatic effects: it hampers creative action abroad by identifying the alien with the unintelligible, and it inspires hysteria at home by generating the anxiety that unintelligible things produce. The Red scare, in other words, is not only our domestic problem: it is our international problem as well.[24]

The identification of the alien with the unintelligible is at the heart of the matter because the unintelligible is frightening. Genuine European conservatism is alien to America. Marxism and socialism are alien to America. Maoism, Titoism, and Castroism are alien to America. All "isms" except liberalism are alien and even liberalism in America is not dimensionally known by American liberals. American liberalism, as the embodiment of self-evident truth, makes other ideologies not only alien, but the embodiment of nontruth. As such, "isms" are dangerous and un-American. One can only react to them negatively, automatically and savagely.

This not only forecloses reason, but assures irrationality and passion and extremism. It also heightens the credal and dogmatic quality of the American national faith.

It is the passionate and irrational commitment to Americanist liberalism which conditions America to so misperceive the un-American world. Vietnam is another version of the Wilsonian demand that the rest of the world accept the self-evident truths of America. If we cannot impose them on the rest of the world, we can isolate ourselves from their fatal errors. Hartz has correctly suggested that the domestic hysterias ". . . are actually a form of isolationism, for they seek, within the context of the descent of the alien world to repel contagion from it. . . ."

We turn now to some possible American futures. I wish to consider the possibility that political hysteria and democratic repression have become archaic, that is, displaced by more sophisticated forms of managing tension and more sophisticated techniques of cooption and repression.

7

THE HIGHER REPRESSION
AND THE ROOTS
OF LIBERATION

MANY years ago, that extraordinary American political figure, Huey Long, predicted that if something like fascism came to America it would not at all look like fascism. The external trappings—concentration camps, elite troops, orgies of violence, emergency legislation, secret police, special judges, etc.—would not be necessary. Sophisticated but relentless propaganda, "public relations," and monopolistic control of communications, Long predicted, would be the critical apparatus of an American fascism. Our study of political hysteria suggests that Huey Long may well be correct, because political hysteria in America engenders a democratic repression—pluralist, fundamentally legal, and, with rare exception, nonviolent. He may even be correct because America is capable of producing so many subtle forms of repression and ways of managing tension and dissent that crude repression and fascism have become archaic.

For a democratic repression to occur in contemporary—pluralist, legal, nonviolent—America, all that would be necessary would be motivated elites, a weakened party opposition that does not oppose the repression, or what is much more likely, a joint two party combination, in which the minority party sees potential political payoffs in competing for the patriotic constituency. For a significant repression to occur in America neither a large police state nor concentration camps would be necessary. Numerous, decentralized, and highly focused local police terrorisms—like the killing of Panthers—would probably be sufficient to frighten most of the potential liberal opposition. A Goebbels-like propaganda agency would not be necessary. Promotional material would be supplied, as it was during the Red scare, by the mass media.

The repression would unfold while the "democratic process" is maintained and "representative government" flourished. Elections would be held as usual. No truly sophisticated proponent of repression would be stupid enough to shatter the facade of democratic institutions. The repression would unfold via Congressional legislation—"no knock," "conspiracy to incite riot," "crossing state lines," "preventive detention," "legal wiretapping"—and it would be enforced by judges and juries.

The stresses that might motivate elites to provoke a political hysteria need not be solely domestic, nor severe, nor imminently threatening. Neither economic recession nor a widespread depression are necessary preconditions.

A combination of moderate dislocation and deviant behavior in America coupled with a dramatic extension of communist power abroad can nudge elites to conclude that their hegemony is threatened or that their self interest can be better served by exploiting the public's susceptibility to a democratic repression than by more traditional pluralist combinations. The Bolshevik revolution of 1917 and communist uprisings in Germany were major factors precipitating the Red scare. They made the American people more susceptible to the ancient Whig-Republican tactic of slandering domestic opponents with the rhetoric of Bolshevism. The American people were—during a period of affluence—in part, susceptible to Senator Joseph McCarthy because of the rise to power of the Chinese Communists, the Russian explosion of an atomic bomb, and the Korean War.

Political hysteria and democratic repression might be an American response to drastic domestic dislocation, but drastic dislocation is not a necessary precondition for democratic repression. As a matter of fact, a drastic dislocation, a major depression, for example, necessitates a functional and pragmatic response. The hysterias of 1919 and the 1950's were not functional. They did not solve significant problems. Though they profited elites and provided pleasure for the masses they did not stabilize the economy or redress political grievances. Is it accidental that the great depression produced the pragmatist F.D.R. and not A. Mitchell Palmer or Joseph McCarthy?

One of the significant questions of our political future may well be whether or not we will resort to Palmer and McCarthy if other nations opt for socialism and if American problems multiply beyond the possibility of incremental and liberal solutions. Although America has undergone great technological, economic, and physical changes, the country has managed to resist fundamental changes in values and political institutions. America has remained liberal since the late eighteenth century, Lockian in its polity, and capitalist. The immobility of liberalism remains the prime characteristic of the political culture. The Civil War excepted, America has been able thus far to deal with economic and political disturbances within the liberal framework and has been able to coopt and absorb what little deviance and transcendence has occured. The question, of course, is whether it can continue to do so as the velocity of history accelerates, producing many and serious strains on the economy and polity. The question is whether America's socialization into Locke and Smith began breaking down in the sixties and will continue to do so. Certainly until that time, little had disturbed the liberal one-dimensionality of America.

In evaluating the possibility of a future political hysteria and democratic repression, it may be illuminating to look briefly at some variations and the themes of the liberal American past.

There have been several Americas out of which the future will develop: a changeless, moderate, incremental, centrist, stable, Lockian and Smithian America; an America of archaic eighteenth century political structures; and an America dominated by vast, overarching, corporate giants; a humane Walt Whitmanesque America; a Populist America; a nostalgic preservationist small town America; an America committed to due process and free speech; a unidimensional, closed, dogmatic, mindless, and hysterical America; a reformist America; and a millennial America convinced that it has found self-evident truth and must, as Gods work, liberalize the world, make it safe for capitalism, and smash communist antitruth. These Americas coexist, overlap, ebb and flow, and affect each other. The once dominant lingers as secondary, but not insignificant. None fully die. These Americas, like the stages of development in the life of a man, fuse, layer upon layer, and sometimes, during stress, a primordial and customarily quiescent America—regressive, hysterical, superpatriotic, punitive—is reawakened.

But the need to mobilize this America arises only occasionally because the dominant America is brilliantly equipped to absorb and coopt deviance and dissent, to manage tension, and maintain its system of oligarchies without hysteria. The dominant America is an America which is flexible enough to manage recession and depression by realigning its parties and policies in incremental and Lockian ways—never losing close touch with its past values, never seriously altering its original political institutions, and never dislodging, in fundamental ways, its dominant powers. It is a delicate and beautiful and profitable balance for those interests that decisively influence its public life.

CONTEMPORARY AMERICA

American politics is dominated by a configuration of colossal corporations and trade unions which are able to decisively effect those public policies that bear on their self-interests. Occasionally they do this by application of intense and focused pressure.

Intense pressure, however, is not customarily necessary because those who hold significant public office hold the same values as those who dominate the great corporations and the great trade unions. In fact, the ideology of trade union leaders is, in essence, little different than that of corporate leadership. They accept the contours of capitalism. The dominance of the large corporation and union is not a consequence of conspiracy, but consensus. They are able to dominate, in part, because their less powerful opponents cannot possibly compete. They succeed, in part, because powerful members of the Congress do not believe that their dominance adversely affects America's interest or the interest of their constituents. Their ability to decisively affect policy is relatively unhampered by disorganized, amorphous, and unselfconscious masses. Their dominance is invariably not violated by the outcome of elections, the significance of which, as a tool of meaningful participation and a technique for exerting leverage on elites has always been vastly exaggerated. Occasionally, a combination of lesser oligarchies frustrates a dominant oligarchy. Occasionally, the state refuses to grant them a particular desire. But the state does not threaten their interests.

Men whose world view has been fundamentally congenial to the leaders of giant corporations have dominated Congress for decades. The corporation, we noted, does not get what it wants through complicity. Men of political power accept, in its essentials, the corporate political economy. They understand the corporations' need for planned, coordinated, and centralized regulation of capitalism. They understand that regulation at the periphery is necessary to curb anarchic influence and excessive and destructive competition. They understand that rationalization of the political economy is necessary for growth and for the continuity of corporate dominance. The more sophisticated have understood, for decades, that the unfettered right to earn had to be selectively curbed, before the few could fully exploit the right.

This mutuality of big business, big labor, and big government—this consensus—nourishes the continuity and liberal immobility of America. This consensus is America. The consensus invariably relieves elites of the need to trigger a political hysteria and repression. Political hysteria would be an admission that elites thought the consensus was threatened.

Men of political power have long accepted the giant corporation's definition of the good society as the society that continues to enlarge its surplus property. They came to believe long ago that to expand prosperity, it was necessary to promote overseas economic expansion—to sell and invest abroad those products and that capital that could not, with profit, be sold or invested domestically. Some of the more sophisticated politicians also understand that despite vast and unremitting social need, the productive capacity of the United States has greatly outstripped the capacity of Americans to absorb its products at a profit. America needs to find a profitable product that it can sell to a customer with adequate purchasing power. The product is tanks, guns, and planes, and the customer is the United States government. Permanent war preparedness—not war—is one fundamental means by which the dominance of economic interests is sustained and prosperity maintained.

For decades American politicians have accepted the oligarchies' excuse for a theory of society—the view that expanding prosperity will automatically solve social problems and create an American *communitas*. Accepting this, they accepted, as a corollary, the view that it is not necessary to think through or confront the problem of justice and community. The view that increasing surpluses, trickling down to the poor, will automatically solve fundamental problems and create equity, is the American substitute for thought. Political thought in America is cliche—Locke is cliche, Smith is cliche. The absence of political philosophy—the mindlessness—is an American motif.

This mindlessness serves the dominant America in important

ways. The triumph of nonthought means the absence of a critical and possibly transcendent theory of society. Critical theory can be a tool for analyzing emerging contradictions, for reaching the essence beyond the appearance, and it therefore can be a powerful vehicle leading toward transcendence. The absence of such critical theory aids the triumph of the present—the triumph of existing practice and priority and values. The quality of life in the present tends to remain unquestioned because a critical theory positing alternate values and ways of living is absent. The American assumption that there is nothing fundamentally wrong with political liberalism and capitalism other than the fulfillment of their ultimate potential appears more credible because alternate theories and theorizing are absent. The triumph of nonthought is the triumph of nontranscendence—the absence of alternatives to Locke and Smith as cliche. It is socialism stillborn.

The dispossessed want only what the possessed have, not a different way of living and relating. They know of no other way of living and relating than the dominant way. This greatly increases the possibilities of inclusion and cooptation. It is much easier to give a man more bread than a life with fraternity. Once the dispossesed are admitted to possession, therefore, the present—its practice, its values, its life—becomes more dominant. America widens its liberal constituency as it produces more material comfort because America can continue to avoid the challenge of redefining, in non-bourgeois terms, what constitutes the good man and the good life. The definitions of the past not only suffice, they become more acceptable. The present is strengthened. Political hysteria and democratic repression are rendered less likely as increasing material comfort mitigates the threat of thought.

In the dominant America, major alterations of public policy, like the New Deal, occur not as a consequence of new theory but rather as a consequence of dislocations, disorders, and systemic dysfunctions that threaten existing power arrangements.

Elites, acting in enlightened self-interest, institute reforms. Reforms designed basically to preserve the system and its domination by elites, nevertheless, do ameliorate the lot of millions. The panoply of New Deal reforms did provide social security, unemployment compensation, the right to bargain collectively, and dozens of other benefits for millions, and it did make life more secure for them.

However, while benefits are extended to working men, the political and economic system, qua system, is strengthened and the dominance of corporate enterprise and values is perpetuated —indeed strengthened. The very structured inequalities that condemn millions of Americans to live a life, more or less broadly bounded by the condition of their birth, are marginally ameliorated, but essentially perpetuated.

The dominant America is structured inequality. Bright conservatives realize this and they realize that the structures they dominate preserve structured inequality. Liberal reformers who recognize this, attempt to ameliorate the inequality, but not the structure that produces the inequality. The American system would be seriously threatened if liberals and democrats attacked the structure rather than the inequality. If they did attack the structure, they, of course, would no longer be liberals and democrats.

William Appleman Williams has astutely remarked that American reformers are "almost unique in the intensity of their commitment to private property." Unlike European reformers, they never developed a theory of society. They are Lockians and Smithians. Commitment to Locke and Smith *is* commitment to the structure. A commitment to widening opportunity, within the framework of capitalism and the ethic of possessive individualism, is commitment to inequality. Reformers rationalize the political economy of the large corporation and the large union. They mask oligarchic reality. They preserve structured inequality. They are, therefore, key agents in the process by which America manages tension and maintains existing power arrangements, with minimal adjustments, and without the need for political hysteria.

American liberalism is an efficient way to foster corporate dominance because it flourishes within a facade of pluralism, of legalism, and utilizes an electoral apparatus that is taken by most Americans as meaningfully representative. As America became more oligarchic between 1880 and 1930, its electoral apparatus became more democratic—initiative, referendum, direct election of Senators, woman's suffrage, etc., and more and more people did vote. The forms of democracy were carefully preserved and improved. In the dominant America, it is the content that becomes increasingly more shallow. The preservation and improvement of the forms, however, preserves the illusion of representation and democracy. This illusion mitigates opposition to the system because it negates the demand for meaningful participatory democracy at the place of work and at the local community. The illusion also masks the decisive influence which corporate power exerts on public policy. The system depends, in part, upon the true distribution of power and influence remaining blurred.

David Rockefeller needs F.D.R., Lyndon Johnson, Edmund Muskie, and Edward Kennedy. When severe socioeconomic dislocations occur and more than the usual millions suffer, they lead a realignment of parties which produces a broad redefinition of electoral alignments and policies. The critical realignment is a major technique for managing tension and maintaining stability. Liberal political formulas are redefined in terms that gain massive popular support—terms that remain liberal. The system of structured inequality has its legitimacy restored.

No critical alignment, however, has seriously threatened the dominance of Lockian-Smithian values. Major economic reversals have shuffled some of the elites that govern America and resulted in substantial economic gains for segments of the population, but no critical alignment has terminated corporate dominance or brought about a democratic and participatory redistribution of power. No critical realignment has seriously altered the position of blacks or whites or made a serious difference for the thirty million poor in America. No critical realignment has resolved the crisis in health care or housing. No critical alignment has affected problems of work alienation, the wastefulness and irrationality of the economic system, or the inadequacy of public and community facilities. No critical alignment has dealt with qualitatively new possibilities of social organization. And no critical realignment has mitigated the irrationality and compulsiveness of our stereotyped anticommunism. If anything, New Frontiersmen have strengthened this sterotype. Critical realignments, like the New Deal, preserve Smith and Alger, preserve the system of private property, preserve structured inequality, more widely distribute parcels of inadequate social security, and sustain corporate dominance.

The success of such realignments lessens the need for political hysteria and democratic repression because it enhances the allegiance of the American people to the system of corporate dominance and pseudopluralism. Threats to the hegemony of elites are thus mitigated. The very subtle relationship of so-called liberals to so-called conservatives is at the heart of the dominant America—the very subtle and complementary relationship of F.D.R. and L.B.J. and the Kennedys to David Rockefeller, of the Chase Manhattan Bank.

L.B.J. and the Kennedys shared so many fundamental values with Rockefeller that he was able to "use" them and relieve himself of the need to cry conspiracy. The Kennedys and Johnson did not believe they were being used. They would have vigorously denied it. But Rockefeller needs them to increasingly regulate an economic system that periodically produces recessions, and he needs them to regulate a society that is becoming increasingly anarchic. A Rockefeller periodically needs a Johnson or a Kennedy as president because this is the only way they and he can generate enough power in the Congress to override Republican opposition to the occasionally regulated economy that Rockefeller needs. Rockefeller also needs them not to become Norman Thomas; but he need not worry much on this account. Liberals not only protect themselves and Rockefeller from Norman Thomas but also from Eldridge Cleaver and Joseph Welch and George Wallace.

Perhaps the ultimate political significance of the 1960's will, in retrospect, turn out to be the fact that David Rockefeller finally discovered that it was in his best interest to become more and more like Johnson and the Kennedys. At that future moment in American history when the irrelevance and dysfunctionality of Locke and Smith become increasingly apparent, Rockefeller too, will maintain Smithian rhetoric while putting his prestige and muscle behind a guaranteed annual wage, a national health insurance plan, and public ownership of seriously ailing industries. Neither Rockefeller nor the liberals have ever needed to abandon Smith to maintain the system and their dominance. The question, of course, is will they be forced to. And will they be farsighted enough to do it. How far they can leave Adam, Smith and the "American Way" before much less sophisticated business and political elites will become outraged and panicky and discover the political capital available through the rhetoric of Bolshevik slander and conspiracy? How far can they go without the American Legion and some future George Wallace finding out about it? The probability of a future democratic repression depends, in part, on these circumstances.

But the probability of elites promoting some future political hysteria and democratic repression is lessened by the fact that America has developed many sophisticated techniques for managing tension and for maintaining the system which is crowned by corporate and labor oligarchies. For the dominant America is a system designed to protect men of power and contain qualitative change. Successful political systems develop techniques for protecting men and groups which monopolize power. Successful systems either prevent attacks on dominant power, or coopt and shunt such attacks. Successful systems manage to prevent malfunctions from becoming so painful to the people that they come to question the authority and legitimacy of the system and of the men in power. Successful systems are designed to permit vested interests to define the comforts of life in a profit maximizing way, convince the people that comforts so defined are eminently desirable, and then provide enough comforts so that the vast majority believe they are receiving what they are entitled to. This binds the people to the system and, unwittingly, to the vested interests that dominate it. The most successful systems are those which are able to mask the power of elites from public view while successfully generating the illusion that the people have power. America has such a system, and it is, from the vantage point of those with dominant influence, enormously successful.

Political hysteria and democratic repression are two ways of managing tension but the former is a technique of last resort. It is an inefficient and crude way of eliminating or curbing challenges to oligarchies. As techniques of social control multiply and become more sophisticated, the political hysteria of the Red scare variety will probably become archaic. It is being and will be replaced by higher and more efficient forms of democratic repression. It is worth examining the dominant America as a system for managing tension.

THE DOMINANT AMERICA

The key to America's tension management is its socialization processes—the techniques by which Americans during their early years are taught the value and truth of Locke, Smith, Alger, and America, and the dangers of socialism. The American parent, the school, and the media devote much effort training young Americans to believe that a "free world" and a "slave world" exist and that America is at the center of the former. The doctrine is inculcated that the theory of representative government in its institutionalized American form works and works well, that elections provide meaningful leverage over the elected representatives, and that elections do involve meaningful choices. The totalitarian nature of communist one-party states is the sixth grade and high school counterpoint to this political philosophy.

Horatio Algerism, in slightly Keynesian dress, is the economic philosophy into which Americans are socialized. The Republican reworking of early nineteenth century Whig doctrine which captivated America at the turn of the century with dreams of boundless wealth, openness of opportunity, and thrift continues, albeit with increasing exceptions, to captivate America. Nixon announced recently that the fundamental American right is the right to earn. Algerism manages tension by sustaining hope and teaching each man that he is where he is because of his intrinsic merit. Whiggish doctrine continues to be the American ethic. America has no classes, no class conflict, and no class structure. American doctrine excludes the very categories of critical thought which could lead to the perception of the pseudoequality of pluralism and the unmasking of oligarchic control. Exploitation, and expropriation, and alienation, and manipulation, and repression, and classes, and class conflict—the categories of European thought—are not categories of American political thought. They are categories used by some American social scientists but not by politicians, or politicial movements, or public figures. American Whiggery has succeeded in preempting them with the doctrine that America has boundless opportunity and little or no stratification or exploitation. The flattening of political language, the denuding of political and economic theory of its oppositional categories, as Marcuse suggested, negated the critical capacity of thought. This denuding is a major technique of tension management because it leaves the dominated and the outcast and the dehumanized without a leader, a langauge, and a theory which could expose the roots of their place and lead to the demand for qualitative change.

The one-dimensionality of language and the unidimensionality and compulsion of the American version of liberalism make it difficult or impossible to gain anything other than the liberal perspective on America. Therefore, what critiques of America are produced are nonsystemic. Liberal ills are to be dealt with by liberal correctives which always assume the sanctity of existing political and economic structures. This is system maintenance.

The more efficient processes of socialization condemn those values and systems of thought which attack and unmask the repressive aspects of what people are socialized into. American socialization does this and thereby manages tension and negates criticism. The categories of exploitation, dominance, structure, repression, class, and socialist perspectives are not only not transmitted to the young, they are presented as antitruth, intellectually shallow, irrelevant, or utopian. This is system maintenance.

The fact that American values and institutions are presented as the embodiment of self-evident truth simplifies the process. In possession of self-evident truth, and affectively committed to it, Americans maintain their system by defining antiliberal versions of the political economy as nontruth so that the dissenter may be defined—as I noted previously—incompetent—excusable but hospitalizable—if he is believed to be simply not bright enough to perceive the truth. Or he may be defined as a heretic and jailed, if he is perceived as having rationally and willfully opted for antitruth. This was Eugene Debs' real crime.

Primitive and crude political socialization in America manages tension and maintains the American system by trainng those who would not be Republicans to be Democrats, that is, to broadly accept American fundamentals. Socialization, in its modern and much more sophisticated form, has shifted from political indoctrination into liberalism to reshaping needs and wants of consumers in accordance with the desires of vested interests. It is the very nature of modern technological society

—Russia as well as America—to remake men into eager consumers not only of the political values which sustain elites but of the commodities deemed most profitable by them. In so doing, it obliterates the opposition between public and private existence, and this makes the private over into the public. "In this society," Herbert Marcuse remarks, "the productive apparatus tends to become totalitarian to the extent to which it determines not only the socially needed occupations, skills, and attitudes, but also individual needs and aspirations. It thus obliterates the opposition between the private and public existence, between individual and social needs. Technology serves to institute new, more effective, and more pleasant forms of social control and social cohesion."[1]

The ability of vested interests and modern technology to reshape the consciousness of men according to the needs of technology and vested interests creates a powerful identification between the individual and his society. And this identification, which is facilitated by the intrusiveness of modern society—largely through television—tends to eliminate opposition to society. This identification in America simply reinforces the compulsive and affective commitment to liberal dogma which existed long before society became so efficiently intrusive. In the Soviet Union this intrusiveness heightens the identification with Marxism in clichéd form. This intrusion and the socialization have succeeded to the point where most Americans share four things, and little else: they are intolerant liberals, not dimensionally committed to the rights of dissenters; they are capitalists; they are consumers; and they are anticommunists. The urge to oppose the status quo is thus mitigated by the intrusions of modernity and the compulsions of America's unanimous liberalism.

As these identifications fuse and reinforce each other, loyalty to the American way renders crude techniques of social control archaic. Terror on a national scale, political hysteria, and large scale democratic repression are rendered unnecessary because the consciousness that could lead to organized threats to the hegemony of elites withers away. A combination of cold war and liberal cliches, advertising, industrial psychology, television, public relations and pseudo-pluralism, in conjunction with increasing increments of comfort, adequately pacify the modern public. These intrusions and comforts have expanded the scope of society's domination over the individual far beyond that of earlier societies. These developments lead Herbert Marcuse to conclude:

Contemporary society seems to be capable of containing social change—qualitative change which would establish essentially different institutions, a new direction of the productive process, new modes of human existence. This containment of social change is perhaps the most singular achievement of advanced industrial society; the general acceptance of the National Purpose, bipartisan policy, the decline of pluralism, the collusion of Business and Labor within the strong State testify to the integration of opposites which is the result as well as the prerequisite of this achievement.[2]

Comfort pacifies. Technology and advertising create needs and aspirations. The will to oppose lessens. The identification with the present expands. Political hysteria is rendered dysfunctional.

These are the major causes and consequences of our pacification. But America now has other and more sophisticated techniques for managing tension and maintaining its oligarchic pluralism—techniques which arise more from the nature of America than from the modern condition.

The nature of American politics also promotes the identification with America. The parties—primary instruments of socialization—heighten the identification by excluding systemic explanations for political and economic difficulties. In so doing, they continuously legitimate and thus reinforce the main contours of the polity and the economy. By concentrating upon institutional gimmickry (departmental reorganization) to solve problems, they legitimate wider political structures and draw attention away from the oligarchic quality of pluralism and the need for participatory politics. By defining Keynesianism as the outer bound of economic policy, the parties legitimate modified capitalism. Socialism remains *the* nondecision of American politics and qualitative and nonincremental change is preempted. The parties, and literally every prominent person, venerate the classical liberal freedoms—speech, press, assembly, etc.—at the moment when modernity and America negate private consciousness through indoctrination, and thus, the will to use speech, press, and assembly to promote qualitative change and to develop the categories of a truely critical theory of society. American politicians also legitimate elections and parties by utilizing rhetoric which portrays elections and parties as instruments of significant choice. Oligarchic reality is thus masked and rationalized and the demand for truly participatory forms of choice are negated.

Though commited to Locke, Americans are commited to Locke as cliche. The American commitment to diversity, to variety, to dissent is not deep. Americans, particularly those of lower socioeconomic status, have low levels of tolerance. The weakness of this commitment contributes to the management of tension by fostering a posture of approving passivity among the masses when the state and other interest groups repress variety and dissent. Opposition to major assaults on civil rights —the internment of Japanese Americans during the Second World War, or Senator Joseph McCarthy's assaults—is neither vigorous nor popular. This low level of tolerance also discourages potential dissenters through forewarning. The antiliberal and would be antiliberal comes to know that he may expect serious opposition and little support. The force of majority opinion for conformity, which de Tocqueville noted, further militates against the development of pockets of opposition to the status quo.

America also manages tension and maintains its oligarchic pluralism by permitting or occasionally fostering critiques upon, and escapes from, the system which do not significantly affect the distribution of power. Right wing critiques of the system in the form of psychotic conspiratorial fantasy, intellectual fantasies obviously not rooted in any reality, are tolerated as harmless, if offensive. The view of the John Birch Society that Eisenhower was a leader of the international communist conspiracy is a classic example. The government makes no attempt to repress the Birch Society. These ultraright critiques drain affect away from systemic analysis of the policy and are thus system preserving. Critiques of the system in the form of utopian fiction and fantasy (Edward Bellamy's *Looking Backward* or Charles Reich's *The Greening of America*) are usually system preserving in that their portrait of utopia is customarily fused with liberal perspectives. The means proposed to achieve utopia are either extremely vague and ideological, or they avoid the need for social struggle as a vehicle for change, or they assume that men of power can be convinced through reason and good will to surrender their power.

This again illustrates how difficult it is in America to develop a nonliberal perspective. The history of Americans who struggled with America and then opted for expatriation—for European socialism or facism or corporatism, or for communal living in Vermont—are cases in point. Expatriation has denuded America of some major critics—Pound, Henry Adams, draft resisters in Canada and Sweden, Cleaver, T. S. Eliot. Exile and expatriation is thus system maintaining. The difficulties of escaping the compulsions of American liberalism are so great and the centrifugal force of liberalism in America is so strong, that great leaps into conspiratorial fantasy, or utopia, or Consciousness III or exotic oriental religion are often necessary to break out of the gravitational pull of America's compulsive liberalism.

The compulsions of America's unidimensional liberalism tend to produce critics and crusaders who operate within liberal bounds. Though Progressives and New Dealers occasionally attempted to step beyond the confines of Locke and Smith, they clearly had neither the heart, will, nor theory to do so. American reform is always bounded by liberal perspectives. The tradition of muckraking—from Lincoln Steffens to Ralph Nader—is a classic example.

America never represses muckrakers, it encourages them, listens to their testimony in legislative investigations, is eager to publish their criticism, and provides them with substantial royalties. This, in part, because the muckraker mentality is a liberal mentality. Muckrakers rarely engage in critiques of the system, qua system, or of dominant values, and therefore, they do not propose major redistributions of ownership, of power or profit, or new ways of living. The cost of whatever reforms are incurred, because of their efforts, are customarily passed on to consumers. The psychological and symbolic value of muckraking for business may even be substantial. Muckrakers receive wide publicity while attacking specific evils and specific companies (occasionally an entire industry) but they do not attack the patterns of property ownership. The illusion is thus created that something fundamental and progressive is occurring. Such attacks siphon emotions away from broader critiques, hinder the development of critical theory, and create the belief that when the specific evil is remedied, all will be well. Big business often responds to their critique of specific evil. By so doing, consumers are benefited. The image of the corporation is temporarily tarnished, but it may be restored by better service. Power remains where it was. This is system maintenance.

The system of oligarchic dominance is also maintained and potentially serious tensions are managed, by permitting, or fostering, expressionist political movements—movements like prohibition—the purpose of which is to permit the expression or acting out of deep seated moral sentiments or moral outrage, rather than to influence or alter the distribution of power. The goal of expressionist politics is moral posturing, and such politics does not involve systemic analysis. Expressionism, in fact, usually postulates a revival of nineteenth century liberal attitudes and is, therefore, oriented towards the maintenance of existing power relations or a return to earlier arrangements. Expressionist politics provide much emotional release without threatening existing elites. Nixon and Agnew made a serious attempt to foster expressionism and moralistic posturing by emphasizing the issue of crime in the streets and cultural deviance—drugs, long hair, profanity, etc. Affect channelled into these issues is affect not channelled into poverty, inflation, urban decay, and Vietnam. Responsibility for malfunctions in the polity and economy is also shifted away from political and economic structure to conspiratorial deviants and radicals.

The oligarchic distribution of power is also sustained by focusing attention on very significant issues like conservation, ecology, and pollution, which, like motherhood, everyone must favor, but, which are not perceived by the masses as a consequence of the pervasive American ethic which permits the rape of the environment in the name of the unfettered freedom to earn and consume. Many ecologists do see the problem as stemming from dominant values, but they do not stress this argument for fear of losing the support of moderates. The critique of the corporate system, therefore, is obfuscated by presenting the problem as an unfortunate unintended consequence of modernity which, in part, it is. The system is thus preserved by tracing the roots of the problem as not related to the system itself.

Discord and potential attacks on dominant power are also shunted aside by the distribution of symbolic rewards to dissident groups. One classic example is the appointment of a black to the Supreme Court. Another is the granting of control of federal funds to local black power groups for the promotion of black capitalism which would identify blacks with prevailing values and institutions. Presidential commissions often are symbolic pacifiers, designed to placate groups which have been or may become disaffected. Symbolic goodies, with rare exception, quiet the noisy and leave the distribution of power where it was prior to the noise.

In the dominant America, recourse to political hysteria and democratic repression as a means of maintaining oligarchic pluralism, becomes increasingly less necessary because of the system's ability to absorb cultural deviance and fit almost everything that happens into a bourgeois life style. One can now purchase a new parlor game called "Dirty Water," the subject of which is pollution. Fashionable clothing stores sell the suede fringe of cultural revolution. Bell bottoms, and long hair, and pot are now suburban phenomena. The prime polluters, if one were to believe their ads, are striving night and day to alleviate pollution. Blacks appear in ads—but they sell the same plastic junk and automobiles that whites sell. Black capitalism is touted and if it succeeds, "Black liberation" will come to mean that a few blacks will join in and help to perpetuate oligarchic control. Universities admit a few students and faculty to governing boards, not enough to alter the structure of power, but enough to create the illusion of change. The cultural revolutionaries, like those they claim to despise, are master consumers —stereo sets, records, granny glasses, pot, second hand fur coats, motorcycles, bandanas, guitars, drums, prefaded dungarees, sandals. America will produce what they want, because the market is there. They will become identified with America, like others, through consumerism. They have already become rigidly conformist to their own peers, and they are in the process of privitising their lives, withdrawing, and thus depoliticising the alleged cultural revolution—replicating, in some important ways, the privitization and political apathy of middle class life.

The ability of America to coopt deviance and contain qualitative change is impressive. The ability of America to maintain ancient liberal values and ancient political institutions while preserving its structures of power, with only peripheral adjustment, is very impressive. America has managed to resist fundamental changes in values and political structures, and it has never been confronted with the challenge of a mass political movement that demanded basic alterations in the distribution of power.

The major problem of American politics may well be whether capitalism and the traditional techniques of tension management will continue to work for existing oligarchies as the velocity of history and technological development, along with population, greatly accelerate producing unintended consequences and instabilities of substantial magnitude. Perhaps no one really knows, but literally every serious economist, historian, sociologist, and political scientist predicts that America will undergo severe stresses in the next three or four decades. Social scientists also agree that America will have to show great flexibility and innovativeness to meet these strains. There is a sense in which America has been wonderfully flexible under conditions of great stress. We have met every stress except the Civil War without resort to revolution. And we have managed to produce an incremental critical realignment of parties and policy—a realignment within the bounds of liberalism—at those moments when the economy of polity was in serious trouble. Though no realignment dismantled dominant oligarchies or eliminated widespread poverty, or racism, or introduced a truly participatory politics, or resolved crises in housing or health care, or introduced anything approaching fraternity and sorority, or eliminated bullying in foreign policy, realignments slowly introduced bits and pieces of very modest equity for organized labor and peripheral groups.

America, in its most important aspects, is essentially changeless. Its liberalism is immobile. America has resisted altering fundamental values and political institutions. American political institutions remain Tudor in character, much as they were in the eighteenth century and American values are liberal now, as they were, at the founding of the Republic. The immobility and unanimity of American liberalism is very impressive.

The liberal tradition may be running out of the time and space it needs to survive. The irrelevance and dysfunctionality of Locke and Smith are slowly becoming apparent. The need for planning is very slowly becoming apparent. The baneful effects of an acquisitive possessive individualism are slowly becoming more obvious—the destructive effect on man's nature, the anarchic effects on the economy, private affluence and public squalor.

But this ethic and liberal tradition in America is the American consciousness and consensus, and its sustaining power is great. The stresses of the next three or four decades—like those of the past—may lead to another critical alignment—a grand New Deal.

The most probable short-term American future may well be a substantially more liberal version of the recent past. The economy will probably become more regulated. The unfettered right to earn could be further curbed. Welfare systems will become more extensive. Income taxes will rise. A guaranteed annual wage, an expanded Social Security system, and a national medical insurance program are likely. Industries that are vital to the well being of the economy, but unable to sustain themselves—like railroads—are being nationalized. Much of the defense industry actually belongs to the government. Substantially greater federal regulations of the securities market will probably be enacted, and a variety of programs providing for opportunities for small business men will be sponsored. Programs for Black and Puerto Rican capitalism will be developed. They should pass the Congress and with much less opposition than might be expected because the velocity of technological and social change will be so great, the unintended consequences and uncertainties of life so compelling, that dominant elites will be forced to resort to these programs to stabilize the economy, to manage increased tension, and maintain their power. The great corporations cannot tolerate high degrees of uncertainty because the products they now produce are so complex and the inputs so numerous that years are necessary to plan production and train consumers. Such plans can only be made on the basis of relatively predictable futures.

I agree with Herbert Marcuse's view that dominant elites will be sophisticated enough to perceive the system maintaining potentials of a grand New Deal. Marcuse writes:

Under these circumstances, the prospects for a streamlined containment of the centrifugal tendencies depend primarily on the ability of the vested interests to adjust themselves and their economy to the requirements of the Welfare State. Vastly increased government spending and direction, planning on a national and international scope, an enlarged foreign aid program, comprehensive social security, public works on a grand scale, perhaps even partial nationalization belong to these requirements. I believe that the dominant interests will gradually and hesitantly accept these requirements and entrust their prerogatives to a more effective power.[3]

Ultra New Dealish programs probably will be America's response to destabilization and stress in the future, as their miniversions were in the past. A grand New Deal, however, will depart only incrementally from Locke and Smith. This realignment will invoke the classic bourgeoisie and reformist ideal of extending economic opportunity to the small man without attacking the economic and political structures that are largely responsible for inequality. The poor probably will, in large part, be slowly lifted into the fringes of the lower middle class. The lower middle class will receive aid and succor in the name of opportunity, not in the name of welfare, and its lot will be improved. The middle classes will become larger and more affluent.

The expanding affluence that will result from more liberal reform and controls, and from technological development, will evoke more demands for more liberal reform. If the Republicans do not comply—and the evidence suggests that they are already beginning to—the Democrats certainly will. Their successes will

temporarily curb the long term trend towards the disaggrega-
tion of party and the growth of independent voters—as did the
first New Deal. The Democratic Party could regain solid control.
What amounts to the first critical alignment since 1932 could
occur as the Republicans suffer Goldwaterian losses. The Southern strategy will be regarded as an anachronism so irrational—in
retrospect—that it will be difficult to understand how professional politicians could have believed it.

The ability of a grand New Deal to accomplish its liberal
and limited objectives may be enhanced by similar developments
in other advanced nations. The containment of qualitative
social change that is the quintessence of advanced nations,
along with the maintanance of existing oligarchies and forms of
dominance, characterize Russian and Chinese societies as well
as American. To contain qualitative change they must also
provide the comforts they define as necessary and this could
lead them to conclude that trade with America and peace are
essential. A rapprochement with America could enhance the
ability of all three great powers to maintain their systems of
power.

America will again be praised. The theme that the system
works will be repeated and exaggerated in a thousand variations
by almost everyone. From the vantage point and values of those
few in America whose decisions affect the many, the system will
work.

However, elites will continue to play decisive roles. They will
continue to merge and consolidate as they have for two decades.
The technological revolution will reap great riches upon America
and reconcentrate wealth. It will endow the rich with bounty
and the poor with increases in the minimum wage. But America
will continue to produce as much plastic junk, and automobiles,
and as many instruments of death, as it can sell at a profit. That
very American counterpoint between private affluence and public
squalor will continue, through the squalor will be mitigated.

America will probably produce more public housing and other facilities, but substantially less than the need warrants and substantially less than would be produced by a society willing to sacrifice for its poor. That is because the aggregate of privatized selfishness and invidiousness that is a big part of America will not sacrifice to the degree necessary. A nation that is not a nation—not a community of citizens with fraternity, but an aggregate of private and competitive persons—will not place communal need at the pinnacle of its priorities. The right to earn will remain a prime right. The allocation of most scarce resources will remain tied to profit rather than social need. Profits, however, could be so great that some important social needs will be met. The intrusiveness of society, however, will permit vested interests to more efficiently shape the needs and priorities of consumers. The comforts of the advanced welfare state will heighten the identification of the consumer with America. Private consciousness—the source of potential opposition to society—will be further whittled away. The urge to transcend and develop new forms of living and participatory politics will be negated. The bourgeois life will be increasingly identified as the good life. The pacification of the masses will be the consequence of a rising standard of living. The long term and compulsive identification with the Americanist ethos will thus be strengthened and the rationality of protest will be weakened.

This America will appeal to millions. The forms of democracy will be preserved and extended in this America just as they were preserved during the first two decades of this century while corporate oligarchies successfully penetrated the leadership cadres of both parties. We are now granting the right to vote to eighteen year olds. The classical freedoms of speech and press and assembly will be preserved though the masses will be more indoctrinated and more identified with the dominant America. More Blacks and Puerto Ricans will be registered. But the cost of campaigning, like other costs, will continue to mount. And the electorate will continue to be presented with alternate choices within the framework of oligarchic pluralism.

A society based on the ethic of privatized selfishness and competition, regardless of how extensive is its welfare provision, must produce inequality, avariciousness, and administered intrusion. It cannot be a true nation—a *communitas*. The true failure of such a state will not be its inequality or its poverty, but its failure to produce men who care about each other and who can cooperate. Such a society cannot generate widespread fraternity and it cannot permit the fulfillment of human potentialities beyond those bounded by the market place.

Adlai Stevenson once described America as a "chaotic, selfish, indifferent commercial society" dominated by the "purposelessness tyranny of a confused and aimless way of life." Were he alive twenty or thirty years hence he probably would be able to say it again—despite the second New Deal. For despite its economic success, the United States will remain a manipulative society which differentially benefits vested interests, perpetuates planned obsolescence, enormous waste, stupefying work, and alienated labor. Despite its economic successes it will continue to foster invidiousness and competitiveness and continue to frustrate the potentiality of needs and the capacities of man beyond those which are socially determined. It will continue to richly reward the men who manage money and it will continue not to relate reward to social service—for social service is not one of its prime priorities.

But the comforts of the future welfare state and the ability of vested interests to indoctrinate and shape the needs and instincts of people is likely to hide those repressions and unfreedoms from all but a few—at least for the near future. The question is, how long can they remain hidden, and how will American elites react when the ideology and institutions that sustain their power are exposed? This could depend on the continued economic success of the system and the depth of the rejection of America by its young. At the present moment, little is known about either.

LOCKE AND LIBERATION

The depth and size of the cultural revolution in America remains a very debatable question. No one really knows the degree to which the socialization process has been altered. No one really knows how deep is the disaffection of American youth with fundamental American values, indeed, with the entire American way of life. Some argue that a genuine counter-culture has developed and that America is truly and irreconcilably divided. Others, myself included, believe that the 1960's will, in retrospect, appear to have been a short-term turbulence —a temporary resistance, a Luddism of Youth and the left— which did not stem the triumph of a technological, intrusive liberal welfare state capable of containing qualitative change.

But the 1960's may be a portent of the post-Second New Deal future. At least it raises some important questions about how American liberalism may deal with qualitatively new demands sponsored by the previously unorganized. The accelerating velocity of history and the increasing strains which are being placed on the American system are not solely the consequences of technological change but of new political mobilizations seeking qualitative new demands, new life-styles, and new power arrangements. Youth, blacks, the poor, students, teachers, women, welfare recipients, homosexuals, those opposed to the war, and migrant workers coalesced and organized in the sixties. This is what threatened pluralist balances, appeared to threaten liberal values, and intensified conflict. The pseudopluralism that sustains oligarchic control depends upon the dispossessed and disgruntled remaining passive, not organizing, and not raising the ante for what passes for social harmony and representative government. Pluralism, in the 1960's began to seriously operate as the disorganized began to organize into pluralist combinations. This more viable and meaningful pluralism is what pluralists and oligarchs found so disturbing.

The conflict appeared to be particularly sharp and was difficult for politicians to deal with because some of these coalitions sought goals other than economic advantage. The issues raised were more profound and disturbing—the liberation of women, the rights of students, sexual freedom, the harshness of the Protestant ethic, the meaninglessness of affluence, indeed, the meaning of freedom and life itself. The issue, oddly enough was political in the most antique and elemental sense—the meaning of human relationships, of justice, and the definition of the good life. Having discovered the answers to these ancient questions in the form of self-evident truth in the eighteenth century and Algerized them in the nineteenth, America foreclosed a discussion of these problems. A variegated pluralism that not only reopens the discussion but rejects traditional answers can be very threatening to the American people who root their identity in the traditional verities, and it can be threatening to American elites whose power and privilege is rooted in institutions based on those verities.

The discussion and the conflict that ensues from it may be temporarily foreclosed but I do not think it is over—despite the likelihood that an expanded welfare state will contain qualitative change and strengthen the identification with America for some time to come. The discussion of fundamentals tends to be raised more frequently as social change accelerates, as traditional ways evaporate, and as people become more disoriented. Of course, the militant defense of ancient ways and values, as a counter to disorientation, is also a natural response. There is a sense in which the American future may be a race between two opposing forces: the cooptive capacity of the welfare state and the deepening of the cultural revolution; and the effort to break out of America's one-dimensional liberalism.

The serious confrontation probably will not occur unless and until the grand New Deal exhausts itself and cannot cope with the growing stress and conflict of American life.

If liberalism becomes increasingly dysfunctional—even in its modified form—some future generation might discover and then reject America. The discovery will be made that America is unique in world politics—the triumph of a unanimous and comprehensive liberalism unchallenged by conservatism and radicalism. The discovery will be made that liberalism has largely become a cliched and dogmatic and restrictive national faith from which the humanist thrust has been drained. The discovery will be made that the liberal compulsion benefits American elites much more than the American people. The oligarchic character of pluralism will be discovered. The discovery will be made that liberals attack the edges of inequality but not the structure that produces it. This will lead to the discovery that the Rockefellers and Muskies and Kennedys of the future are of a piece, and that political choice and change is always marginal, and always preserves the fundamental divisions of power. The discovery will be made that America has no political philosophy—merely Locke and Smith as cliche. The discovery will be made that modern society is enormously intrusive and that vested interests do shape the needs and very instincts of the people—to the advantage of vested interests. The discovery will be made that freedom and traditional liberties are less meaningful, as indoctrination becomes more efficient and complete. These discoveries would amount to an explosion of self-consciousness, and self-consciousness—consciousness of servitude —could be a step towards liberation.

These discoveries may be made even if the welfare state continues to dispense traditional comfort for decades, because America inevitably will increase its contacts with alien cultures and Third World revolutions. These contacts could speed and sharpen the discovery of America by making it possible to compare and contrast the unanimity of America's liberalism with cultures that are not so possessed. America has entered the world—the alien world—that is not mesmerized by the American version of self-evident truth. The sight of European, African, and Asian change and variety may hasten the discovery of America's liberal immobility, which is America's constraint. The discovery of constraint may excite the aspiration for variety and lead to the rediscovery of political philosophy and ultimately to alternative ways of organizing the polity and the economy.

The transcendent temper may be nourished by other explosions of self-consciousness. The discovery may be made that the repression of America is not the customary kind—jailings, convictions for political activities, political murders, systematic witch hunting, and organized elimination of dissent. The discovery may be made that America's repression is more pervasive and subtle. If the sophisticated perceive repression as the manner and degree to which a society closes and limits the life space, thought space, value space, options and possibilities of its citizens, then compulsive liberal Americanism may be seen as repressive. The degree to which this compulsion commits America to one and only one set of political and economic values and life-styles will be defined as its constraint.

The philosophers of the age of American discovery define one aspect of repression as the absence of free will and a deeper aspect as the lack of consciousness of the absence of free will. They will come to see the fullness of America's philosophic tyranny. Its unidimensionality is imposed without the presence of alternate choices, without the knowledge that such imposition is restrictive, and with the conviction that what is imposed, is freely chosen. The nonchoice, perceived as choice, is even perceived as self-evident truth. When the intrusion of political culture on consciousness is profound, voluntarily entered into, and lovingly embraced, the victims of the culture see themselves as free men.

The discovery that what one always thought was freedom, is, in fact, a limit upon freedom, can be politically explosive.

The discovery of American intrusiveness and unidimensionality is only the first step toward liberation. The demand for private mental space must grow, and efforts to escape the intrusion must grow, and this requires what Marcuse calls "the great refusal"—saying "no" and refusing to listen. But saying "no" is not enough. One must develop and utilize the categories of critical thought to define all those potentials for freedom that are frustrated and to delineate the limited use of traditional freedom within the context of indoctrination. One must point out, for example, that every political choice offered by the electoral system—no matter how much it may improve the lot of the less fortunate—and some choices do—nourishes and sustains a wider network of power that produces inequality and frustrates human potentials. All the capacities of man that lead to a wider fraternity and a lessening of alienation, which are frustrated by society, must constantly be put forward as ideals. New institutional and sexual arrangements—in great variety—must constantly be counterpoised to present arrangements—communes, cooperatives, collectives, local control of schools, and participatory decision-making. A plea must be made for human arrangements that permit each man and woman to find his unique way.

But this is not enough. If much of the dominance, nonfreedom, and waste of the present stems from private control over the means of production, and the absence of planning and the presence of cruel and blind national priorities, then humane socialist alternatives must be constantly posed. It is not enough to understand the roots of one's nonfreedom. It is not enough to understand the limits and cruelities of liberalism—all the missed opportunities. The alternative of a humane and decentralized and participatory socialism must be offered. And there are now no existing political systems that could serve as a model.

That we have amassed the mightiest productive apparatus in the history of the world and yet are what we are, and have only the faintest idea of what we might become—this is our sadness. But cries of socialism, in America, evoke cries of treason.

In the sixties, large numbers of Americans raised questions. Many were full of doubt about America. But the overwhelming majority felt that something was very wrong. They were frightened, disquieted, and angry. They did not like to hear the questions which might have led to a reshaping of their America. The ultimate stress in a man's emotional life occurs when he is forced to renounce a truly significant and old relationship—a relationship which largely makes him what he is. But those who discover America in the future will ask America to renounce Locke as cliche and capitalism. Resistance to renunciation and separation is always profound. It evokes anxiety and loneliness, and people try to protect themselves from these pains. It will not be easy for us to renounce what we have so strongly identified with and what has become the tenacious American nationalism.

If the discovery of America continues and the yearning for transcendence does not die still-born, but grows, "un-Americanism" could become *the* issue of American life. And then elites, in trouble, would be very tempted to excite the fierce and regressive commitment of the masses to the old America. A man committed to his bondage, perceiving it to be the essence of a self-evident truth, will not take kindly to those who seek to liberate him.

NOTES

Chapter 1

1. Fred R. Marvin, "Are These Your Friends?" Pamphlet (The Americanization Press Service, 1922), p. 3.

2. Rev. M. D. Shutter, D.D., "Some Recent Developments in Socialism," reprinted from *The Minneapolis Tribune* by The Women's Association, 1921, p. 6.

3. Woodworth Clum, "America Is Calling," Pamphlet, 7th edition, (Los Angeles: The Better America Federation of California, 1922), p. 1.

4. William Hornaday, "The Lying Lure of Bolshevism," Pamphlet (American Defense Society, 1919), p. 4.

5. Arthur Dunn, "The 'Reds' in America; From The Standpoint of The Department of Justice," *The Review of Reviews*, 61, no. 2 (February 1920): 161.

6. Quoted in *The Literary Digest*, 60 (November 22, 1919): 15.

7. Charles Parkhurst, "The Leper in the House," Pamphlet (National Security League, 1920).

8. Ralph Easley, "Bolshevism—What Is It? What Is the Extent of Its Menace to This Country? How Can It Be Dealt with?" Statement to the Executive Council, The National Civic Federation (July 27, 1923), p. 1.

9. Clayton Lusk. "Radicalism under Inquiry," *The American Review*, 61 (February 1919): 167.

10. *The Literary Digest*, "Rooting Out The Reds," 60 (November 1919): 15.

11. "Behind The Veil," The Better America Federation of California, Pamphlet (Los Angeles, ca. 1920), p. 2.

12. *Ibid.*, p. 2.

13. When Nicholas Romanoff, Czar of Russia, was dethroned, the archives of the government were seized by Kerensky. The letters and documents which had passed between the late Kaiser Wilhelm Hohenzollern of Germany and the Czarina of Russia, were discovered, which proved the Czar of being guilty of an intrigue to corrupt Russia. While the Brest-Litovsk peace was being made between Germany and Soviet Russia, spies employed by the aristocracy of Russia secured letters that

showed the large sums of money which Lenin and Trotzky had received from Germany as her paid agents. Later, when the Kaiser fled Holland, further proof of the great conspiracy was unearthed in the German archives. William Hornaday, "The Lying Lure of Bolshevism," Pamphlet (American Defense Society, November 1919), p. 8.

14. Royal A. Baker, *The Menace of Bolshevism* (Detroit: Liberty Bell Publishers, 1919), pp. 12, 20.

15. *National Civic Federation Review,* "Serious Conditions and Need of Proposed Work Discussed at Conference," 5, no. 2 (April 1, 1920): 19.

16. Quoted in *The Literary Digest,* 60 (June 14, 1919), p. 11.

17. Arthur Dunn, "The 'Reds' in America . . ."

18. *The Literary Digest,* "Rooting Out The Reds," 60 (November 22, 1919): 16.

19. Address by Charles Patterson, "Red and Radicals in America," (New York City: The Lawyers Club, January 10, 1920), p. 9.

20. "Behind the Veil," p. 7.

21. Ole Hanson, *Americanism Versus Bolshevism* (New York: Doubleday, Page and Co., 1920), pp. 283–284.

22. American Constitutional League of Wisconsin, "Looking Straight At Socialism," 1920, p. 2 (Library of Congress Pamphlets on Socialism, Communism, Bolshevism, Microfilm Shelf 21396 vol. 7).

23. William Hornaday, "The Lying Lure Of Bolshevism," p. 11.

24. Fred R. Marvin, "Are These Your Friends?" p. 11.

25. Clayton Lusk, "Radicalism Under Inquiry," p. 172.

26. W. J. Ghent, "Bolshevism In The United States," *National Civic Federation* Review, 4, no. 14 (May 15, 1919): 16.

27. Ralph Easley, "Bolshevism, What is it . . . ," p. 10.

28. William Hornaday, "The Lying Lure of Bolshevism," p. 10.

29. Royal A. Baker, "The Menace of Bolshevism," pp. 28–29.

30. George B. Lockwood, "Radicalism—Menace or Myth?" *The National Republic* (no date).

31. William Hornaday, *Awake America* (New York: Moffat, Yard and Co., 1918) p. 83.

32. *Ibid.,* pp. 106–107.

33. National Civic Foundation, Untitled pamphlet, 1919.

34. Ole Hanson, *Americanism Versus Bolshevism,* p. 238.

35. Joseph Cashman, "America Asleep: The Menace of Radicalism," Pamphlet, The National Security League (February 1923), p. 6.

36. *Ibid.,* p. 13.

37. National Civic Federation, Untitled pamphlet, 1919.

38. "Questions For Every Good American To Consider," Author and Source Unknown, date about 1919, Collection of the Library of Congress, Microfilm Shelf 23196.

39. George B. Lockwood, "Red Radicalism—Menace or Myth?" p. 3.

40. Rome G. Brown, "Americanism vs. Socialism," Address delivered

before the Middlesex Massachusetts Bar Association, 1919. Library of Congress Microfilm Shelf 21396, p. 1.

41. American Constitutional League of Wisconsin, "Looking Straight at Socialism," p. 3.

42. *Ibid.*, p. 4.

43. George C. Cartwright, "The World's Greatest Blunder," Address delivered before the convention of the National Association of Sheet Metal Contractors, 1921, p. 14.

44. Mitchell Palmer, U.S. Attorney General, telegram to *The Literary Digest. The Literary Digest*, "Extent of Bolshevik Infection Here" 64 (January 17, 1920): 13.

45. Otto H. Kahn, "Labor and the Golden Rule," *National Civic Federation Review* 4, no. 14 (May 15, 1919): 4.

46. Martin J. Wade, Judge, U.S. District Court, Southern District of Iowa, 1919 (opinion). (Davenport, Iowa: Scott County Council of National Defense.)

47. National Civic Federation Review, (no author cited) "Plan To Create National Service Committees," 5, no. 4 (July 10, 1920): 6.

48. George W. Cartwright, "The World's Greatest Blunder," p. 18.

49. Nicholas Murray Butler, President, Columbia University. "Is America Worth Saving?" *National Civic Federation Review* 4, no. 14 (May 15, 1919): 15.

50. Ralph Easley, "Bolshevism," p. 8.

51. *National Civic Federation Review* 5, no. 5 (September 25, 1920): 3.

52. William Libbey, "Report of the Committee Appointed to Draft a Protest Against Red Propaganda in this Country" (New Jersey: Council of the Society of Colonial Wars, June 2, 1923), p. 2.

53. (Addendum to point 5) quoted in *Literary Digest* 64 (January 17, 1920): 14.

54. William Hornaday, "The Lying Lure Of Bolshevism," p. 28.

55. *Ibid.*, p. 25.

56. Rome G. Brown, "Americanism vs. Socialism," p. 26.

57. Ole Hanson, *Americanism Versus Bolshevism*, p. 298.

58. H. C. Block, "The Enemy Within Our Gates" (Washington, D.C.: National Association for Constitutional Government, 1919), p. 23.

Chapter 2

1. Stanley Coben, A. *Mitchell Palmer* (New York: Columbia University Press, 1963), p. 204.

2. *Life*, 84 (October 9, 1919): 630.

3. Robert Murray, *Red Scare: A Study of National Hysteria 1919–1920* (New York: McGraw Hill, 1964), pp. 126–129.

4. *The New York Times*, September 12, 1919.

5. The Commission of Inquiry: The Interchurch World Movement, *The Report on the Steel Strike of 1919* (New York: Harcourt, Brace and Howe, 1920), p. 29.

6. *Ibid.*, p. 225.

7. Murray, *Red Scare*, p. 145.

8. *Ibid.*, p. 202.

9. *Ibid.*, p. 208.

10. *Ibid.*, p. 215.

11. National Popular Government League, *Report Upon the Illegal Practices of the United States Department of Justice* (Wash. D.C., 1920), p. 11.

12. *Ibid.*, p. 13.

13. *Ibid.*, p. 39.

14. *Literary Digest*, 64 (Jan. 17, 1920): 13.

15. Murray, *Red Scare*, p. 232.

16. Paul Murphy, "Sources and Nature of Intolerance in the 1920s," *The Journal of American History*, 51 (January 1964): 65.

17. Murray, *Red Scare*, p. 90.

18. Norman Hapgood, *Professional Patriots* (New York: Albert and Charles Boni, 1927), pp. 55.

19. Murray, *Red Scare*, p. 97.

20. *Ibid.*, p. 178.

21. *Ibid.*, p. 252.

22. John Higham, *Strangers in the Land: Patterns of American Nativism* (New York: Atheneum, 1968), p. 232.

23. *The New York Times*, Feb. 1, 1920.

Chapter 3

1. Stanley Coben, A. *Mitchell Palmer* (New York: Columbia University Press, 1963), p. 208.

2. George Creel, *How We Advertised America* (New York: Harper and Brothers, 1920), p. 5.

3. John Higham, *Strangers in the Land: Patterns of American Nativism* (New York: Atheneum, 1968), p. 223.

4. Edward Shils, *The Torment of Secrecy* (Glencoe: The Free Press, 1956), p. 78.

5. Investigation of the Activities of the Department of Justice, 6 Congress I Sess. Senate Document 153.

6. Max Lowenthal, *The Federal Bureau of Investigation* (New York: William Sloane Associates, 1950), p. 88.

7. William Preston, *Aliens and Dissenters* (New York: Harper and Row, 1966), p. 120.

8. Robert Murray, *Red Scare: A Study of National Hysteria* 1919–1920 (New York: McGraw Hill, 1964), p. 5.

9. Mark Sullivan, *Colliers*, 64 (August 3, 1919): 8.

10. Frederick Lewis Allen, *Only Yesterday* (New York: Perennial Library, Harper and Row, 1964), p. 4.

11. Franz Newmann, "Anxiety and Politics" in Franz Newmann, *The Democratic and Authoritarian State* (Glencoe: The Free Press, 1957), p. 279.

12. U.S. Senate, Committee on Education and Labor, Report, Investigation of Strike in Steel Industry, 66 Congress, I Sess., 1919, p. 14.

13. *The New York Times*, April 25, 1920.

14. Lusk Committee, *Revolutionary Radicalism: Its History, Purpose and Tactics*, Report of the Joint Committee Investigating Seditious Activities; The Senate of the State of New York, (Albany: J.B. Lyon and Co., 1920).

15. Lusk Committee, 2, pp. 2004–2006.

16. *Ibid.*, 1, pp. 501–502.

17. See Richard Hofstadter, *The Paranoid Style in American Politics* (New York: Vintage Books, 1967), p. 36.

18. Lusk Committee, 2, p. 44.

19. *The New York Times*, September 12, 1919.

20. *Literary Digest*, 42, September 20, 1919.

21. Murray, *Red Scare*, p. 65.

22. *The New York Times*, February 9, 1919.

23. *Ibid.*

24. *Literary Digest*, 63, (October 18, 1919).

25. quoted in Murray, *Red Scare*, p. 139.

26. quoted in Murray, *Red Scare*, p. 140.

27. *Boston Evening Transcript*, October 28, 1919.

28. *Literary Digest*, 63 (March 8, 1919).

29. *The New York Times*, May 1, 1919.

30. Murray, *Red Scare*, p. 142.

31. *Ibid.*, p. 146.

32. *Ibid.*, p. 77.

33. *The Washington Post*, January 4, 1920.

34. *Literary Digest*, 64 (October 2, 1920).

35. *Report on the Steel Strike of 1919*, p. 242.

Chapter 4

1. *Saturday Evening Post*, 112 (March 1, 1919.)

2. *The Washington Post*, February 16, 1919.

3. *Congressional Record, 66th Congress*, I Sess., October 14, 1919, pp. 68–69.

4. Leo Lowenthal and Norbert Guterman, *Prophets of Deceit* (New York: Harper and Brothers, 1950), p. 36.

5. *Ibid.*, p. 37.

6. George Simmel, *The Sociology of George Simmel* (Glencoe: The Free Press, 1950), p. 334.

7. *Ibid.*, p. 330.

8. Edward Shils, *The Torment of Secrecy* (Glencoe: The Free Press, 1956), p. 34.

9. Simmel, *Sociology*, p. 331.

10. Ole Hanson, *Americanism Versus Bolshevism* (New York: Doubleday, Page and Co., 1920), p. 284.

11. Royal A. Baker, *The Menace of Bolshevism* (Detroit: Liberty Bell Publishers, 1919), p. 29.

12. Hanson, *Americanism*, p. 284.

13. Robert Lane, *Political Ideology* (New York: The Free Press, 1967), pp. 126–127.

14. Richard Hofstadter, *The Paranoid Style in American Politics* (New York: Vintage Books, 1964), p. 34.

15. *Ibid.*, p. 9.

16. Lowenthal and Guterman, *Prophets*, p. 55.

17. William T. Hornaday, *Awake America* (New York: Moffat, Yard, and Co., 1918), pp. 141–142.

18. Herbert Marcuse, *An Essay on Liberation* (Boston: Beacon Press, 1969), p. 75.

19. Franz Neumann, "Anxiety and Politics," in Franz Neumann, *The Democratic and Authoritarian State* (Glencoe: The Free Press, 1957), p. 279.

20. Murray Edelman, "Myths, Metaphors, and Political Conformity," *Psychiatry: Journal for the Study of Interpersonal Process*, 30 (August, 1967): 224.

21. Peter Collins, "Bolshevism in America," *Current Opinion*, 68 (March 1920), p. 327.

22. Leonard Berkowitz, *Some Implications of Laboratory Studies of Frustration and Aggression for the Study of Political Violence* paper delivered at the 1967 Annual Meeting of the American Political Science Association, Chicago, September 5–9, p. 7.

23. Edelman, "Myths," p. 217.

24. Murray Edelman, *Public Policy and Political Violence*, University of Wisconsin Institute for Research on Poverty, mimeo, 1968, p. 37.

25. Rome G. Brown, "Americanism vs. Socialism," address delivered before the Middlesex (Massachusetts) Bar Association, 1919. p. 1. (Library of Congress, Microfilm Shelf 21396).

26. For hundreds of formulations of this kind, see the collection of superpatriotic pamphlets in the Library of Congress: Microfilm Shelf 21396.

27. Gordon Alport, *The Nature of Prejudice* (Garden City: Doubleday, 1958), p. 406.

28. Stanley Coben, "A Study in Nativism: The American Red Scare of 1919–1920," *Political Science Quarterly*, 79 (March 1964): 54–55.

29. Edelman, "Myths," p. 225.

30. Theodore Lowi, "The Wheel of Panic," *The Nation*, 208 (May 19, 1969): 625.

Chapter 5

1. For an interesting treatment of extremism in America, see Seymour Martin Lipset, *The Politics of Unreason* (New York: Harper and Row, 1971).

2. The Commission of Inquiry: The Interchurch World Movement, *The Report on the Steel Strike of 1919* (New York: Harcourt, Brace and Howe, 1920), p. 29.

3. Sidney Howard, *The Labor Spy* (New York: Republic, 1924), p. 91.

4. *Report on the Steel Strike of 1919*, p. 229.

5. Paul Murphy, "Sources and Nature of Intolerance in the 1920s," *The Journal of American History*, 51 (January 1964): 17.

6. Philip Graham, Jr., *The Origins of Hysteria: Certain Aspects of The Red Scare of 1919*. Undergraduate Honors thesis, Department of History, Harvard College, 1964, p. 31.

7. Foster Rhea Dulles, *The Road to Teheran: The Story of Russia and America* (Princeton: Princeton University Press, 1945), p. 154.

8. Murphy, "Sources," p. 66.

9. Robert Murray, *Red Scare: A Study of National Hysteria 1919–1920* (New York: McGraw Hill, 1964), p. 67.

10. National Popular Government League, Report Upon the Illegal Practices of the United States Department of Justice (Wash. D.C., 1920), p. 52.

11. Louis Post, *The Deportations Delirium of Nineteen Twenty* (Chicago: Charles H. Kerr and Co., 1923), p. 80.

12. *Ibid.*, p. 82.

13. *Report, Investigation of Strike in Steel Industry*, 66 Congress, 1st session, op. cit., p. 911.

14. Sidney Howard, *The New Republic*, (September 10, 1924): 10.

15. *Report Upon the Illegal Practices of the United States Department of Justice, op. cit.*, pp. 64–66.

16. U.S. Senate, Committee on Education and Labor, Report, Investigation of Strike in Steel Industry, 66 Congress, I Sess., 1919, p. 167.

17. Congressional Record, 65th Congress, 3rd session LVII, 5, p. 6865.

18. Lowenthal, p. 76.

19. *Ibid.*, p. 83.

20. R. M. Whitney, "The Reds in America," in Hapgood, pp. 69–70.

21. *Ibid.*, p. 70.

22. *Ibid.*, pp. 73–74.

23. *Ibid.*, pp. 83–84.

24. *Ibid.*, p. 84.

25. *Ibid.*, p. 26.

26. *Ibid.*, p. 100.

27. *Ibid.*, p. 101.

28. *Ibid.*, p. 119.

29. For a brilliant exposition of the uses of random terror as the basis of authority and legitimacy, see E. Victor Walter, *Terror and Resistance* (New York: Oxford University Press, 1970).

30. Zachariah Chaffee, Jr., *Free Speech in the United States* (New York: Atheneum, 1969), p. 214.

31. Gabriel Kolko, *The Roots of American Foreign Policy* (Boston: Beacon Press, 1969), p. 8.

32. For a discriminating treatment of pluralism and mass politics as it relates to McCarthyism see: Michael Paul Rogin, *The Intellectuals and McCarthy* (Cambridge: The Massachusetts Institute of Technology Press, 1967).

Chapter 6

1. Louis Hartz, *The Liberal Tradition in America* (New York: Harcourt Brace, 1956).

2. *Ibid.*, p. 300.

3. Erik Erikson, *Childhood and Society* (New York: W. W. Norton, 1963), p. 285.

4. Alexis de Tocqueville, *Democracy in America*, ed. Philips Bradley (New York: Alfred A. Knopf, 1948), Vol. 2, p. 99.

5. *Ibid.*, p. 10.

6. George Pierson, *Tocqueville and Beaumont in America* (New York: Oxford University Press, 1938), pp. 236–237.

7. Marvin Meyers, *The Jacksonian Persuasion* (Stanford: Stanford University Press, 1957), p. 40.

8. Tocqueville, *Democracy*, Vol. 2, pp. 129–130.

9. *Ibid.*, Vol. 1, p. 294.

10. *Ibid.*, Vol. 2, pp. 138–139.

11. *Ibid.*, Vol. 2, p. 136.

12. *Ibid.*, Vol. 2, pp. 136–137.

13. Erikson, *Childhood*, pp. 285–286.

14. Tocqueville, *Democracy*, Vol. 2, p. 255.

15. *Ibid.*, Vol. 2, p. 257.

16. Hartz, *Liberal Tradition*, p. 3.

17. *Ibid.*, p. 6.

18. *Ibid.*, p. 9.

19. *Ibid.*, p. 19.

20. Louis Hartz, *The Founding of New Societies* (New York: Harcourt, Brace and World, Inc., 1964), p. 5.

21. *Ibid.*, p. 6.

22. *Ibid.*, p. 19.

23. Tocqueville, *Democracy*, Vol. 1, p. 290; Vol. 1, p. 13.

24. Hartz, *Liberal Tradition*, p. 285.

Chapter 7

1. Herbert Marcuse, *One Dimensional Man* (Boston: Beacon Press, 1964), p. xv.

2. *Ibid.*, p. xii.

3. *Ibid.*, p. 38.

BIBLIOGRAPHY

BOOKS

Allen, Frederick Lewis, *Only Yesterday. An Informal History of the 1920's* (New York: Harper and Row, 1964).

Allport, Gordon, *The Nature of Prejudice*, (Garden City: Doubleday, 1958).

Chaffee, Zachariah Jr., *Free Speech In The United States*, (New York: Atheneum, 1969).

Coben, Stanley, *A. Mitchell Palmer*, (New York: Columbia University Press, 1963).

Commission of Inquiry of the Interchurch World Movement: Report on the Steel Strike of 1919, (New York: Harcourt, Brace and Howe, 1920).

Creel, George, *How We Advertised America*, (New York: Harper and Brothers, 1920).

Dulles, Foster Rhea, *The Road to Teheran; The Story of Russia and America*, (Princeton: Princeton University Press, 1945).

Erikson, Erik, *Childhood and Society*, Second ed. (New York: W. W. Norton, 1963).

Graham, Philip Jr., *The Origins of Hysteria: Certain Aspects of the Red Scare of 1919*, Undergraduate Honors Thesis, Department of History, Harvard College, 1964.

Hanson, Ole, *Americanism versus Bolshevism*, (New York: Doubleday, Page and Company, 1920).

Hapgood, Norman, *Professional Patriots*, (New York: Albert and Charles Boni, 1927).

Hartz, Louis, *The Founding of New Societies*, (New York: Harcourt, Brace and World, Inc., 1964).

Hartz, Louis, *The Liberal Tradition in America*, (New York: Harcourt, Brace and Company, 1955).

Higham, John, *Strangers in the Land: Patterns of American Nativism 1860–1925*, (New York: Atheneum, 1968) .

Hofstadter, Richard, *The Paranoid Style in American Politics and Other Essays*, (New York: Vintage Books, 1964).

Howard, Sidney, *The Labor Spy*, (New York: Republic, 1924).

Kolko, Gabriel, *The Roots of American Foreign Policy*, (Boston: Beacon Press, 1969).

Lane, Robert, *Political Ideology: Why the American Common Man Believes What He Does*, (New York: The Free Press, 1967).

Lipset, Seymour Martin, *The Politics of Unreason*, (New York: Harper and Row, 1971).

Lowenthal, Leo and Norbert Guterman, *Prophets of Deceit: A Study of the Techniques of the American Agitator*, (New York: Harper and Brothers, 1950).

Lowenthal, Max, *The Federal Bureau of Investigation*, (New York: William Sloane Associates, Inc., 1950).

Marcuse, Herbert, *An Essay On Liberation*, (Boston: Beacon Press, 1969).

Marcuse, Herbert, *One Dimensional Man*, (Boston: Beacon Press, 1964).

McGiffert, Michael, Ed., *The Character of Americans*, (Homewood: The Dorsey Press, 1964).

Meyers, Marvin, *The Jacksonian Persuasion*, (Stanford: Stanford University Press, 1957).

Morrison, Elting, Ed., *The American Style: Essays in Value and Performance*. (New York: Harper and Brothers, 1958).

Murray, Robert, *Red Scare: A Study of National Hysteria, 1919–1920*, (New York: McGraw-Hill, 1964).

Pierson, George, *Tocqueville and Beaumont in America*, (New York: Oxford University Press, 1938).

Post, Louis, *The Deportations Delirium of Nineteen-Twenty*, (Chicago: Charles H. Kerr and Company, 1923).

Preston, William, *Aliens and Dissenters*, (New York: Harper and Row, 1966).

Report Upon the Illegal Practices of the United States Department of Justice, (Washington, D.C.: National Popular Government League, 1920).

Rogin, Michael Paul, *The Intellectuals and McCarthy*, (Cambridge: The Massachusetts Institute of Technology Press, 1967).

Shils, Edward, *The Torment of Secrecy*, (Glencoe: The Free Press, 1956).

Simmel, George, *The Sociology of George Simmel*, (Glencoe: The Free Press, 1950).

de Tocqueville, Alexis, *Democracy in America*, 2 Vols. Phillips Bradley, Ed., (New York: Alfred A. Knopf, 1948).

Walter, E. V., *Terror and Resistance*, (New York: Oxford University Press, 1970).

ARTICLES

Berkovitz, Leonard. "Some Implications of Laboratory Studies of Frustration and Aggression for the Study of Political Violence." Paper de-

Berkovitz, Leonard, "Some Implications of Laboratory Studies of Frus-
Association, Chicago: Mimeo.

Blum, John, "Nativism, Anti-Radicalism, and the Foreign Scare, 1917–
1920." *Midwest Journal*, 3 (winter 1950–1951).

Coben, Stanley, "A Study of Nativism: The American Red Scare of 1919–
1920," *Political Science Quarterly*, 79 (March 1964).

Davis, David B., "Some Themes of Counter-Subversion: An Analysis of
Anti-Masonic, Anti-Catholic, and Anti-Mormon Literature," *Mississippi
Valley Historical Review*, 47 (Sept. 1960).

Edelman, Murray, "Public Policy and Political Violence," (University of
Wisconsin: Institute for Research on Poverty, mimeo, 1968).

Edelman, Murray, "Myths, Metaphors, and Political Conformity," *Psychiatry: Journal for the Study of Interpersonal Processes*, 30 (August
1967).

Howard, Sidney, "Our Professional Patriots," *New Republic*, 40 (Sept.
3, 1924).

Lowi, Theodore, "The Wheel of Panic," *The Nation*, 208 (May 19,
1969).

Murphy, Paul, "Sources and Nature of Intolerance in the 1920's," *The
Journal of American History*, 51 (June 1964).

Neumann, Franz, "Anxiety and Politics," in Neumann, Franz, *The Democratic and Authoritarian State*, (Glencoe: The Free Press, 1957).

SUPERPATRIOTIC PAMPHLETS AND BOOKS

A substantial collection of superpatriotic literature is collected in the Library
of Congress: Microfilm Shelf 21396, under the title: "Collected Pamphlets
Issued By or Relating to the Communist International, IWW Leaflets, and
Pamphlets on Socialism, Communism, and Bolshevism." Several super-
patriotic books and pamphlets are also available in the collections of the
Harvard and Yale University libraries and the Boston Public Library.

American Constitutional League of Wisconsin. "Looking Straight at
Socialism" Pamphlet, 1920. Library of Congress, "Collected Pamphlets
Issued By or Relating to the Communist International, IWW Leaflets,
and Pamphlets on Socialism, Communism, and Bolshevism," Microfilm
Shelf No. 21396, Library of Congress. (Hereafter cited as "Library of
Congress Documents")

Anonymous. "Questions for Every Good American to Consider." Date about
1919. Library of Congress Documents.

Anonymous. "Plan to Create National Service Committees," *National
Civic Federation Review*, Vol. 5, July 10, 1920.

Baker, Royal A. *The Menace of Bolshevism*. Detroit: Liberty Bell Publishers, 1919.

Block, H. C. "The Enemy Within Our Gates," Washington, D.C., National Association for Constitutional Government, 1919. Library of Congress Documents.

Brown, Rome G. "Americanism vs. Socialism," Address delivered before the Middlesex [Massachusetts] Bar Association, 1919. Library of Congress Documents.

Cartwright, George W. "The World's Greatest Blunder," address delivered at the convention of The National Association of Sheet Metal Contractors, 1921. Library of Congress Documents.

Cashman, Joseph. "America Asleep: The Menace of Bolshevism." Pamphlet, The National Security League, February, 1923.

Clum, Woodworth. "America is Calling." Pamphlet, The Better America Federation of California, 7th edition, 1922.

Dunn, Arthur. "The 'Reds' in America; From the Standpoint of the Department of Justice." *The Review of Reviews*, Vol. LXI (Feb. 1920).

Easley, Ralph. "Bolshevism: What Is It?" Pamphlet, "Statement to the Executive Council of the National Civic Federation," National Civic Federation, 1923.

Hanson, Ole. *Americanism Versus Bolshevism*. New York: Doubleday, Page and Company, 1920.

Hornady, William. *Awake America!* New York: Moffat, Yard & Company, 1918.

Hornady, William. "The Lying Lure of Bolshevism." Pamphlet, American Defense Society, 1919.

Kahn, Otto H. "Labor And The Golden Rule." *National Civic Federation Review* Vol. 4, May 15, 1919.

Libbey, William. Report of the Committee Appointed to Draft a Protest Against Red Propaganda in This Country. New Jersey, Council of the Society of Colonial Wars, June 2, 1923.

Lockwood, George B. "Radicalism: Menace or Myth?" *The National Republic* (no date). Library of Congress Documents.

Lusk, Clayton. "Radicalism Under Inquiry." *The American Review*, Vol. LXI, Feb. 1919.

Marvin, Fred R. "Are These Your Friends?" Pamphlet, The Americanization Press Service, 1922.

Parkhurst, Charles. "The Leper in the House." Pamphlet, National Security League, 1920.

Patterson, Charles. "Red and Radicals in America." Pamphlet, The Lawyers Club of New York City, 1920.

Shutter, Rev. M.D. "Some Recent Developments In Socialism." Reprinted from *The Minneapolis Tribune* and issued by The Women's Association, 1921.

Wade, Martin J. U.S. District Court, Southern District of Iowa (opinion). Published by the Scott County Council of National Defense, Davenport, Iowa, 1919.

Whitney, Richard. *Reds In America*. New York: Beckwith Press, 1924.

GOVERNMENT DOCUMENTS

Investigation of the Administration of Louis Post, Assistant Secretary of Labor, in the Matter of Deportation of Aliens, Hearings before the House Committee on Rules (Washington, D.C.) 1920.

Lusk Committee, *Revolutionary Radicalism: Its History, Purpose and Tactics, Report of the Joint Legislative Committee Investigating Seditious Activities; The Senate of the State of New York.* 4 Volumes. Albany: J. B. Lyon Company, 1920.

U.S. Senate, *Committee on Education and Labor Report, Investigation of Strike In Steel Industry,* 66th Congress, 1st Session, 1919.

NEWSPAPERS AND MAGAZINES 1919–1920

The American Legion Weekly
The Baltimore Sun
The Boston Evening Transcript
The Boston Herald
The Chicago Tribune
The Cincinnati Enquirer
The Cleveland Plain Dealer
Colliers
Current Opinion
Life
The Literary Digest
The Los Angeles Times
The Nation

The New Republic
The New York Times
The New York Tribune
The Pittsburgh Post
The Rocky Mountain News
The Salt Lake City Tribune
The San Francisco Examiner
The Saturday Evening Post
The Seattle Post-Intellegencer
The Seattle Star
The Seattle Union Record
The Wall Street Journal
The Washington Post

INDEX